# When God Weeps

## OTHER BOOKS BY JONI EARECKSON TADA

*Joni*
*Heaven: Your Real Home*
*Diamonds in the Dust: 365 Sparkling Devotions*
*Barrier-Free Friendships*
*The Life and Death Dilemma*

# When God Weeps

## Why Our Sufferings Matter to the Almighty

## Joni Eareckson Tada
## Steven Estes

ZondervanPublishingHouse
*Grand Rapids, Michigan*

*A Division of HarperCollinsPublishers*

In this book, the authors have placed certain words from Scriptural quotations in italics without individually marking each instance with such words as "italics mine." The reader should be aware, however, that these italics are not found in the original texts but are added by the authors for reasons of emphasis and clarity.

*When God Weeps*
Copyright © 1997 by Joni Eareckson Tada and Steven Estes

Requests for information should be addressed to:

📖 ZondervanPublishingHouse
*Grand Rapids, Michigan 49530*

**Library of Congress Cataloging-in-Publication Data**

Tada, Joni Eareckson.
        When God weeps : why our sufferings matter to the Almighty / Joni Eareckson Tada
    and Steven Estes.
            p.    cm.
        Includes bibliographical references.
        ISBN: 0-310-21186-7
        1. Suffering—Religious aspects—Christianity. 2. Theodicy. I. Estes, Steven. II. Title.
    BT732.7.T33  1997
    2448.'8-dc 21                                                                                    97-25826
                                                                                                            CIP

This edition printed on acid-free paper.

Published in association with the literary agency of Wolgemuth and Associates, Inc.

*Interior design by Sherri L. Hoffman*

*Printed in the United States of America*

00 01 02 03 04 05 06 07 /❖ DC/ 20 19 18 17 16 15 14 13

*To Verna—*
*Eight kids later and still*
*the most fun companion on earth*


*To Ken—*
*You make me forget this chair . . .*
*and that's saying a lot*

# CONTENTS

# SPECIAL THANKS TO. . . .

Sometimes a fresh word may, in fact, be a very *old* one. Truths that are timeless often need only the "time" brushed away in order to reveal the polished patina that has gleamed all along. And so we acknowledge those fathers of theology on whose shoulders we have built this book. People like Calvin and Luther and Latimer, Jonathan Edwards and George Whitefield, Loraine Boettner and Martyn Lloyd-Jones. Not many pull the writings of Jeremiah Burroughs off the shelf for a little casual reading these days, and so *When God Weeps* is meant to give a fresh and contemporary treatment of doctrines hammered out by theologians of old. We give thanks to God for these men of faith who continue to shape the thinking of many.

We extend a hearty handshake to our friend, Dr. John MacArthur, who researched the Scriptures for Appendix B. (And he did so long before you could click on a computer icon and—zip!—have the answers!).

Our profuse gratitude goes to Scott Bolinder of Zondervan who graciously accommodated our schedule, and John Sloan, our editor, with Bob Hudson, who picked up our slack. Thanks, also, to Robert Wolgemuth of Wolgemuth & Hyatt who kept us on track. This book was a team effort and sometimes the writers (Steve and Joni) had the defense and offense scrambling. Bless you, friends.

We can't leave this page without writing a few individual acknowledgments. Joni, who can't type a key or turn a page without help, would like to thank Judy Butler and Francie Lorey for generously serving as her hands on *When God Weeps*. She can't miss saying an extra thank you to Ken for cheering her on through late nights and Saturday afternoons. The JAF Ministries staff was gracious in respecting Joni's closed office door and shortened administrative meetings—all to give her time to think, pray, and write. A special thanks to Bunny Warlen, Steve Jensen, Judy Butler, Francie Lorey, and a host of intercessors, including the Wednesday night group at Church in the Canyon, who lifted the manuscript, day by day, up in prayer.

---

Steve would like to send out his heartfelt thanks to:

Jesus Christ knows me yet still loves me. I cannot get over this.

The elders of Community Evangelical Free Church, Elverson, Pennsylvania, for granting a six-month leave that stretched into eight, and for the generous conditions of that leave. They and the staff bore the weight of additional work during that period, especially Arleigh Hegarty who so competently filled the pulpit.

My congregation who made me feel as if I were engaged in the world's most important project—when *they* were the ones so engaged by their daily plugging away in the work of God's kingdom. They loved me, sent me notes, had our family for dinner, and prayed, prayed, prayed.

Paul and Carolyn Montgomery. You know all you gave me. It helped this book so much.

Dave Godown for your enthusiasm about this project, backed up by a gesture of real self-sacrifice.

Merle and Dave Stoltzfus for putting at my disposal a most pleasant office and staff. What would I have done without this gesture—and without your friendship which I prize beyond words? Why did God give me such brothers-in-law?

Emily, Ashley, Debbie, and Paula who were 4/5 of that helpful staff. They cheerfully helped me in a hundred and one ways.

Steve Beard whose flexibility last September helped me in this project more than he knows.

Whistling Al Marple whose weekly cleaning visits cheered me. He always inquired about the book's status and prayed daily for Joni and me.

Rev. Tom Hall and the Elverson Methodist Church for access to their building where I could find quiet spots to walk and pray throughout this project.

The Wednesday Soup Kitchen members.

Verna, who listened to every whine as I wrote this but helped, loved, and fed me anyway. 5' 0" of smiling selflessness.

Jeb, Gail, Leah, and Sarah Bland who hosted Verna and me for an autumn weekend in Rhode Island. How we needed and loved it!

Ben Mountz who carried tons of books and shelving up flights of stairs to my writing office. Turns out I didn't need most of it. Sorry.

Bob Hughes, who one day told me, "Give me your office key, tell me when you'll be out for a day, and don't ask any questions." I returned to find my old bookshelves whisked away, new ones moved in, and the thousands of books transferred. I now have the nicest bookshelves on the east coast, hand built by Bob as a labor of love—stocked with John Owen, Francis Turretin, and other books he bought me. Sherri helped him all the way. I will always remember them, now moved to Florida.

Larry Everhart for insight into thunderstorms, as background for Chapter 6. An easy-going, low pressure kind of guy.

The mother of the young man I have called Paul Ruffner in Chapter 5, for many hours of uplifting phone conversation in which she described God's remarkable grace to her family during some heart-breaking years.

John Frame of Westminster Seminary, California, for faxed thoughts on God's emotions as I worked on Appendix C, although he never had opportunity to see the appendix.

Vern Poythress and Sinclair Ferguson of Westminster Seminary, Philadelphia. Separate theological conversations with these men have helped my life and thinking enormously, even though their insights had only indirect impact on this book.

Laurie O'Connor who re-wrote Appendix C out of sloppy sense-lessness into coherence when my back was against the wall for time, and who prayed for me like a trooper.

Diane Stoltzfus who cheerleadered me through Chapters 2 through 6 in some bleak moments. Thank you, thank you.

And finally, Curt Hoke, who on the countless occasions I called for help made me feel like I was doing *him* the favor. Nobody helped more with this book than he. I love the man.

# BEFORE YOU BEGIN

I first met Joni in the summer of 1969 in a church parking lot. Several hundred other teenagers and I had just exploded from the building. The youth meeting was over, and everyone was scattering, engines starting, radios cranked up—laughter and good-hearted tomfoolery everywhere.

A white station wagon had pulled up to the side steps. Somehow, with my friend Diana holding the keys, it avoided looking like a middle-aged person's wheels. Diana had the world's most carbonated personality. She stood by the front passenger door, next to an empty wheelchair she had pulled from the back seat to unfold. She wanted me to meet the paralyzed friend she had told me about. From my angle up on the steps, I couldn't see the face of the tall girl in the seat. I could see the braces on her wrists.

"Steve, I want you to meet Joni."

"Hi, Joni."

The face in the front seat bent down to peer out. Stylishly short blonde hair. Freckle-faced and cute. Ski-slope nose. A bright but bittersweet smile—sweet because, if you know Joni, that's just her. Bitter because she looked as if that chair had taken something precious out of her.

"Hi, Steve! Good to meet you." Enthusiastic but tentative.

"You two have a lot to talk about," Diana effervesced. We agreed it would be fun to get together.

A week later I walked into the stone-and-timber home that I'll always think of as a vestibule into heaven. Antlers over every fireplace, Indian rugs scattered about. Candles, candles. Simon and Garfunkel on the turntable, laughter in every room, and the bubbling friendliness of the parents and sisters from whom Joni had stolen that winning smile.

But once we were alone, it wasn't ten minutes before the question came.

11

"So, Diana says you're big into the Bible. Tell me, do you think God had anything to do with my breaking my neck?" She casually brushed a wisp of hair from her forehead with the back of her wrist, but those eyes were anything but casual.

Here is the crux of the book you're about to read.

I am a sixteen-year-old nobody, a paper boy, sitting across from perhaps the most popular girl of her huge high-school class from two years earlier. The crowd she ran with I saw only from across the gymnasium. Now look at her. I tap my foot to James Taylor in the background; she just bobs her head. I eat my own lunch; someone has to feed her. I'll be walking out that screen door in about thirty minutes; she'll stay sitting in that chair till the Grim Reaper comes. And she wants to know if I think God put her there? Who am I to open my mouth?

I know what the Bible says about her question. A dozen passages come to mind from years of church and a Christian dad who taught his kids well. But I've never test-driven those truths on such a difficult course. Nothing worse than a D in algebra or puppy-love-gone-sour has ever happened to me. But I think, *If the Bible can't work in this girl's life—it never was for real.*

I clear my throat and jump off the cliff.

"God put you in that chair, Joni. I don't know why, but if you'll trust him instead of fighting him, you'll find out why—if not in this life, then in the next. He let you break your neck because he loves you."

Oh, it sounded trite to me—but apparently not to her. We looked at a few verses, and I went home. From that day on I had to study hard just to keep one step ahead of the girl; she always had her nose in that Bible.

This book is about God weeping over human heartache, his entering our anguish himself, and the *love* that drives him to let us suffer. It's about experiencing the friendship of God along difficult paths we didn't even know he walked. Much of it is written from Joni's perspective because her life is a remarkable laboratory that proves God knows what he's talking about.

But *your* life is the important laboratory to put God's Word to the test as you read. Do God's thoughts about suffering sound trite to you?

Steve Estes
March 31, 1997

W here do the years fly?

I can still see Steve Estes, humped over his Bible by the hearth, looking up only long enough to put another log on the fire. He'd flip furiously between the Old and New Testaments, finding a page, tracing his finger down a column, and jabbing the very verse to answer my latest query.

"Okay, Jon, now follow me. Listen to this in Ephesians chapter three:'The purpose is that . . . ,'" he'd say, as if revving an engine with little taps on the accelerator. Off we'd go, heading down a road of questions, bumping over them, stopping, backing up, and then starting again, taking a detour or two, then shutting down after the last log on the fire had burned into embers. He was as raw and youthful as I, hungry to see truth work. And so we'd be at it again, next Bible study, charging ahead—he, excitedly pointing out the sights through Scripture, and I, keeping pace, not missing a thing.

> *If God is loving, why is there suffering?*
> *What's the difference between permitting something and ordaining it?*
> *When bad things happen, is God in cahoots with the Devil?*
> *How can he expect me to be happy this way?*

"Hold that thought!" Steve would yell over his shoulder, running to the kitchen to grab another RC Cola.

Never were there sweeter days than those early years we spent journeying through Scripture. Our adventure was to go down that road of knowing God in suffering as far as it would take us. Thirty years later we've passed a few milestones and suffered the bumps and bruises of growing older and wiser. Thankfully we both have marriage partners, Verna and Ken, who keep cheering us on. Much has changed, but one thing remains constant: our friendship still orbits around the Son.

Something else is constant. Suffering. In some respects, it's even harder. My bones are aching from sitting so long in a wheelchair, and I'm weary from battling the encroaching limitations of my paralysis. Yet it's still an adventure (although what I'm learning is but an echo of those early days, as though I were simply taking soundings at greater depths).

Never would I have dreamed, long ago, sitting by that fire, the hour late and the cola bottles empty, that the answers I discovered then would have such powerful repercussions now. Through decades of quadriplegia and almost as many years of encountering people in situations as bad if not worse than mine, I continue to pass on these truths.

They are not so much truths about suffering as they are about God. And so I introduce this book with the premise: *When God Weeps* is not so much about affliction as it is about the only One who can unlock sense out of suffering. It's not why our afflictions matter to us (although they do), but why they matter to the Almighty. Another premise: we believe the Bible to be God's Word, the Hebrew Bible unfolding into the New Testament, each book an immovable stone in the foundation of truth. The Bible is the proven road map we will use in this book.

I knew I couldn't handle a potent topic like this alone. It begs for experience and scholarship. I lend experience, and Steve Estes, with his many years of seminary study, brings the scholarship. He has graciously lent his writing gifts and learning so that, together, we could "disciple" you through the same tough questions.

For one leg of the journey—chapters 2 through 6—the research and writing are Steve's. Your heart and mind will be stirred, as was mine when he first shared the insights in "Who Is This God?" by the side of my wheelchair. In the twelfth chapter, Steve writes about hell, and I follow it with the concluding chapter on heaven. Appendices A and C are his too. We hammered out the book's outline together (many times!) and tweaked one another's work, having stimulated each other on the subject of suffering for years.

One more thing. "Weeping endures for a night, but joy comes in the morning": joy for those who suffer—but especially for God. It's Steve's and my prayer that through this book you will better understand why our weeping matters to a loving God. A God who, one day, will make clear the meaning behind every tear.

Even his tears.

Joni Eareckson Tada
Spring 1997

# One

# I'M HURTING BAD

The African night smelled and looked like pitch. Only the beam of a flashlight guided the way. I shook off my nausea at the smell of rancid trash, wanting to enter cautiously, but my companion thought nothing of striding ahead. Lifting the flap of the canvas lean-to, he beamed his light into the darkness and entered. I followed in my wheelchair.

When the flap dropped behind me, a dozen slum-street noises were muffled. My eyes would now do most of the learning. He held his flashlight high, spotlighting a young woman with hair and skin as black as the shadows. She had no hands. Splayed beneath her on the straw mat were her stick-thin legs. These did not hold my gaze. I had seen the alleys full of people who, from polio, or amputation, had stubs for hands or callused stumps for feet. All of them, homeless. Quadriplegics, like me, don't survive in Ghana, equatorial west Africa, let alone on the sidewalks of this miserable pesthole in the capital of Accra—only disabled people who are strong enough to fend for themselves on the streets. Streets wet with urine and rotting garbage.

The glow from my companion's flashlight illumined the tiny lean-to, and when the young woman saw me, she smiled African-style, broad and full of tooth. Her dark eyes glinted from the light when she flashed her smile at my companion. She knew well this African pastor who made it his ministry to go out into the streets and the alleys to find the blind and the lame.

The pastor cleared his throat for introductions. "Ama," he began with an accent and a British air, "I would very much like you to meet my American friend, Joni." She returned the greeting in her tribal tongue. I

15

was told that Ama, a citizen of this former British colony, understood English, and so our conversation ensued as though we were having tea around a table. Yes, I was pleased to meet her and her friends on the street. Yes, our trip was long, but we were delighted to come. Our group from Joni and Friends (JAF Ministries) was here to give wheelchairs to her and some of her friends. Would she care to join us up the street? She would. For that matter, would she care to point her smile my way so I could see it for the rest of the evening? We laughed. She did.

I was hooked. My heart was captured, yes, by the African girl who came to symbolize for me the disabled street Christians of Accra, but also by her flashlight-toting pastor who had chosen to spend his days with the scourings of the earth. The stench of things rotting lay heavy over the streets, but a few minutes with Ama, like a miracle, made it a fragrance of life.

I backed out of the canvas lean-to and was swallowed by the night. I followed the flashlight across the dirt street, lurching around chunks of asphalt. My JAF friends—the ones who brought our crutches and wheelchairs—hoisted me up on the opposite sidewalk. Where are we going? Stay with the flashlight!

Out of a shadowed alley crawled two teenagers dragging their twisted legs. Polio survivors, I thought as they joined our group. We overtook a woman in tribal dress inching along in her rickety wheelchair. An eighty-year-old man, legless and no more than three feet high, hopped up on the curb and flashed a smile my way. I stopped. He waddled over and extended his stump of an arm to shake my hand. I leaned over to press my paralyzed fingers against his stump and we grinned at our odd handshake. We were pulled on by the singing and clapping up the street. As our group approached, the orphaned and homeless parted to welcome us in under the glare of a neon light. We had arrived in the center of a sidewalk worship service.

We westerners sat upright on benches, facing the ragtag crowd. "And now, Christian brothers and sisters," shouted the pastor, "let us give a warm welcome to our most gracious friends from America who have traveled very far to bring us wheelchairs and Bibles!" Cheers erupted; then, a welcome song. The full rich drone of African harmony twisted my heart, and tears fell freely as we listened to the disabled people applaud each other's testimonies and to the readings of Scripture. A half hour of constant praise passed easily, and then I was asked to speak.

"Thank you, friends, for welcoming us," I said as I wheeled into a clearing on the sidewalk. My JAF friend pushed a wheelchair-gift alongside of me. "God is good!" someone shouted as the first child was placed into it. Another chair, another disabled person. Hands began clapping in rhythm as a flow of crutches and wheelchairs were passed from our group to theirs. More syncopated clapping, loud and snappy. Ama bobbed her head in time, beaming a proud smile as she rubbed her stumps on the leather armrests of her chair. The teenage boys with polio started a dance in the clearing.

"Look," I said to a team member, "even the people who know there aren't enough wheelchairs to go around—they are so happy for those who get something."

The rising moon was lightening the eastern edge of the night. As we readied to leave the slums, the Africans bid us farewell with one more song:

Because he lives, I can face tomorrow.
Because he lives, all fear is gone.
Because I know, I know he holds the future;
And life is worth the living just because he lives!

*Is it the neon glare?* I wondered, as I squinted at their smiles. No. It was joy out of this world.

My pastor friend lit the way back to the van. As we jostled across the street, my thoughts were jumbled. So much gladness in the midst of misery. Joy, like a fresh daisy, sprouting up from manure.

"What happens to Ama when it rains? Who takes care of her?" I asked.

The glow of the flashlight gave a sheen to his smile. "God takes care of her."

*Oppressive heat. People penniless. A girl with no hands, no legs to walk, no bed, and not even a fan, living on concrete. It doesn't sound like God's doing a very good job.* I recall hearing something; a boy who lived in a box by the trash heap said, "You westerners are the ones we can't understand. God has given you so much, you have been so blessed . . . why are so many people in your country so unhappy?"

## OUR SIDE OF THE WORLD

We have our ranch-style homes and unemployment insurance, three-meals-a-day on the table, and supermarket double coupons, if not food stamps, but isn't it odd how we still want more? If we're single, we want marriage. If we're married, we want the perfect spouse. If we have the perfect mate, we want the time to enjoy life.

Other times we have too much. Sky high medical bills. Fourteen visits to the Mayo Clinic and eight surgeries. A stroke renders our husband speechless or chromosomes retard our grandchild. The funeral was yesterday, and we wonder how we'll face the future alone. We collapse under the burden, baffled at why the abundant life eludes us and lands in the laps of others.

We want what we do not have.

We have what we do not want.

And we are unhappy.

A story about noble Africans who suffer joyfully is inspiring, but God—we convince ourselves—wouldn't want to cramp our style as he might with poor people in Ghana. Our God exists to make our lives happy, more meaningful, and trouble-free. *Our* God deals differently with us. Maybe we're conditioned by the Puritan ethic, bent on finding a fix-it. Our Western culture—and the God who inspires it—has built hospitals and institutions to alleviate suffering. We're civilized and so is our view of God.

He is our Father, as he describes himself in his Word, and fathers want the best for their children—not used clothing bartered off the streets or shelter that collapses under a downpour. He is our Savior, securing for us peace and well-being while crushing underfoot the deeds of the Devil, including disease and disasters. He promises abundant life (and God always keeps his promises). He is our deliverer, releasing us from the bondage of sin and its effects. With his stripes we are healed.

And to be healed of suffering is to be happy.

This line of thinking is the path I took not long after the diving accident in which I became paralyzed in 1967. Lying on my back in a Stryker frame with my head immobilized in steel tongs, I could look only up. A natural position for talking to God. I tried to imagine what he was thinking. If God were God—I was convinced he was all powerful and loving—he had to be as anxious to relieve my pain as I was. A heavenly Father had to weep over me as my daddy often did, standing by my bedside, white-knuckling the guardrail. I was one of God's children, and God would never do anything to harm one of his own. Didn't Jesus say, "Which of you fathers, if your son asks for a fish, will give him a snake instead? Or if he asks for an egg, will give him a scorpion? If you then . . . know how to give good gifts to your children, how much more will your Father in heaven!" (Luke 11:11–13).

A God this good is worth pursuing. And so, when I was released from the hospital, my friends would drive me to Washington, D.C., so I could be first in line at the door whenever the famous faith-healer, Kathryn Kuhlman, came to town. Miss Kuhlman breezed onto the stage in her white gown, and my heart raced as I prayed, *Lord, the Bible says you heal all our diseases. I'm ready for you to get me out of this wheelchair. Please, would you?*

God answered: I never walked away from my chair. The last time I wheeled away from a Kathryn Kuhlman crusade, I was number fifteen in a line of thirty wheelchair-users waiting to exit at the stadium elevator, all of us trying to make a fast escape ahead of the people on crutches. I remember glancing around at all the disappointed and confused people and thinking, *Something's wrong with this picture. Is this the only way to deal with suffering? Trying desperately to remove it?*

When I looked in the mirror after I got home, I saw their sullen expression staring back. I was just as perplexed as the people near the elevator. *Okay, let me get this straight: God is good. God is love. He is all powerful. Plus, when he walked on earth, he bent over backward to relieve the sufferings of people, everyone from the hemorrhaging woman to the centurion's servant. So why does my five-year-old niece, Kelly, have brain cancer? Why did my brother-in-law abandon my sister and their family? Why does Daddy's arthritis not respond to medication?*

Good questions.

As answers elude us, as God's ways stymie us, the fire of suffering is stoked. We feel the heat of wanting what we don't have and having what we don't want. God appears unmoved. Happiness escapes us. We are discontent and restless.

I wonder how many of those sullen-faced folks at the elevator after the healing crusade still believe in God? That was almost thirty years ago. Are they still waiting in line? Still hoping? "Hope deferred makes the heart sick," and a heart can break only so many times.

If God is a God who dangles hope like a carrot only to snatch it back, little wonder our appetite for him—our confidence in him—wanes.

## WE ARE WEAK BUT HE IS STRONG

We could learn a lesson from those Africans. They wish they had the burden of food stamps! Oh, for a ranch-style home to vacuum! A power vacuum? It would be handy inside Ama's canvas lean-to. Healing? They'd love for legs and feet to sprout from stumps! Their suffering is a pit, a yawning abyss. Yet as hurting and harangued as they are, they seem to trust God with absolute abandon.

Don't think I'm glorifying them. This isn't a snobby one-upmanship on whose purple heart medals shine the brightest. Before we cast Ama and her friends into plaster-of-paris sainthood, remember they are more like us than we realize. They too want what they do not have.

The difference is the way they look at God.

On a hot and windy evening, as we prepared to board our jet to leave Ghana, I talked on the tarmac with an African airport employee. When I told her about the hurting yet happy people we met in the slums, she replied, "We have to trust God. Our people have no other hope." She flattened her whipping hair with her hand and gave me a knowing look, her eyes unblinking, her broad smile, unflinching. She meant every word. I asked how she kept smiling. She shrugged her shoulders. "I too have God."

She made it sound so simple. *Maybe it is,* I pondered. She has the same God as we do. The same Bible. And when it comes to suffering, she has the same text as do we all. Second Corinthians 12:9–10 plainly states: "Therefore I will boast all the more gladly about my weaknesses, so that Christ's power may rest on me. . . . I delight in weaknesses, in insults, in hardships, in persecutions, in difficulties. For when I am weak, then I am strong."

Hardships press us up against God. It's a universal truth we all learned in the old Sunday school song, "We are weak, but he is strong."

This is what I saw that night in Africa. Our pastor-friend spread wide his arms and beamed, "Welcome to our country where our God is bigger than your God." It was a happy-hearted fact: God always seems bigger to those who need him the most. And suffering is the tool he uses to help us need him more.

*Know God better through suffering?* That's a quaint thought. Then again, there's that high school buddy who never *did* take God seriously until trouble hit. Bagging a football scholarship to a Big Ten university consumed all his attention, but in his sophomore year at Michigan, he got slammed on the five-yard line. Two surgeries and three sidelined seasons later, he had done some serious thinking: life was short; where were his priorities? Today, he is still into sports (he coaches the Tiny Tornadoes after work), but his priorities are straighter. Bible study and prayer get their chunk of time in his schedule.

*Closer to God through trials?* Another curiosity. Then there's the couple down the street who tend to be just a tad materialistic. But then last year when he lost his job, they prayed harder, got by with less, and learned some lessons. They found that family means more than possessions, that community college wasn't so bad for their Princeton-bound daughter, and that God took care of them while they climbed back to their feet.

*Discover God's hand in heartbreak?* One more peculiarity. But then there's the twenty-six-year-old man whose girlfriend had returned the engagement ring. He let it sit on his dresser for months as a monument to his failed love life. He dealt with the grief by pouring himself into a troubled kid who lived two doors down and had never known a father. Took him to the stables on weekends and taught him to horseback ride. It made him grow up. He learned that his problems were super-small.

Two years later, the man ducked into a bookstore to buy a present and spied a honey-blonde girl with a knock-out smile flipping through a calendar of palomino horses. They got to talking and discovered they had more in common than just equines. He took her riding the next weekend, joined the singles group at her church, and not long afterward, she said a big yes when he popped the question on her front porch swing. Today, he shudders to think that he could have missed her.

When we are weak, God is strong? Sure, we'll buy that.

So why do we squirm when we feel the crunch? Why do we keep asking why? A clue is hidden in the questions we ask: "Will I ever be happy again?" and "How is this fitting together for my good?" The questions themselves are technical and me-focused. Even when we hit upon good reasons why—like the Michigan football player who got his priorities straightened or the materialistic couple who learned to get by with less or the guy whose pain led him to Miss Perfect—even good reasons can be me-focused:

> "Suffering sure has helped me get my spiritual act together."
> "I see how this trial is improving my character and prayer life."
> "Think what I would have missed had it not been for that heartbreak."
> "This tribulation has really strengthened my marriage."

Notice all the me's.

God notices too.

## SUFFERING BEYOND THE LIMITS

Wave upon wave, field daisies sway on the embankment just feet from where we sit. Pine branches bob in the wind, my hair is tossed, and my spirits lift. Has a backyard ever held so much sunlight? John McAllister and I sit in our wheelchairs, rigid in the breeze. He faces the far away mountains with a faraway look, a wool wrap tucked high around his neck. He resembles a statue of someone noble and famous—or a scholar meditating in his garden.

"I need to come here more often," I sigh. "I love this view, this day. I appreciate your friendship."

"Ha-a-ahh," he guffaws, laying aside the compliment as he would a gift to relish later. I compare our situations. Almost three decades of paralysis has taken a toll on my frame. But a degenerative nerve disease is guilty of open extortion on his. A six-foot-three-inch oak is bent and withering in front of me.

A nurse-friend approaches with a syringe and a plastic container of creamy liquid. He and I keep chatting as she undoes the lower buttons of his shirt. His white abdomen is exposed, along with a patch and a permanent feeding tube. Into the tube she plunges lunch. He doesn't seem embarrassed, but still, I cover the moment: "It must be hard to know when to say grace when you get fed through a tube!"

He nods. I think about stronger days when he was more mobile, able to volunteer at a nursing home, always looking for ways to keep active, keep serving, keep doing. The nurse unplugs the syringe and wipes his abdomen, as she might a mouth with a napkin. I'm grateful she's tidy. John craves to keep clean. Showers are the one normal thing he clings to. Everything else is yesterday.

Months pass. The air is chillier, the days shorter. John's wheelchair sits unused in the corner. He's too weak to sit in it much. His bed stands in the center of the living room. John is in it. Nighttime is no longer friendly. Shadows cast jerking, jagging shapes across the room. Gravity is his enemy as the weight of the air settles on his chest. Breathing is heavy labor. Calling out is impossible.

He needs to call out tonight. In the darkness an ant finds him. The scout sends for others and they come. First hundreds, then thousands. A noiseless legion inches its way down the chimney, across the floor, secretly crawling up his urine tube, up, over and onto his bed. They fan out over the hills and valleys of John's blanket, tunneling under and onto his body. He is covered by a black, wriggling, invasion.

I'm across the ocean in England when the fax arrives at my hotel, relaying the story. John's wife, along with a nurse, found him in the early morning with ants still in his hair, mouth, and eyes. His skin was badly bitten and burned. *Pray for him,* the fax conveys, *we've never seen him so depressed.* I'm not at the hotel when the message arrives. I'm speaking at a conference, conveying the plight of disabled people. I'm speaking of God's mercy and his protection over the weak and the vulnerable.

I sit by the receptionist's desk and want to read the fax a second time but can't. My stomach's sick. John is a Christian. His God can see in the dark.

Why, in the name of heaven, why? *God, who are you?* I almost want to say.

If you knew John, you'd say the same. This isn't a story about torn ligaments on a football field. This isn't a polite refusal letter for financial aid to Princeton. This isn't heartache over a returned engagement ring. This is crazy. This is suffering stalking a person down and ripping into his sanity. This is affliction spinning out of control. Suffering like this would never draw me *to* God, you think. It would push me *away* from him.

Are we to assume suffering like this helps a person know God better? That its purpose is to move one up a few notches closer to God? Is this God's idea of accomplishing something deep and profound in our lives?

Is there anyone out there who can make sense of this? Who actually believes this?

## BACK TO THE BIBLE

Stripped to his waist and forced on his stomach by the authorities, Paul shut his eyes. A pair of sandals shuffled in the dirt behind him. He heard the crowd quiet down, heard the breath taken, the whistle of the leather, and—snap!—felt its bite. The guard found his rhythm and the beating began in earnest.

The flogging was characteristically Jewish: thirty-nine applications of a triple lash. Thirty-nine, not forty. Mosaic law permitted up to forty, but better not to risk overstepping the bounds.

By the thirtieth blow, Paul's tongue lagged in the sand. Before his career's end, he would taste the dust outside of five such synagogues. He would also know scar-opening sessions under the rod of Rome, barely elude assassination, cling to ship's wreckage in the open sea for a day and a night, mark years in chains, and be left for dead after stoning-by-mob (2 Corinthians 11:24–27).

He could avoid it all. A few disclaimers would do, even just a discreet silence at critical moments. But Paul never could hold things in.

His enemies came to hate his endless spewing of quotations, not to mention his formidable intellect. They couldn't fool Paul. He knew their deeper objection. What his enemies truly loathed was the unseen figure behind every debate and discussion he entered—the one, as the Baptizer had put it, whose sandals he wasn't good enough to untie. It was the memory of this unseen man that kept Paul going.

Of course, what always set everyone off was that thing about "three days in the tomb and *then* . . ." Hadn't the Greeks guffawed over that one! A corpse hopping off his stone slab? A stiff traipsing about town? Hah! But what entertained the Greeks incensed the Jews. How dare a mere mortal claim the same rank with the Almighty! Especially a bastard rabbi from the backwoods who polluted the Sabbath with his so-called healings and infested teachings![1] He was double a fool for having gotten himself crucified!

But Paul had seen this Rabbi. *After* the burial. Less than a decade afterwards. This Rabbi had appeared to Paul and his caravan on the road to Damascus—enveloped in eye-sizzling glory, speaking from the third heaven, and majestic beyond words. Unquestionably risen from a stone-cold tomb. This incident alone convinced Paul that Jesus of Nazareth was indeed the long prophesied Son of God—come to meet death for the sins of the world in order to grasp life again and lavish it on others.

Hours later this same risen Christ had appeared in softer tones to a Christian man in Damascus, telling him to find and baptize Paul. The message ended with an announcement: "This man is my chosen instrument to carry my name before the Gentiles and their kings and before the people of Israel. *I will show him how much he must suffer for my name*" (Acts 9:15–16).

The proclamation proved true. Paul was destined to spread the fame of Jesus more than the other apostles combined. Yet he suffered intensely in the process.

How we admire him! How often we quote him! We yearn to live that nobly, speak that boldly, fight our vices that manfully. We long to mirror his heart and soul, totally recast by Christ's death-plundering power.

Some friends of Paul in his own day longed for the same. "We want to be like you, Paul. What's your secret? How can we know God like you do?" The apostle confided to them in a letter. He described what fueled his remarkable spiritual life and what *he* craved:

All I care for is to know Christ,
to experience the power of his resurrection,
and to share in his sufferings,
in growing conformity with his death . . .

(Philippians 3:10, NEB)

"All I care for is to know Christ," Paul wrote.

Yes, we say in our best moments; we want the same. Life is happiest when we're on good terms with our Maker.

"All I care for is . . . to experience the power of his resurrection."

Absolutely! Bring it on. We want to rise above our circumstances just like he rose from the dead. We could use a good soul-scrubbing. Heaven knows the help we need to wrestle down our vices. We all want to do better.

"All I care for is . . . to share in his sufferings."

Uh, wait. Perhaps the apostle overstates himself a bit. We don't actually *want* a share of sufferings, Christ's or anybody else's. On further thought, however, we grant that hard times in moderate doses can be a good tonic for the soul. This topic of suffering, no doubt, is an important part of Christian living that we all should know more about. Just keep the heat down to a manageable level.

"All I care for is . . . growing conformity with his death."

What? Becoming like Christ in his *death?* we ask. As in martyrdom by crucifixion? As in a living death where we "carry our cross" and God slowly wrenches from us everything we hold dear? You mean likeness to Christ's death as in being force-fed things I don't want while wanting things I don't have? Having suffering shoveled down my throat by God-who-says-he-loves-me? Ugh!

Wait a minute, you say. If the apostle Paul is our prototype, if God points to Paul to show us we can do the same, does he—or the God he represents—have an inkling of the pain I have endured?

Has a husband walked out on him and left him a mountain of bills? Was he born with a facial scar that drew playground taunts and stares? Has he groaned and burned with longing for simple, sensual pleasures I will never know again? Does God sit in an Iranian jail, blindfolded and bewildered? Does he slowly freeze to death in January on a New York sidewalk? Live with the memory of abusive parents, incest, or rape? Has he watched people he cherishes—children, for God's sake— twitch with torment in body and soul? Get real!

Who is this God I thought I knew?

Who is this God who bids us crawl over broken glass just for the pleasure of his company?

# Section I

## WHO IS THIS GOD?

# Two

## ECSTASY SPILLING OVER

Long, long before matter existed, before the cosmos took its first breath, before the first angel opened his eyes, when there was nothing—God had already lived forever. He had not just lived forever. He had been *contented* forever. And whatever God was, he still is and always will be.

An odd thought for us moderns. Who says God is contented? Assuming it's true, is it good news? After all, the entire human race is trudging through pain. Should God be allowed to watch it all happen with his feet up in a hammock? Maybe the notion of a satisfied, untroubled Creator disturbs you. But it shouldn't. For if God is to rescue anyone from heartache he had best not be bleeding himself.

Few people today believe in a contented God, not even his alleged fans. Consider the recent fireside discussions about Genesis hosted by public television's Bill Moyers. In the show, biblical scholars are seated around the room discussing Moses' book. Look at the God most of them discover there. He is worried, unsure, petty, jealous, even vindictive. Adam and Eve caught him off guard by eating the fruit, and now he has Big Problems on his hands. First he's biting his nails, then he's blowing his stack, overreacting, making heads roll. He'll probably feel bad about it in the morning.

But the Bible calls him "the blessed God" (1 Timothy 1:11). Not a threatened, pacing deity starving for attention but "the blessed and only Ruler, the King of kings and Lord of lords, who alone is immortal . . ." (1 Timothy 6:15–16). One translation actually reads "the blissful God."[1]

31

Ancient Greeks used the word to describe the rich and powerful—society's upper crust—and to label the gods, who could have whatever they wanted and do as they pleased. Jesus used it when he said, "Blessed are the meek . . . the poor . . . the peacemakers." He meant that such people are fortunate; we should envy them; they're the truly happy ones.

This is the word the Bible picks to describe God. So to be accurate, *contented* doesn't say it strongly enough. God is actually *happy*. Scan the Bible's big picture and you'll find that he's rapturously happy. He doesn't just get by—he flourishes.[2]

What's God so happy about? Think about it. Unlike us, he lacks for nothing. He'd be that hard-to-shop-for person at Christmas. He once reminded some worshipers who thought they were doing him a favor, "I have no need of a bull from your stall or of goats from your pens, for every animal of the forest is mine, and the cattle on a thousand hills" (Psalm 50:9–10). No teachers, bullies, bosses, coaches, drill sergeants, OSHA inspectors, or wacked-out guys with loaded pistols order him around, for "Our God is in heaven; he does whatever pleases him" (Psalm 115:3). He's not behind schedule, low on energy, short of clout, or awaiting bank approval and a zoning permit to fulfill his plans, because "no one can hold back his hand or say to him: 'What have you done?'" (Daniel 4:35).

Imagine the pleasure he must take in everything he's made. You've seen the satisfaction in the child's face whose crayon masterpiece "House With Tree" is taped onto the fridge. You know how *you* feel after serving the lauded dinner, typing the compelling term paper, coaxing up the eye-pleasing flowers, or finalizing that corporate merger. We keep returning to admire that brick sidewalk we laid, the model clipper ship sailing proudly across the bookshelf, the restored '64 Ford Mustang in the garage. We grin ear to ear after pulling off the perfect prank on Uncle Frank. How did Robert Frost feel holding the first copy of his collected works? Or Michelangelo gazing up at the last bit of drying paint on the Sistine Chapel dome? What runs through Steven Spielberg's mind at the premiere of his latest film?

Small potatoes all, for God. What do you think surged through him the minute after a billion galaxies came into being? With typical understatement, the Bible tells us: "God saw that it was good" (Genesis 1:18). After standing back to take in the panorama, he rested—not to catch his breath from exhaustion but to savor the moment.

That's contentment.

Any job well done is doubly gratifying with someone around to notice. God had this as well. He told Job that as the earth's foundations were laid "all the angels shouted for joy" (Job 38:7). How they fell prostrate at the sight! Is it possible to grasp that heavenly scene? With everything God ever did, from ages past:

> Day and night the smoking incense of praise ascended before him from golden vials held by spirits who bowed in reverence; the harps of myriads of cherubim and seraphim continually thrilled with his praise, and the voices of all those mighty hosts were ever eloquent in adoration . . . Can you imagine to yourselves the sweetness of that harmony that perpetually poured into the ear of . . . God?[3]

Such pleasure and worship to drink in! But we still haven't considered what utterly steals his heart.

If you were God, where could you go to be impressed? After all, you have created everyone and everything. It's all wonderful, doubtless, but lesser than you. Conversation with any of your creatures, even the grandest, costs an infinite lowering of yourself. What could truly entertain your limitless mind? What idea would intrigue you? Whose company would charm you? Whose character and accomplishments take you aback? Where could you find beauty and grace enough to ravish *you*?

There is only one answer. Nothing can satisfy an infinite being but an infinite being. For God, the real intoxication comes as he stares in the mirror.

Where is this mirror?

It's in the Trinity.

Eternities before the cosmos, before the angels, prior to heaven itself—the one and only God existed as three persons. Father, Son, and Holy Spirit. To deny this, you cannot be a Christian. Yet to fathom it, you would have to be one of the Three.

God has therefore never been alone. Three-As-One, he draws life and being and ultimate enjoyment from no one but himself. He sustains his own existence and fans the flame of his own emotional life. He is his own best friend.

The Spirit is the quiet One. Sharing equal deity and status with the others, he nevertheless eternally flows from the Father and Son. His task is to honor the Son by applying to us the benefits of Jesus' death and resurrection. The Father and Son both "send" him. The Spirit doesn't resent this. He has never resented it. The Three have eternally agreed to this. It's the Spirit's very nature to point to the Son. He knows exactly how the Son and Father think, and burns with love to them, for the Three are God together. The Father and Son love the Spirit for this.

But in the Bible, it's the Son who commands center stage. He is God, absolute divinity, on a par with the Father and the Spirit in every way. The Father never tires of bragging about him:

"Here is my . . . chosen one in whom I delight . . ." (Isaiah 42:1).

"This is my Son, whom I love; with him I am well pleased" (Matthew 3:17).

The two are so close that the Son is "in the bosom of the Father"— that is, resting his head on his chest, as close friends did while reclining on carpets around a low dinner table in the Middle East (John 1:18 KJV). Furthermore, God has taken the universe and turned the shop over to the Son: "All things have been committed to me by my Father" (Luke 10:22).

Why does the Father treasure him so? Because he sees himself in his Son. His own perfections are flawlessly reflected there. The Son is God standing in the mirror. In him God sees the fountain of all the intelligence, grandeur, and goodness that ever was. *We* look in the mirror and are almost always disappointed. God looks in the mirror and is riveted. To put it almost ridiculously, if the Father ever had any "cravings," they are more than met by the Son. The eternal Threesome revels together in a swirling dance of mutual love. The Trinity enjoys pleasure beyond comprehension.

Does this blow your mind? It should.

But how does it help the cancer patient coughing up blood? Or the prisoner sitting on death row? Or John McAllister as the ants wage war on him?

Think of it this way. Your car breaks down a hundred miles from home on a back road, and you're no mechanic. The kids are whining and hungry in the backseat. You have misplaced your wallet. You walk half a mile to the nearest town. As you walk, you feel a flu coming. From a phone booth you dial friends, collect—no answer. The auto shops are closed. You scan Main Street for someone to drive you to your car, possibly to peek under the hood, but definitely to find your family a place indoors to wait until someone can wire money.

Whom will you approach? That elderly gentleman stepping from the funeral home, wiping his eyes? Those teenagers shouting put-downs at each other across the street? The middle-aged man storming from that row house, cursing as the door slams? The woman in the tattered coat shuffling down the sidewalk with a dirty-faced kid in tow? Or those two neighbors on adjoining front porches, gossiping and chuckling?

You'll pick the neighbors. Why? Because the others have worries of their own—some of them might even snap your head off. But the neighbors seem in a good mood. People in a good mood are most likely to help others.

God, we might say, is in a good mood. He's not depressed. He's not misery seeking company. He's not some bitter, cosmic Neanderthal with his finger on a nuclear weapon. *God is joy spilling over.* This is where his mercy comes from. The full tank of love he enjoys is splashing out over heaven's walls. He swims in elation and is driven to share it with us. Why? Simply, as he put it, "so that my joy may be in you" (John 15:11).

But God is nobody's water boy. As the solemn Monarch of all, he shares his gladness on his own terms. And those terms call for us to suffer—to suffer, in some measure, as his beloved Son did while on earth. We may not understand his reasons, but we are insane to fight him on this.

He is in ecstasy beyond words.

It is worth *anything* to be his friend.

———————————

Okay, so God likes being God. He's enjoying himself. But does he care about us? Sunshine in Hawaii doesn't stop sleet over Boston—what about sunshine in heaven? Lovers at a candlelit table are notoriously oblivious of others—the café has closed, everyone's gone home, they don't even notice. God too is in love. The Trinity is happy. But we're down here drowning in misery. How do we know he even thinks about us?

We know his Son.

The Son "is the image of the invisible God" (Colossians 1:15). He's "the exact representation of [God's] being" (Hebrews 1:3). "No one has ever seen God, but God the One and Only, who is at the Father's side, has made him known" (John 1:18).[4] Take this reverently: snap a photo of Jesus and you've got God on film.

What did God look like as he walked in our sandals? He was likable. People enjoyed the kid who worked with his dad at the carpenter's shop in Nazareth. An intelligent boy, yes, but it didn't spoil him—his parents noticed how well he listened. "All spoke well of him" and admired his gracious way with words (Luke 2:51–52; 4:22).

Reaching manhood, he swam against a life of self-indulgence like a salmon to the spawning. Watch him spend his days. Chapter 1 of Mark is a documentary, a typical day in the life. On a Sabbath morning he is attending synagogue at Capernaum-on-the-Lake. There he feeds hungry hearts with a kind of bread no one can buy. Halfway through his sermon a maniac shrieks from the crowd. "Come out!" the Teacher shouts. The offending demon instantly and hatefully obeys, and the poor man is restored. The service ends, and now it's to Simon and Andrew's modest home. But Simon's mother-in-law is bedridden with fever, a common killer. Jesus doesn't speak from across the room—he goes to her, takes her hand, and helps her up. Her brow becomes cool and she serves them food.

The sun sets. This means that the Sabbath is over and work is now allowed—work like carrying one's sick in a stretcher to the house down the street. Did you hear that she was cured today by you-know-who? They come, "all the sick and demon-possessed. The whole town gathered at the door, and Jesus healed many who had various diseases. He also drove out many demons. . . ."

But early next morning, before anyone knows, he slips out into the dark and finds a quiet field away from town. His companions have to search for him. There he is—praying again. Don't you know every-body's looking for you?

He knows. But, "Let's go somewhere else—to the nearby villages—so I can preach there also. That is why I have come." So begins the most selfless three-and-a-half years ever lived.

A leper throws himself on the ground. "Lord, if you are willing, you can make me clean." Breaking all protocol and natural revulsion, Jesus reaches forward. "I am willing." Not for a very long time has the man been touched. Sickly white skin blushes, and a neighbor can return home (Luke 5:12–13).

A somber crowd funnels out through the town gate at Nain. They carry a dead man, the only son of his mother, a widow. Who will care for her now? Jesus and the disciples are approaching the town. As the two groups pass each other, Jesus stops. Eyes shift nervously. He's actu-ally going to *touch* the bier. Some in the crowd are protective. What right does a stranger have? But they don't know his mind or his power, for "when the Lord saw her, his heart went out to her." He speaks to the woman—"Don't cry"—then to the dead man—"Get up." And he does (Luke 7:11–15).

That is how it goes with blind beggars, spine-twisted women, and people who have run out of wine at weddings.

A boat drifts on Lake Galilee. How quiet except for the wind snap-ping the sail. Lately, there have been so many people—the Master and his close friends scarcely have time to eat. So they've taken this little getaway together. But the crowd has figured out where they will land and runs around the water's edge to meet them. The outing is ruined, but "When Jesus landed . . . he had compassion on them, because they were like sheep without a shepherd. So he began teaching them many things" (Mark 6:34).

As the sun dips, many sick people feel perky again, many deaf folks are hearing a day's gossip for the first time, and everyone's soul is filled. But their stomachs are empty. "Send them away to buy supper," his dis-ciples urge him. But he says, "This is a lonely place; where would they go? What food can you find?" Some kid's mom has packed him a lunch he didn't eat. Jesus looks in the basket, they have a prayer, and five thou-sand people need a good stretch and a belly-rub before heading home.

Who does Jesus do all this for? Polite society? Most of them get upset and leave after they hear a thing or two he says. It's the everyday people who really take to him—some fishermen, a tax-raker, two spinsters and their unmarried brother. Jesus goes out of his way for folks carrying just a little too much baggage. There was that lady with the bleeding problem—you hate to even mention it. He was pushing through the crowd to reach some little girl who was failing fast when the woman grabs his robe, hoping not to be noticed. He turns around and she sets to crying and it makes a scene. But he's not angry at all. "Daughter," he called her, "your faith has healed you. Go in peace" (Luke 8:48).

Then there was that graveyard man—the one who ran around naked and screaming and made everyone not want to attend funerals. But Jesus had a way with him, and by the time Jesus was done the fellow had clothes on and everything, sitting like a kindergartner with folded hands on desk. No one ever begged so hard for Jesus to take him along.

Condemned criminals, half-breeds, short guys with too much money, women whose homes you visited only after dark—these were the people he went after. He washed their feet and went to their parties. But you never got the sense that his hands were dirty afterwards. Children liked to tug on his clothes and crawl on his lap. He saved his anger for the self-important, or for his followers when they tried to shoo kids away, or for when they got to talking about "calling fire down from heaven" on folks who weren't buying the message.

That doesn't mean he went easy on sin—no store-front preacher in Harlem ever so vividly stoked a congregation's image of a brimstone lake. But people who were sorry about themselves and sick with how they had acted never met with such mercy. Take that incident the night Peter tried to blend in at the courtyard—the denials, the rooster crowing. Three days later when Jesus sent word to the Eleven that everything was all right, he made sure that one hurting pup in particular got the message: "Go, tell his disciples *and Peter* . . ." (Mark 16:7). Later still, he predicted in front of the fisherman's friends that the elderly Peter would one day distinguish himself by a brave death for the Master's sake.

He healed the severed ear of the very one arresting him. He rescued the soul of that pitiful wretch who was crucified next to him. He tread lightly on the sorry doubts of Thomas on the evening of his rising, in the room with the bolted door. How he wept at the graveside of a friend and spoke the gentle word to the most timid among us! He fulfilled in every way the ancient and sacred promise: "A bruised reed he will not break, and a smoldering wick he will not snuff out" (Isaiah 42:3).

"Very impressive of Jesus," we say. "But what about the Father? There's a little too much Old Testament in him for my taste—all that lightning and thunder on Mount Sinai. He's in heaven enjoying himself. But does he care about us?"

Listen to the eye-opening words of the Son of God: "I tell you the truth, the Son can do nothing by himself; *he can do only what he sees his Father doing*, because whatever the Father does the Son also does" (John 5:19).

Does the Father care?! The healer from Galilee never lifted a bent blade of grass without watching his Father do it first. Jesus was moved at the sight of the straining, clueless crowds—but a millennium earlier it was written of Jehovah: "As a father has compassion on his children, so the LORD has compassion on those who fear him; for he knows how we are formed, he remembers that we are dust" (Psalm 103:13–14).

We know Jesus took pity on the orphans, but Hosea said of the Father: "In you the fatherless find compassion." Yes, Jesus wept at the tomb of Lazarus, but of the Father we learn, "His loved ones are very precious to him and he does not lightly let them die." Christ defended the poor, railed against the oppressions of the rich, and overturned tables of dirty money in the temple—but centuries before, Jehovah hurled his prophets at a partying, poor-be-damned culture: "Woe to those who make unjust laws, to those who issue oppressive decrees, to deprive the poor of their rights and withhold justice from the oppressed of my people, making widows their prey and robbing the fatherless. What will you do on the day of reckoning when disaster comes from afar?" (Hosea 14:3; Psalm 116:15 LB; Amos 5:7–12, 18).

The Lamb of God turned his cheek to the smiters and pled clemency for his murderers—but we read of Jehovah: "The LORD is compassionate and gracious, slow to anger, abounding in love. He will not always accuse, nor will he harbor his anger forever; he does not treat us as our sins deserve or repay us according to our iniquities" (Psalm 103:8–10).

It was the God of Moses, the Holy One of Israel, the subject of Ezekiel's visions and Daniel's apocalypses, who forbade Israel to curse the deaf or trip the blind. *He* took pity on Hagar sobbing in the desert, her water skin empty, sitting a bowshot from her baby because she said, "I cannot watch the boy die." *He* promised a son to Hannah who wept so bitterly that she appeared drunk over disappointment with empty arms and an empty womb. He says to anyone with a heart to believe: "*The LORD longs to be gracious to you;* he rises to show you compassion" (Leviticus 19:14; Genesis 21:15–17; 1 Samuel 1; Isaiah 30:18).

Yet he also says, "It has been granted to you on behalf of Christ not only to believe on him, but also to suffer for him" (Philippians 1:29).

Our call to suffer comes from a God tender beyond description. If we do not cling to this through life's worst, we will misread everything and grow to hate him.

But now to something about him even more profound.

## Three

# THE SUFFERING
# GOD

Five centuries before Christ, Xerxes, King of Persia, organized the largest land-and-sea force ever witnessed and crossed the Dardanelles into Europe. His goal was to thrash Greece for its role in a rebellion against his father, Darius the Great. No suffering was too extreme to require of his subjects during the campaign, although his own safety and comfort were paramount.

Five centuries later the Son of God, King of Kings, by himself crossed the chasm between divinity and humanity and walked onto earth. His goal was to endure the thrashing due his creatures for their rebellion against his father, Jehovah. To this day he requires suffering of all his followers, some of it intense—but only for their good, and never equaling what he himself passed through.

Consider the contrast.

Near the start of Xerxes' march, Pythius of Lydia, rumored to be the second-richest man on earth, lavishly entertained the king and his army. He then made an astounding offer—to furnish Xerxes' complete war expenses. Taken aback, the king warmly thanked Pythius but declined. Soon afterwards the wealthy Lydian sought Xerxes again with a small favor to ask. All five of his sons were serving in the campaign against Greece, and he himself was getting along in years—could the eldest son alone remain home to care for his father? The historian Herodotus gives the king's reaction:

> Xerxes at once gave orders that the men to whom such duties
> fell should find Pythius' eldest son and cut him in half and put the

two halves on each side of the road, for the army to march out between them. The order was performed.

And now between the halves of the young man's body the advance of the army began.[1]

This was typical of the Persian king—a minor glitch in the schedule, a decision to be settled before lunch. All in a day's work. Yet he boasted that his expedition was "for the benefit of all my subjects."

Now consider the Son of God. His gentle kingdom is described in the four gospels. The scenes will mean more to us, however, if we don't flip the pages too fast getting there. Let's not burst into the room where he sits with his disciples. Let's watch his reign through the keyhole first. Let's stand back twenty centuries or so before Jesus ever came and see what led up to God becoming man—see things that foreshadowed his arrival—things that hint about the tone of his rule. Let's start, of all places, in Genesis.

In Genesis 15 God appears to Abraham.[2] He promises him a baby boy and more great-grandchildren than Abraham can see stars. But the nomad's beard is not as dark as it was, and the midwife has never shooed him out of the tent and told him to go boil some water. God also promises him a country, the very one they are speaking in. But other people already live there. How can the old shepherd be sure?

"So the LORD said to him, 'Bring me a heifer, a goat and a ram, each three years old, along with a dove and a young pigeon.' Abraham brought all these to him, cut them in two and arranged the halves opposite each other" (Genesis 15:9–10).

The sun is setting. Abraham dozes off uneasily. A blackness thicker than night settles on him, and a deep dread. It is God come close. This time the Lord repeats his promise with words more solemn than before. Still, they are only words. But look! A little stove appears—like the everyday earthenware bread-baking jars where the coals glow inside and the dough is pressed against the outside. A burning torch rises from inside the stove. Abraham shudders—he senses that God is inside the stove and torch. The Lord is about to "cut a covenant." Having promised Abraham something, he will now bind himself to it with chains that cannot snap. The stove and torch rise by themselves and move toward the carcasses. Abraham cannot believe what he sees. The Dreadful One, so great that he has never even told Abraham his name, passes between the bloody pieces. He is speaking by his actions. "If I fail to keep my word to you and your descendants," he is saying, "I will make myself like these animals—*I will saw myself in two.*"

"Say what?" Xerxes would say if he knew.

But there was no need for any sawing. The Lord kept his word. Abraham had a boy, who in turn had a boy, who had bunk-beds full of boys, who each married nice Jewish girls—and soon there was an Israel. God carried the nation from birth "as a father carries his son." When Egypt enslaved them he "heard their groaning" and "was concerned about them." He loved them and engraved their names on the palm of his hand. He gave them the country he had promised to Abraham. When they fell into trouble, he rode to the rescue because he "delighted in" them and "could bear Israel's misery no longer." He "caused them to be pitied by all who held them captive." They were his "sheep," his "wife," his "inheritance"—"the apple of his eye," "the people close to his heart." Mothers would forget their nursing babies before he forgot them—he swore it.[3]

But *they* forgot *him*. Even though he had adopted them forever at Mount Sinai. Even though he had handwritten their family agreement on pages of stone. They had stood, knees shaking as the mountain breathed fire, swearing up and down to stick to his wishes. Like a bride at the altar who can scarcely wait for the "I do"—they couldn't spit the words out quickly enough: "We will do everything the LORD has said; we will obey" (Exodus 24:7).

But they lied. The nation that was given rest in Canaan grew restless. Jehovah and his commands started feeling like a coat a few sizes too small. *Normal* countries—Israel began mumbling—had less demanding gods, visible ones you could see and know were there and could carve into a shape that suited you. *Their* worship services ended with dessert, pleasure on the heels of prayer, brotherly-sisterly fellowship with those lovely priests and priestesses who tended so well to the worshiper's libidino-spiritual needs.

In no time the nation's hand was in the cookie jar. One sin led to another, and soon there wasn't a commandment that Israel hadn't broken. They set their children on fire at the shrine of that grisly god Molech. They sank lower than the degenerates who had infected Canaan before them. They got creative with sin. Why didn't they just urinate on the tablets of Moses?

"The LORD, the God of their fathers, sent word to them through his messengers again and again, because he had pity on his people and on his dwelling place. But they mocked God's messengers, despised his words and scoffed at his prophets" (2 Chronicles 36:15–16).

The one race equipped to shine truth into the world eclipsed the very sun with its own evil example. Who *now* deserved to be sawn in two?

But it wasn't just Israel. Every nation on earth spurned what little light it had—countries where God's rain had softened the fields and his sun had ripened the grapes. God's kindness failed—it failed to fan any spark of human righteousness—there was none to fan. Jews and Gentiles alike sickened the stomach of their maker, causing him to write: "There is no one righteous, not even one; there is no one who understands, no one who seeks God. . . . They have together become worthless" (Romans 3:10–12, quoting from Psalms 14:1–3; 53:1–3; Ecclesiastes 7:20).

God brooded. His anger began to stir the lid. Is this how his kindness is repaid? There must be an accounting. One by one he let the nations fall into war. Each in turn was overrun and exiled—Egypt, Moab, Phoenicia, Edom, and the powerhouses of the east: Assyria, Babylon, Persia. All the while they kicked Israel between them like a stone on a dirt road. It did no good. None of them truly repented. Every nation cursed its fate and whatever gods it had invented. War, exile, hell-on-earth—and after death, eternal hell—these satisfied God's justice, but that was all. They did for people what jail-time does for a criminal—the gavel falls, the sentence is read, and the prisoner goes tuition-free to a barbed-wired Graduate School of Evil. There, in the humid darkness, the sick fungus in his heart flourishes as he rubs against other infested souls.

For God, this was not good enough. He had created humans to mirror him, not to be miniatures of Lucifer. Something was needed to cut through the stench and salvage this pathetic race. Some medicine more potent than anyone knew of. Some procedure. Some life-giving surgery.

The king became Great Physician. Summoning his compassion and his plumbless wisdom he conceived of a surgery. How to save the patients without trivializing their guilt? (They had *knowingly* spread the fatal sickness among them.) How to cure them without letting the horror of the disease ever be forgotten? How to mingle mercy with justice? How to slice the cancer from their souls and leave no scar?

He prepared for the procedure by donning not gloves and a lab coat but a mortal body. Did it feel a few sizes too small? He stretched himself upon the operating table.

His hand reached for a saw.

---

His last true comfort was that final moment before slipping from his mother's womb. Then, a borrowed feeding trough met him, and the story of his pain began. "Since the children have flesh and blood, he too shared in their humanity" (Hebrews 2:14).

Did he taste tension in the milk of his mother as she hastily fled in the night from those searching to murder him? What did he feel when he grew up to learn what his presence had cost the baby boys of Bethlehem? How old was he before realizing what people thought about his mother and her morals? Did the young boy with his family in Egypt feel like a refugee?

Nazareth became his home town when the danger had passed—a chalk-soiled frontier perch, overlooking the great trade routes of the Esdraelon Valley below but never a part of them. Nothing much happened there. The village never received mention with the hundreds of towns listed in the roll calls of the Old Testament. "Nazareth! Can anything good come from there?" (John 1:46).

As he wielded the mallet and plied the adz in his father's shop, he grew used to soldiers passing outside the window. Their plumed helmets and pagan insignia reminded him daily that foreigners owned his country. In another era he himself might have ruled, for he was royalty, or so his genealogy ran.

We never read that as a young man he drew appreciative glances from the girls in his neighborhood. There is no story of courtship or mention of romance, and he was never to marry. "He had no beauty or majesty to attract us to him, nothing in his appearance that we should desire him" (Isaiah 53:2). Instead, he was known for his solitary strolls in the hills. By the time he was thirty, those long walks had done their work. He sensed it was time to go public.

Some curious fellow wearing camel-skins began drawing crowds in a remote spot near the River Jordan. He was fiery, this one. The man was preaching sermons about Someone who was coming; people needed to get ready. The rugged preacher had never met Jesus—possibly didn't even know his name.[4] But his sole purpose in life was to prepare everyone for the Someone just around the corner.

Jesus rounded the corner. He went to the Jordan and stood in line behind hundreds who carried consciences with memories of things he had never even *thought* about. One by one they bowed to the baptizer's cleansing water, but when Jesus stepped up the man balked. His eyes searched. Certainly there was no need. People might misunderstand. So they might—but Jesus said, "It is fitting for us," and bent low (Matthew 3:15 TCNT).

Then the Spirit compelled him into the wastelands to know hunger of more than one sort. For forty days and nights he traced the ravines and heard the wild animals—a day for every year his race had failed their test while plodding sinfully through a different wilderness. No manna here. But at the end there was bread by the loaf, piping hot, dripping with butter, simply for his commanding it to be. A presence suggested to him: "Can you smell it in your mind? But what's that sound? Ah, it must be the complaining of your stomach. Your face is pale; your knees must be so very weak." (Charm itself smiled and urged.) But no, the Bread of Life must not indulge today, not in this way. Well then, what did he think of this flight to the temple heights? Ah, the sight of people again, down below. How they would marvel at the spectacle of his leaping from the pinnacle, only to be floated down by adoring seraphs, proving beyond all question his identity. Did he recall the attention and esteem that had bathed him in that former world so far away and long ago? No, he must refrain; this was not the time. Very well. But then, certainly he would enjoy this whirlwind tour of the planet and its kingdoms from the perspective of, say, the southern Alps or perhaps the Himalayas. Ooh, the splendor of India, the courts of China, the intrigue of Persia—Scythia, Gaul, the far-off coasts of Britain. Subjects to be had by the millions. It would take only a dropping to the knee, a slight but respectful genuflection, nothing much.

But he looked away. No, no . . . he must not. He could not.

He did not.

So the enticer vanished. He would call again at an appropriate time. He had a perfect occasion in mind.

This was how the Rescue began, the most unexpected, set-on-its-head campaign a king ever launched. Very unlike Xerxes. For as long as sovereigns have reigned, citizens have been asked to sacrifice for king and country—their lands, their money, their children. But this king stepped from the merriment of his palace, abandoned the cheery fireplace and the spread table, resigned his luxuries and lands, and set out to perish for his citizens.

The people at first found him delightful, the way New Englanders welcome winter's first snow before it becomes inconvenient and stays too long. They flocked so enthusiastically that merely getting around soon became cumbersome. "See that no one knows about this," he strictly urged two men who had been blind until just minutes ago. "But they went out and spread the news about him over all that region" (Matthew 9:30–31). "See that you don't tell anyone," he ordered a leper with brand new baby skin. "Instead he went out and began to talk freely, spreading the news. As a result, Jesus could no longer enter a town openly but stayed outside in lonely places. Yet the people still came to him from everywhere" (Mark 1:45).

They poured out of Galilee's highlands and Judea's nooks and crannies to enjoy the free medical services, eat his spectacular lunches, and watch him make fools of the Pharisees. "How that fellow does put a sanctimonious nose out of joint!" people remarked. It seemed that every day a different poor stooge from the temple elite would stand in the crowds and yell out questions, trying to trip him up. But they always went away with egg on their faces. Sometimes the big brass themselves would come, icily cordial, armed with quotes and cross-references. But they too crashed and burned, their faces glowing hues of red that no one had ever seen before.

Back at the high priest's mansion they would gather for hushed discussions. What should they do with this Galilean embarrassment? They kept coming back to one rather extreme suggestion. The public would have been horrified to know of it, but Jesus knew, and the knowledge accompanied him everywhere.

The first adult casualty of the Rescue happened in one of King Herod's dungeons. No one saw it coming, not even the elite, not even Herod. But at a black-tie affair in the palace, Herod's step-daughter took to the floor and began catching the rhythm of the music. The girl's body became liquid, and the king was seized by the eyes. He found himself showing off for her in front of his guests—gushing words the way a man does when his brain's not calling the shots. "And is there anything I can do for *you*?" Her eyes questioned him. "Really," he said, "anything." An almost feral look came over her face. Time to score big-time with her mother, her mother who hated a certain outdoor preacher. "Yes," said the girl with a toss of her hair. "There is something." Before the evening was over the baptizer's head was presented to the party on a platter. The forerunner was gone; now the full weight of public attention fell on his Master.

Meanwhile Jesus preached. "Repent, for the kingdom of heaven is near."

"Repent" had a quaint tone to it. It smacked of Amos and Isaiah and other national heroes of yesteryear. Many listeners thought, "I know some people who should take this to heart." But sometimes the Preacher got to implying that they themselves—good, tax-paying, Torah-reading citizens—needed repentance as well, thus missing the target with his wit and hurting innocent bystanders.

His hometown was the first to lose confidence in him. Sometimes folks who know a person when he's young, before he becomes famous and things go to his head, later have the best read on his character. "Many who heard him were amazed. 'Where did this man get these things?' they asked. '. . . Isn't this the carpenter? Isn't this Mary's son and the brother of James, Joseph, Judas and Simon? Aren't his sisters here with us?' And they took offense at him" (Mark 6:2–3).

The eyebrow-raisers included his own brothers. One time when he entered the room they quickly became all seriousness; suppressing grins they winked at one another and urged him "go more public with his important message." Such skepticism led Jesus to heal fewer people in his old neighborhood than anywhere—naturally confirming the neighbors' doubts—and the gossip began. No doubt even without this attitude in Nazareth, popular opinion would have begun dividing. "Among the crowds there was widespread whispering about him. Some said, 'He is a good man.' Others replied, 'No, he deceives the people'" (John 7:12).

His goodness actually scared people. One village asked him to move on just after he had healed their town's most notorious psychotic. Some whom he greatly helped didn't even turn to thank him. It became common to hear people wonder out loud why Jesus attended parties when the baptist had contented himself with wild honey and fried locusts. His rich and well-connected admirers found themselves in a catch–22. They loved him, but anyone following him could count on getting ejected from the synagogue—and "they loved praise from men more than praise from God" (John 12:42–43). A few ugly incidents increased their fears—times when his sermon insights got an audience so incensed that the congregation started fingering large stones. But Jesus never backed down. He kept to the furrow he was plowing.

Because his work meant steady travel, plodding the serpentine paths between towns, and since he tried to avoid autograph seekers, he often slept in odd places—a boat, an olive grove. As he traveled—preaching, debating, healing, and listening—the entire universe leaned every hour on his divinity. The North American brown bear took his Creator's cue to begin hibernation. The Arctic tern awaited signal to leave its breeding grounds eight degrees latitude south of the North Pole and go winter in the Antarctic. A female water spider listened to his echoes in her brain tell how to trap air bubbles and house her eggs in silk at the pond's bottom. But the teacher himself, God now-become-human, often went without shelter. "Foxes have holes and birds of the air have nests, but the Son of Man has no place to lay his head" (Matthew 8:20).

No place to lay his head? The Jewish High Council had come to definite opinions about where the man's head might best be laid. For them, it was no longer a question of "if" but of "when." No one could deny that this fellow pulled off miracles. But his power clearly came from the dark side. How could anyone with a decent feel for Moses advise some panhandler to run around waving his mat on the Sabbath? What would possess him to eat from the same plate as undesirables? If he were any sort of prophet he'd know what kind of vermin were always hanging on to him. Who did he think he was? Oh yes, his "Father" sent him. Ugh! He wouldn't know the Holy One if he saw him. Why should we let this twisted genius upset the population? Why jeopardize our tenuous relationship with the Roman governor? If we're not careful, this self-appointed world-fixer will have us cleaning our teeth on Italian spear tips.

Then again . . . the Roman presence wasn't an altogether bad thing. True, the Gentiles had final say regarding punishment in capital cases. But if the authorities could be convinced to act, this trouble-maker's last few hours at the hands of Roman justice could be satisfactorily unpleasant. Just as bad as a good stoning, really, and last far longer.

How best to make it happen?

---

By the flicker of oil lamps he looked up from dinner and studied the faces around the room. Twelve familiar expressions. They were his friends, all but one. The miles they had walked together! Yet how could they fathom his thoughts tonight? Can the child ever really understand his father? Solomon was right: "Each heart knows its own bitterness." These were the ones he had come for—natives of this sad planet who had never tasted what had delighted him in that other Place—so slow to learn—so dull in the most urgent of matters—always scrapping about who deserved top honors in a coming world they couldn't possibly grasp. But he loved them.

Very deliberately he broke the loaf, keeping his composure as he watched the crumbs fall. The wine ran down his throat as the true wine began to run cold in his veins. Divinity in a human body ate and drank with his friends. He sensed that familiar presence he had met in the wilderness—the time was close. Judas stood to leave; their eyes met. Do it quickly. The presence that had awaited outside in the dark now stole invisibly into Judas's very essence. For the next few hours, the most distilled evil in the universe would personally operate through the body of a disciple of Jesus.

The Master spoke quietly to them a final time, they sang a psalm, and it was time to go. Out into the darkness they slipped. Through a city gate, down the steep ravine, up into the hill of olive trees. Eleven lambs and a shepherd in the night. What would become of these friends, his only earthly support in this hour? Satan already had the twelfth one, the absent one, by the throat—soon he'd be swinging under a tree limb, gasping and white, facing much worse after his breathing stopped. One of the eleven would soon race terrified into the shadows, stark naked in his haste, scraping his shins, bloodying his soul. All of them would turn tail, near-wetting themselves with fear, shrinking into corners. The loud, friendly fisherman was being invisibly outwitted even now—being set up for a special roughing-up tonight. Clueless, he had just bragged of the noble deeds he would surely rise to. But before morning he would slice off a man's ear, intending far more—he would say unerasable things to a servant girl by an open fire, he would shiver at a rooster's call, and would consider, through his sobbing, whether to find a tree like Judas did. Prophecy-fulfilled was at the doorstep: "Strike the shepherd, and the sheep will be scattered" (Zechariah 13:7).

They reached the olive press. Would his three closest friends mind coming just a little further to pray a stone's throw away? Three of the gospel writers would later tell of Jesus' foreboding just then—about his warning the disciples to pray for inward strength against the tempter—prayers for *their* sakes. But Matthew noticed and would one day record a particular phrase that the others didn't. "My soul is ready to die with sorrow," the Shepherd had said. "Wait here and stay awake with me" (Matthew 26:38).[5]

Stay awake "with me."

For the only time in his life the Shepherd was asking for something from them. *He wanted human comfort that night.* But somebody's yawn tipped the first domino, and in no time everyone's prayers had degenerated into dreams.

Now, the Son of God dropped to the dirt in an olive grove and vomited in his soul at the prospect before him. Eleven men who would later change world history—some, accustomed to working all night on their fishing boats—could not keep awake for the scene. Yet sixty feet away their eternal destinies were being fought over. Except for the heaving of those shoulders that bore the weight of the world, nothing could be seen in that shadowy spot where the Son of God groaned. But the bleachers of heaven filled to capacity that night—and hell strained its neck to see how the spectacle in that lonely acre would end. The Father gazed down and gave his sober nod. The Son stared back, and bowed his acceptance. A line of men and torches snaked down from the city, through the blackness, toward the garden. God in the flesh saw them coming through tear-blurred eyes that refused to blink.

"It's time to get up," he quietly told the eleven.

The torches arrived. The sheep fled. The shepherd stood. The hurricane struck.

Who can describe the whirlwind of the succeeding hours? Could so many lies really be told at a single trial? Could so much sin be poured into one court room? The drowning ones he had come to rescue screamed that he be thrown from the lifeboat. God had claimed to be God—what could be worse! God had kept his sworn promise to send a Messiah—how ridiculous! In the wee hours of that morning, Sodom and Gomorrah came to look virginal next to Jerusalem. Later, in the brighter light of day and to the background of a pressing crowd screaming insanities, Pilate washed away centuries of Roman justice in his finger bowl.

The Savior was now thrown to men quite different from the eleven. The face that Moses had begged to see—was forbidden to see—was slapped bloody (Exodus 33:19–20). The thorns that God had sent to curse the earth's rebellion now twisted around his own brow. His back, buttocks, and the rear of his legs felt the whip—soon they looked like the plowed Judean fields outside the city. "On with the blindfold!" someone shouts. "That's it—now spin him. Who hit you? Heh, heh." By the time the spitting is through, more saliva is on him than in him. No longer can he be recognized. "Cut him down from the post! Send him toting his crossbar to the playground." Up Skull Hill to the welcome of other poorly paid legionnaires enjoying themselves.

"On your back with you!" One raises a mallet to sink in the spike. But the soldier's heart must continue pumping as he readies the prisoner's wrist. Someone must sustain the soldier's life minute by minute, for no man has this power on his own. Who supplies breath to his lungs? Who gives energy to his cells? Who holds his molecules together? *Only by the Son* do "all things hold together" (Colossians 1:17). The victim wills that the soldier live on—he grants the warrior's continued existence. The man swings.

As the man swings, the Son recalls how he and the Father first designed the medial nerve of the human forearm—the sensations it would be capable of. The design proves flawless—the nerve performs exquisitely. "Up you go!" They lift the cross. God is on display in his underwear, and can scarcely breathe.

But these pains are a mere warm-up to his other and growing dread. He begins to feel a foreign sensation. Somewhere during this day an unearthly foul odor began to waft, not around his nose, but his heart. He *feels* dirty. Human wickedness starts to crawl upon his spotless being—the living excrement from our souls. The apple of his Father's eye turns brown with rot.

His Father! He must face his Father like this!

From heaven the Father now rouses himself like a lion disturbed, shakes his mane, and roars against the shriveling remnant of a man hanging on a cross. *Never* has the Son seen the Father look at him so, never felt even the least of his hot breath. But the roar shakes the unseen world and darkens the visible sky. The Son does not recognize these eyes.

"Son of Man! Why have you behaved so? You have cheated, lusted, stolen, gossiped—murdered, envied, hated, lied. You have cursed, robbed, overspent, overeaten—fornicated, disobeyed, embezzled, and blasphemed. Oh, the duties you have shirked, the children you have abandoned! Who has ever so ignored the poor, so played the coward, so belittled my name? Have you *ever* held your razor tongue? What a self-righteous, pitiful drunk—*you*, who molest young boys, peddle killer drugs, travel in cliques, and mock your parents. Who gave you the boldness to rig elections, foment revolutions, torture animals, and worship demons? Does the list never end! Splitting families, raping virgins, acting smugly, playing the pimp—buying politicians, practicing extortion, filming pornography, accepting bribes. You have burned down buildings, perfected terrorist tactics, founded false religions, traded in slaves—relishing each morsel and bragging about it all. I hate, I *loathe* these things in you! Disgust for everything about you consumes me! Can you not feel my wrath?"

Of course the Son is innocent. He is blamelessness itself. The Father knows this. But the divine pair have an agreement, and the unthinkable must now take place. Jesus will be treated as if personally responsible for every sin ever committed.[6]

The Father watches as his heart's treasure, the mirror-image of himself, sinks drowning into raw, liquid sin. Jehovah's stored rage against humankind from every century explodes in a single direction.

"Father! Father! Why have you forsaken me?!"

But heaven stops its ears. The Son stares up at the One who cannot, who will not, reach down or reply.

The Trinity had planned it. The Son endured it. The Spirit enabled him. The Father rejected the Son whom he loved. Jesus, the God-man from Nazareth, perished. The Father accepted his sacrifice for sin and was satisfied. The Rescue was accomplished.

God set down his saw.

*This* is who asks us to trust him when he calls on us to suffer.

# Four

# DOES HE REALLY EXPECT ME TO SUFFER?

No doubt some believers will say:

*Precisely! Thank you for reminding us that Christ suffered immeasurably for us. But his whole reason was so that we wouldn't have to suffer. The Trinity is blissful in heaven and wants us to be joyful too. Jesus' compassion drove him to open blind eyes and rouse lifeless limbs—he never glorified illness or eulogized pain and sorrow. Since "Jesus Christ is the same yesterday and today and forever," it's ludicrous to think he has now changed his mind. Why would Christ ask us to buy with our tears what he has already paid for? Isaiah 53 says: "He took up our infirmities and carried our sorrows," and that "by his wounds we are healed." Suffering is the work of the Devil—Jesus came to destroy the work of the Devil. Satan is totally bad—God is totally good. God doesn't stoop to using Satan's tools. Although he can turn our trials into good, he doesn't wish hard times on us, let alone send them. What he really wants is to bless us. He wants us to believe his good promises—and free him to shatter the prison of misery that Satan builds around us and thus glorify himself.*

All over the world you meet with this view. Russia, Romania, Budapest, Baltimore, Africa, Appalachia, London, Little Rock. Many Christians who hold it are of sterling character. They study their Bibles, volunteer in their churches, nurture their families, donate their money, help hurting neighbors, reach out to the poor, care about non-Christians, and show love for Christ and his kingdom everywhere they go. So it's not lightly or mean-spiritedly that these next words come. But the following two chapters are to convince you that the above is a hopeless mixture of truth and error, and misses the core of why Jesus came. Here's the terrain we'll cross.

First, despite Christ's compassionate death for our sins, God's plan—not plan B or C or D, but his *plan*—calls for all Christians to suffer, sometimes intensely. To encourage us, he may write some light moments into the script of our lives—he may include adventure or romance. An amusing situation will get us chuckling, and an occasional twist of plot may delight us to tears, for God loves to give. But without fail, some scenes are going to break your heart, some of your favorite characters will die, and the movie may end earlier than you wish.

Second, God's plan is specific. He doesn't say, "Into each life a little rain must fall," then aim a hose in earth's general direction and see who gets the wettest. He doesn't reach for a key, wind up nature with its sunny days and hurricanes, then sit back and watch the show. He doesn't let Satan prowl about totally unrestricted. He doesn't believe in a hands-off policy of governing. He's not our planet's absent landlord. Rather, he screens the trials that come to each of us—allowing only those that accomplish his good plan, because he takes no joy in human agony. These trials aren't evenly distributed from person to person. This can discourage us, for we are not privy to his reasons. But in God's wisdom and love, every trial in a Christian's life is ordained from eternity past, custom-made for that believer's eternal good, even when it doesn't seem like it. Nothing happens by accident . . . not even tragedy . . . not even sins committed against us.

Third, the core of his plan is to rescue us from our sin. Our pain, poverty, and broken hearts are not his ultimate focus. He cares about them, but they are merely symptoms of the real problem. God cares most—not about making us comfortable—but about teaching us to hate our sins, grow up spiritually, and love him. To do this, he *gives us salvation's benefits only gradually, sometimes painfully gradually.* In other words, he lets us continue to feel much of sin's sting while we're headed for heaven. This constantly reminds us of what we're being delivered from, exposing sin for the poison it is. Thus evil (suffering) is turned on its head to defeat evil (sin)—all to the praise of God's wisdom.

Last, every sorrow we taste will one day prove to be the *best possible thing* that could have happened. We will thank God endlessly in heaven for the trials he sent us here. This is not Disneyland—it is truth.

## GOD'S PLAN INCLUDES SUFFERING

Everyone who takes the Bible seriously, and many who don't, agree that God hates suffering. Jesus spent much of his short life relieving it. In scores of passages God tells us to feed the hungry, clothe the poor, visit inmates, and speak up for the helpless. So when we feel compassion for people in distress, we know that God felt it first. He shows this by raising sick people from their beds—sometimes to the wonder of doctors—in answer to prayer. Every day he grants childless women babies, pulls small-business owners out of financial pits, protects Alzheimer's patients crossing the street, and writes happy endings to sad situations. Even when he has to punish sin, he says it gives him no pleasure (Ezekiel 18:32). In heaven, Eden's curse will be canceled. Sighs and longings will be historical curiosities. Tears will evaporate. Kleenex will go broke.

But it simply doesn't follow that God's *only* relationship to suffering is to relieve it. He specifically says that all who follow him can expect hardship.

*But didn't Jesus hang on a cross so we wouldn't have to suffer hell?* Yes, but not so we wouldn't have to suffer *here*—on earth. Hear the Bible on this:

> "I will show [Paul] how much he must suffer for my name" (Acts 9:16).
> "For it has been granted to you on behalf of Christ . . . to suffer for him . . ." (Philippians 1:29).
> "The sufferings of Christ flow over into our lives . . ." (2 Corinthians 1:5).
> "We must go through many hardships to enter the kingdom of God" (Acts 14:22).

The Bible goes even further. After calling Christians "heirs of God and co-heirs with Christ" it adds—"*if* indeed we share in his sufferings" (Romans 8:17). In other words, no one goes to Christ's heaven who doesn't first share Christ's sufferings.

*But surely*, someone says, *such suffering by Christians is not God's plan, God's best, God's will.* No?

"Those who suffer *according to God's will* should commit themselves
to their faithful Creator and continue to do good" (1 Peter 4:19).
"[Don't] be unsettled by these trials. You know quite well that we
*were destined* for them" (1 Thessalonians 3:2–3).

*But perhaps such passages refer only to religious persecution. Jesus warned
that the world at large would hate his disciples. The high schooler who men-
tions Jesus in English class may later take some verbal hits in the cafeteria.
Outspoken believers in past centuries spent their last moments on earth burning at the stake. A midnight knock on the door from the police still comes to
Christians in some countries. When the Bible promises suffering, it means these
things—not life's other problems. Persecution aside, Christians who live by biblical principles can expect to be happy and healthy.*

To rephrase: Christians can expect mistreatment—but not measles.
The world may hate us—but it can't make us sick. We can't avoid
dying—but we can stave off illness, disabilities, and months of therapy
after car crashes. All this, provided that we claim by faith God's promises
of health.

What's the logic behind this viewpoint? In part, it goes:

1. Disease flows from the curse God pronounced on us after Adam's
   sin in Eden.[1]
2. Jesus came to reverse this curse.
3. Therefore, Christians shouldn't have to live with disease.

Let's examine these points, kick the tires a bit, and see if we still
want to buy them. Number 1 is certainly true. "In Adam's fall, we
sinned all," chanted colonial New England children from their primer.
Until the first sin, no one ever heard of migraine headaches, athlete's
foot, tooth decay, or diabetes. Baseball star Lou Gehrig had no disease
named after him. Dr. Down wasn't honored by a syndrome. Lyme,
Connecticut, wasn't famous for a tick-borne malady studied there. But
one bite of fruit ruined everything. The Evil One, who had prodded
humans to rebel, now became God's tool for punishing that rebellion.
Satan received the nod to do his worst with us. Before long he had Job
in his oven. Jesus blamed Satan for keeping a pitiful woman hunch-
backed for eighteen years (Luke 18:11, 16).

Number 2 is also true. "The reason the Son of God appeared was to destroy the devil's work." Jesus once likened himself to a burglar who ties up a muscular homeowner so he can rob him blind. Satan is the owner. We're the possessions that Jesus steals from under his nose (1 John 3:8; Matthew 12:29).

But the logic breaks down at number 3. We'd all like to think that "Jesus came to take up our diseases—therefore we don't need to put up with them anymore." But that's akin to saying: "There's an oak in every acorn—so take this acorn and start sawing planks for picnic tables," or "Congress just passed a Clean Water Act—so Manhattan residents can start drinking from the East River tomorrow."

Forty years will pass before that white oak is ready for lumbering. Purging industrial ooze will take time, even if Congress can guarantee the outcome. So, with the Rescue. What Jesus began doing to sin and its results won't be complete until the Second Coming. "It is finished" he uttered from the cross—the *purchase* of salvation was complete, the outcome settled with certainty. But the *application* of salvation to God's people was anything but finished.

Think about it. The Messiah came so the lion might one day lie down with the lamb—meanwhile that lion crunched the bones of first-century Christians in the Roman Colosseum. The Bible says we "*have* redemption"—but the day of our redemption is still future.[2] God "*has* saved" us—yet we are still "being saved."[3] Jesus came to "save his people from their sins"—yet "If we claim to be without sin, we deceive ourselves and the truth is not in us."[4] First Corinthians 15:45 calls Jesus the "last Adam" who came to undo the curse triggered by the original Adam—but this summer you'll again wrestle weeds in your garden, and giving birth to your next child will be no picnic. Only in Paradise will it be said, "No longer will there be any curse" (Revelation 22:3).

Yes, Jesus "carried our sorrows." But Paul knew "sorrow" when his prison companion became ill—he confessed to "great *sorrow* and unceasing anguish in my heart" over the spiritual lostness of his race— and he described Christ's apostles as "*sorrowful*, yet always rejoicing."[5] Jesus' death for us didn't keep the Corinthians from being "*sorrowful* as God intended" over their sins (2 Corinthians 7:9). It didn't hinder Jesus himself from saying, "Blessed are you who weep now"—or James from advising us to "grieve, mourn and wail" when we sin.[6]

Yes, Jesus "took up our diseases" (Isaiah 53:4). His cross is our ship to heaven; his miracles gave us glimpses of Paradise; he ladles out foretastes of bliss by a thousand blessings large and small. But they are all just that—glimpses, foretastes. We're not in heaven yet. So, godly Timothy had stomach ailments and "frequent illnesses." Epaphroditus, who hand-delivered Paul's Philippian epistle, "was ill, and almost died." Paul left his friend Trophimus "sick in Miletus." The apostle himself admitted to his Galatian readers, "It was because of an illness that I first preached the gospel to you"—apparently he had detoured to Galatia to recuperate.[7]

Some Christian teachers have explained this by saying, "Paul and his friends lacked faith." But do we really want to go that route? It's more accurate to say, "We and our friends lack humility—we prefer pointing the finger at Christ's apostle rather than considering the possibility that we've been misreading Scripture."

*But doesn't the Bible specifically say that God "heals all my diseases"* (Psalm 103:3)?

Yes, David writes that in Psalm 103. David, who spent months in caves hiding from King Saul, who lost his best friend in war, whose infant son fell ill and died despite David's prayers, whose other son tried to murder his dad and overthrow the government, and who watched in horror as seventy thousand of his subjects died of the plague. But yes, David apparently recovered each time he had gotten sick and was thankful for it.

*But David's sufferings were avoidable—punishments for his sins* (2 Samuel 12:10, 14). *If we live godly lives, we shouldn't have to go through the same.*

Let him who is without sin cast the first stone at the shepherd whose slingshot killed Goliath! Do we really suppose we are spiritual superiors to this "man after [God's] own heart" whose writing makes up part of the Bible (1 Samuel 13:14)? Didn't Jesus imply that our secret lusts and hatred are a match for David's adultery and murder (Matthew 5:21, 27–28)? Are we above the other psalmist who confessed in prayer, "Before I was afflicted I went astray, but now I obey your word" (Psalm 119:67)? Think twice if you feel superior to these men—you don't know your own heart. "The Lord disciplines those he loves, and he punishes everyone he accepts as a son" (Hebrews 12:6).

*Yet surely healing and prosperity are included in Jesus' promise: "I will do whatever you ask in my name . . . You may ask me for anything in my name, and I will do it"* (John 14:13–14).

Profound verses. They rebuke us all. May we all repent and pray more fearlessly. But let's examine his promise closely. "I will do whatever you ask." Sounds pretty good. "I will do whatever you ask *in my name.*" What does that mean? Surely, more than mouthing "In Jesus' name" at a prayer's end just before the Amen. Rather, it's to pray admitting that God hears me only because I'm the guest of his Son. It's to pray in the bold but respectful way that Jesus did while here. It's to pray for the things Jesus taught us to. What things were they? He summarizes them in the Lord's Prayer: spiritual things, eternal things. "May Your kingdom spread . . . May Your plans be accomplished on this rebellious planet . . . Forgive the way I've treated You . . . Keep me from falling for the evil that allures me" (see Matthew 6:9–13). Only one request in six deals with earth-bound matters, and there he taught us to pray, "Give us this day our daily bread"—not, "Bless the Dow Jones Average and please be with the NASDAQ."

Of course it's not *wrong* to pray beyond our basic needs—to pray that Susie will find her lost kitten, that I'll have fun at my birthday party tomorrow, that none of us will catch colds this winter, and that Christmas will hurry up and get here. God loves to hear pre-schoolers pray. He also invites grownups to "Cast all your anxiety on him," and "Pray about everything" (1 Peter 5:7 NIV; Philippians 4:6 LB). But do we really think Jesus gave us a blank check for an easy life? Do we imagine we can pray our way clear of trials? "In regard to evil be infants, but in your thinking be adults" (1 Corinthians 14:20).

Imagine yourself chaperoning a troop of sixth-grade Boy Scouts to a play at a local community college. Refreshment tables in the foyer greet the audience during intermission. A little sign says: HELP YOUR-SELF. Jimmy-the-Plate-Licker begins stuffing his pockets with pastries. His buddy Weasel slides a tray full of macaroons down his shirt. Never one to be shy, Eddie Wisniewski is appreciatively sampling his sixth glass of generic-brand fruit punch.

Disgusted, you stride up to the tables. "Excuse me, boys?"

Surprised innocence returns the stare. "But the sign *said!*"

Yes, the sign said. But you'll still yank them into a corner and threaten them with a slow, painful death for reading the sign but not reading the situation. What will you say?

"These are refreshments, not Thanksgiving dinner!"

"The cookies are free for you, but somebody had to pay for them!"

"If everyone acted this way, only the first five in line would get something!"

"Your parents had settings like this in mind when they taught you to watch your manners!"

In other words, "Read the sign like someone with an IQ above forty."

Let's use our *heads* about Jesus' promise to grant whatever we request. Peter warns us against distorting the Scriptures. Paul urges Timothy to "correctly handle" the Bible. Apparently these men knew teachers who incorrectly handled it. We avoid this by comparing one Scripture with another—this always throws additional light. Parallel passages are like rails holding a train on course. They're like canals giving direction and flow to teachings that our wishful thinking would otherwise let become swampy and vague.

First John 5:15 is such a canal: "If we ask anything *according to his will*, he hears us." That channels our thinking a bit. For us to receive a go-ahead, God must already want what we're requesting; no one will twist his arm in a prayer meeting or convince him against his better judgment. Some people don't find this thought to be even a mere speed bump. They have a clear handle on God's will: "Surely God will get more glory healing my disease than giving me grace to bear it." But the apostles weren't so clairvoyant. Paul once begged relief from a certain "thorn in the flesh"—surely he could minister better if he were undistracted. "But [God] said to me, 'My grace is sufficient for you.'" Another time he tried to preach the gospel in Bithynia—surely God would want the Good News proclaimed there. "But the Spirit of Jesus would not allow them to." This is why James advised believers not to presume beforehand what God intends, not to make their plans too confidently. "You ought to say, 'If it is the Lord's will, we will live and do this or that.'"[8] No one has the Almighty in his lunch box.

John 15:7 is another canal: "*If you remain in me . . .*, ask whatever you wish, and it will be given you." Quite a tall order. Apparently, the way I live affects God's hearing. Not even an offering-plate full of sincerity can replace a careful life of obedience when it comes to getting prayers answered. Jesus added another condition: "If you remain in me *and my words remain in you,* ask whatever you wish, and it will be given you." This gets even more specific. I can have enough faith to move mountains—enough faith to make the annual congregational meeting interesting—and still my prayers will flop if Christ's words don't remain in me and I ignore his teaching. Have we really grasped this link between getting our prayers answered and steeping our minds in Christ's words? The longer the tea bag sits in the cup, the stronger the tea. The more God's word saturates our minds, the clearer our grasp on what's important to him and the stronger our prayers.

Mark's gospel sheds light on this. Remember his account of Christ's remarkable twenty-four hours at Capernaum? "That evening after sunset the people brought to Jesus all the sick and demon-possessed. The whole town gathered at the door, and Jesus healed many who had various diseases, he also drove out many demons . . ." Understandably, the next morning everyone was looking for the Great Physician. But they found him away from the crowds, praying alone, almost hiding. "Let us go somewhere else," he answered, "—to the nearby villages—so I can preach there also. That is why I have come" (Mark 1:32–39).

So I can *preach*, he says. *That* is why I have come. Not that he didn't care about the cancer-ridden and feverish in Capernaum who had gotten word too late to come for healing the night before. But their illnesses weren't his focus—the gospel was. His miracles were a backdrop, a visual aid, to his urgent message. That message was: Sin will kill you, hell is real, God is merciful, his kingdom will change you, I am your passport. Whenever people missed this point—whenever the immediate benefit of his miracles distracted them from eternal things—the Savior backed away. To a crowd that walked for miles to track him down, he said: "I tell you the truth, you are looking for me, not because you saw miraculous signs but because you ate the loaves and had your fill. Do not work for food that spoils, but for food that endures to eternal life, which the Son of Man will give you" (John 6:26–27). The *words* of Jesus interpret his miracles and must guide our prayers.

Some Christian teachers assure us, "God wants to heal your disease so the world will take note and believe." God says, "If they do not listen to Moses and the Prophets, they will not be convinced even if someone rises from the dead." Prosperity seminars teach, "God wants to bless you with financial abundance." Jesus taught, "Blessed are you who are poor"—and warned, "It is hard for a rich man to enter the kingdom of heaven." Scripture-distorters stump, "God wants to see his children happy." Jesus says, "Blessed are you who weep now" (Luke 16:31; 6:20–21; Matthew 19:23).

Did Jesus die to give the good life to everyone with faith enough to grab it? You be the judge. Our Savior himself was poor, and most of the early Christians were poor. "Not many were influential; not many were of noble birth." The Macedonian believers faced "extreme poverty." James had his head cut off. Peter was imprisoned. Stephen was stoned. John died in exile on a barren island. The Jerusalem Christians were hounded from their city. Aquila and Priscilla were expelled from Rome. Mark quit under the rigors of his missionary journey. Peter described Christians all across Asia Minor as suffering "grief in all kinds of trials." Many were slaves. Many were women with unbelieving husbands who didn't understand them. Many were singles, filled with longing but afraid to marry due to the uncertain times. Many were "publicly exposed to insult and persecution." They fell sick. Their property was confiscated. They felt the pull of temptation, knew what it was to sin, knew the pain of a bruised conscience. All belonged to churches with real problems. All needed constant encouragement to keep going. Perhaps a page from Paul's diary says it best:

> [I have] been exposed to death again and again. Five times I received from the Jews the forty lashes minus one. Three times I was beaten with rods, once I was stoned, three times I was shipwrecked, I spent a night and a day in the open sea, I have been

constantly on the move. I have been in danger from rivers, in danger from bandits, in danger from my own countrymen, in danger from Gentiles; in danger in the city, in danger in the country, in danger at sea; and in danger from false brothers. I have labored and toiled and have often gone without sleep; I have known hunger and thirst and have often gone without food; I have been cold and naked.[9]

Having what they didn't want—wanting what they didn't have. In all this they merely obeyed their Savior who said, "If anyone would come after me, he must deny himself and take up his cross daily and follow me" (Luke 9:23). Yet by sharing his sufferings they tasted "the power of his resurrection."

The Bible could be no clearer. God *does* ask his children of every nation and walk of life to suffer. Only two places on this planet are exempt—a few acres in southern California, and a few in Florida, both run by a friendly talking mouse who wears suspenders.

# *Five*

# ALL TRIALS GREAT AND SMALL

**BEFORE YOU READ CHAPTER FIVE ...**

Thirty seconds after the 1995 terrorist bomb exploded in Oklahoma City, people lay writhing everywhere in pools of blood. Some of you were there. For those who weren't, imagine yourself there. Near you lies a woman—face, torso, and arms shredded with glass shrapnel. An artery has obviously been hit, but you can't tell exactly where from a few feet away. The horror of the sight may make you feel faint. You may feel confused and panicked. You may feel afraid that another bomb will go off. You may feel like cursing or praying. You may feel a thousand things—but if you don't stop *feeling* and start *thinking* about how to stop her flow of blood and attend to her shock, this woman may die.

But shouldn't people have feelings after such a blast? Oh, yes. Intense suffering calls for deep emotions. In the aftermath, Oklahoma and the nation would weep and weep. We *should* weep. God weeps. "To everything there is a season ... a time to weep." But there is also a time to think. Neither can replace the other.

The next two chapters are difficult emotionally. They deal with a doctrine many Christians stumble over. If any reader is reeling from unspeakable loss, choking on the bitterest of pills, heartsick beyond comforting and unable to look upward—God understands. Please, close this book and weep before the Lord. If you read anything, read the Psalms. This is not the time to gag down closely reasoned arguments.

But when you are able, even though your pain is still great, the Bible is full of commands to "think," "ponder," "consider," "weigh," "judge." Jesus often turned questions about life, death, and suffering back onto the questioner. "What is written in the Law?" he would ask. Folks would blink, flip the pages, think out loud, and come up with the relevant passages. But this didn't end the discussion. Now came the real work: "How do you read it?" he would ask. That is, what do you think it *means*? No room for sloppy or sentimental thinking there.

What we think about God influences our friendship with him. It affects how much glory we give him. But our imaginations about God aren't reliable—ancient speculations about the kind of birthday present he might like led cultures into human sacrifice. Nor can we simply trust our emotions about him—if we conceive of God as we'd like him to be, we're sure to recreate him in our own image. We're liable to become like the people Paul described: "They are zealous for God, but their zeal is not based on knowledge" (Romans 10:2).

The Bible is our only safe source of knowledge about God—and it requires thinking. God's persistent invitation in every age remains: "'Come now, let us *reason* together,' says the Lord" (Isaiah 1:18).

---

This is the chapter that will raise eyebrows. It's the section about God being in control even when troubles come. For understandable reasons, most non-Christians and many Christians clear their throats uncomfortably at the notion of a God who claims to be holding the reins. After all, the horses often seem out of control and the stage coach ready to run off the road. For some, the coach has already flipped and landed on them. From underneath the wreckage, perhaps someone is thinking as follows:

*Okay, we can agree that God's plan for Christians includes suffering. That was your first point on page 56. But the second point has some of us concerned, the one about his plan being "specific" for each person, about trials being "distributed" to us. Surely you can't mean that God himself actually makes humans suffer. The Bible says God is love—but if the trials I'm facing come from him, we must be using different dictionaries to define love. A God who actually* decrees *rape, murder, earthquakes, and heart disease is not the God I worship. To say that he in any way causes such things paints him as a monster. It makes me afraid of him. It makes me feel like a pawn—as if some decision-making Machine in the sky has already slated me for broken bones and nasty lawsuits whether I'm careful or not, and whether I pray or not. The way I see it, God's holiness forbids him from urging anyone to sin against us. He doesn't make anyone do anything—we're not robots. He doesn't plan mishaps—they just happen, or perhaps Satan causes them. In his mercy and because we pray, God sometimes prevents tragedies and sorrows, but when they hit he didn't send them. Rather, he usually lets happen what will happen, then after the fact turns bad things into good for those who love him.*

There's certainly a lot of hay in that bale. Who could argue against much of it? We *should* be repulsed at any suggestion that we're pawns. The universe is not a grand marionette show. God does despise suffering. He never sins and never tempts anyone else to sin. How blasphemous for anyone to portray him as a monster! How absurd to imagine our prayers as futile and our actions as meaningless!

But how sad that we deny God's own words about himself in our efforts to defend him against such nonsense. For God clearly claims to run the world—not "could" run it if he wanted to or "can" step in when he has to but *does* run it—all the time. Even when it sins. Even when we suffer. He claims that nothing touches us without first receiving his nod and that "All the days ordained for me were written in [his] book before one of them came to be" (Psalm 139:16). He says without blushing, "Is it not from the mouth of the Most High that both calamities and good things come?" (Lamentations 3:38).

Yet here's the wonder. He claims to do all this without forcing our hands, bypassing our wills, or making us less than human. When it comes to the physical world, his working is so discreet, so regular that normally we can't tell he's involved. In fact, the so-called "laws of nature" are merely our descriptions of his usual dealings.

Thus according to the Bible, when people sin against us they alone bear the responsibility, and God will one day judge them. When hurricanes strike, it's not irreligious for the National Hurricane Center to give a scientific explanation. When disease stalks, there's a traceable medical reason. When animals cause problems, they're acting on instinct. When accidents happen, it's okay to call them accidents—even the Bible does. When babies die and whole populations starve and cocaine junkies blow away frightened convenience-store clerks, God weeps for his world. All these things are true. But the Bible insists on another truth simultaneously. All during these sins, typhoons, illnesses, mishaps, snake bites, crib deaths, famines, and gas-station robberies— *God hasn't taken his hand off the wheel for thirty seconds.* His plans are being accomplished despite, yes, even through, these tragedies. They *are* tragedies. He considers them so. He loathes the wickedness and misery and destruction itself—but he has determined to steer what he hates to accomplish what he loves.

"How can this possibly be?" someone asks.

Welcome to the world of finite humans pondering an infinite God.

But to keep from becoming too theoretical, let's consider all this through the lenses of a pair of true stories.

## GOOD PEOPLE IN PAIN

### Story Number 1

Travel in your mind to an area of the world that for many has become virtually synonymous with terrorism—the Middle East. Below is a sketchy but accurate account of one man's private horror there.

He was a public figure in his country, although not well-known internationally. Due to his wide-ranging charitable work spurred by his religious convictions, he became a hero among the lower class and many sophisticates. But in certain political quarters he was viewed as a threat. The group that took responsibility for his seizure acted at night. As with many desperate organizations, they sought to paint their actions with a veneer of legality. A kangaroo court was convened, the charges stated, the defendant declared guilty. He was taken down a hall and thrown to thugs who beat him skillfully to a pulp. Then they attached him to a crude torture instrument where he was stretched unmercifully and had various body parts skewered. As intended, the widely loved man did not survive the procedure. Outraged and grief-stricken friends remembered him as a humble, helpful person who always had time for others. His murderers were never brought to justice.

### Story Number 2

August 6, 1978. Determined to talk that husband of hers out of going through with the divorce, she hopped in the car and headed south from Georgia. The dog came along for company—the vodka, for courage. By mid–Florida the yellow road lines didn't seem straight anymore. In a misty rain on Highway 441 just north of Ft. Lauderdale she drifted into oncoming traffic and plowed into a green sport-utility vehicle carrying five young people. The boy in the back middle seat got the worst of it.

Seventy-seven days later the doctors decided that the young man would live. Paul Ruffner (not his real name), age nineteen, left the Intensive Care Unit to return home and begin learning how a person gets along without feeling or motion below the neck.

Waiting for him was a natural-wood addition to the house, complete with ramps, built by his dad and brothers. There he basked in the same family closeness he had always known. There he grew skillful with his chin-controlled power wheelchair—went fishing with dad, attended a year's college with his brother as his hands. There he deepened the faith he had shown since age five when he poked his head under the newspaper Mommy was reading and asked how to become a Christian. During those early recovery years, tears and laughter often visited on the same day. Yet friends mentioned how easy it was to drop by because of the pleasant atmosphere.

Five years after his injury Paul became an overnight multi-millionaire through a settlement with the auto company whose faulty design had contributed to his paralysis. It was time to broach an issue with his folks. "My brothers have each grown up and left home— please, let me do the same. I want to have my own place and carry my own weight." This was his first real request since the accident. Dad and Mom agreed, and Paul moved to North Carolina next door to the Ruffners' summer home. The family would still be a part of his life.

Who could see inside the mind of the girl who answered Paul's want ad for a nurse-attendant? A friend had recommended her, assuring him, "She's a Christian." But the nurse brought with her a small and secret problem for which Paul was the solution. Soon she had Paul's heart as tightly wrapped around her as hers was around his checkbook. The other attendants always went home after their shifts, but Janet (not her real name) moved in. Her sweet tooth for marijuana could now begin getting the attention it craved. Paul had a weakness here. During rehab an intern had recommended grass as a muscle relaxant. Now, the first young woman in Paul's life since the accident was urging him back to it—and to more serious candy.

A cold Smoky Mountain winter drove the couple back south to Florida. They settled a three-hour drive from Paul's folks, where Paul bought a waterfront home and the two soon married. "Sure, we'd love a visit," his new wife cooed to the Ruffners. But at the last minute it never suited. Paul would call and say, "I know we planned this, but Janet can't handle seeing anyone today—PMS, you know. Could we get together some other time?" Or Janet would crack the front door open without loosening the chain lock, sorry that Paul wasn't feeling well, and suggest they call him from the boat-house phone in the backyard before starting the trip back. In five years Paul's folks saw the couple only three times. Phone conversations always had the hollow sound of a speaker phone—Janet was monitoring everything. Should they do something? But what? Independence from his parents had been his only request.

Several years into his marriage Paul called his parents. "Mom and Dad, I've been running from God. From now on I'm making decisions in line with Scripture and in a right relationship with the Lord Jesus Christ. My lifestyle's going to change." It did change—the family sensed it. Paul again began talking freely about his faith to workers who came to the house; several became Christians through his influence. Janet changed too, for a time. But the pulling away soon returned. Paul was pleasant when he rang (his family had learned to wait until he did the dialing)—he was clearly off drugs and his folks could tell he wanted to see them—but the calls came less and less. Getting together was never convenient for Janet. Rottweilers in the yard greeted anyone trying to visit. Parcel-delivery vans must honk from outside the fence. Yet all this while a small, white seafood truck bearing more than mere fish filets continued to stop regularly.

Where was Paul? The elder Ruffners assumed that Janet's mother, who lived near the young couple, checked in at least occasionally. But she too was unwelcome. Janet's prescription of emotional control and isolation from family was succeeding only too well with her patient.

On September 9, 1990, Janet uncharacteristically called for her mom's help. "Paul's having chest pains and is having trouble breathing." The mother raced over, took one look, and said, "You don't need me— you need 911."

Rescue workers to this day don't relish describing what they found: the nauseating smell everywhere in the house except Janet's room. Filth-covered mattress. The young man's gangrenous and bloated body. Matted, uncut hair. Curled fingernails. Bones showing through skin. Sickness. And hours later, death.

During the investigation leading to the neglect trial, which ended in a fifteen year prison sentence, prosecutors questioned Janet. "Ms. Ruffner, how many dollars worth of cocaine would you say you personally went through while married?"

The former $15,000-a-year attendant had to think for a moment. She cleared her throat. "Somewhere around a million."

## WAS GOD AT THE PLANNING MEETINGS?

Two true yet unthinkable stories. A tender philanthropist tortured to death for political reasons. A teenager paralyzed by a drunken driver and slowly milked to death for his money.

Did God *intend* these incidents? Obviously he allowed them. But were they decreed? Were they "part of the plan"? Was the philanthropist's murder on a divine blueprint? Could the Ruffners accurately say, "Our family was meant to endure this"? Or in God's mind could another boy just as easily have been sitting in the back middle seat— could a different husband have been homicidally neglected? In the Ruffners' case we have no direct answers from God—the family isn't mentioned in the Bible. But the philanthropist is.

The philanthropist is Jesus.[1]

The New Testament doesn't blink in answering our questions about the Philanthropist's slaying. It strikingly puts the murder of Jesus and the decree of God on the same page. Hear the apostle Peter preaching to a Jerusalem crowd: "Jesus of Nazareth ... was handed over to you *by God's set purpose and foreknowledge*; and you, with the help of wicked men, put him to death by nailing him to the cross. ... Repent ..." (Acts 2:22–23, 38).

"Repent"—their guilt is real and judgment is threatening. "By God's foreknowledge"—God saw the crucifixion coming. "By God's set purpose"—God saw it coming *because he had decreed it.* The phrase literally reads "by God's having-been-decided counsel." Hard as it is to grasp, God willed, ordained, yes, determined history's best-known and most heinous torture-murder. This point is made even clearer just two chapters later where the early Christians are praying: "Herod and Pontius Pilate met together with the Gentiles and the people of Israel in this city to conspire against your holy servant Jesus, whom you anointed. They did *what your power and will had decided beforehand should happen*" (Acts 4:27–28).

"Your power and will had decided beforehand"—does this square with the objections raised several pages ago?

"A God who actually decrees ... murder ... is not the God I worship!"
"When [tragedies] hit, he didn't send them."

No, it doesn't square. God sent this tragedy. He decreed this murder. The above-quoted Scriptures won't allow us to say, "A loving God could never decree horrible acts of sin and violence." Nor will they allow the "robot argument"—that is, the objection that a decree by God would make Paul Ruffner's wife or the drunken driver mere puppets—unless we're prepared to say that the murderers of Jesus were mere puppets. But see Pilate nervously wash his hands after pronouncing the verdict! Hear the crowds scream, "Let his blood be on us and on our children!" Clearly, the guilty parties sensed that they were acting freely (Matthew 27:25). Yet God had planned it all.

*Ah*, says someone, *this is a set-up. Jesus' crucifixion was something unique—the salvation of mankind rested on it. God may override the world's*

*AUTOMATIC PILOT and switch to MANUAL whenever something monumental is at stake—the salvation of humanity, the fate of entire nations, or other rare and special occasions. But that doesn't mean his hand is behind absolutely everything large and small.*

Let's make a biblical checklist of what his hand *is* behind. Since most Christians have little trouble crediting God with life's sunny days, we'll limit ourselves to life's hail storms and to a few things unexpected. We'll start with Leviticus. There God gave instructions to Israel for dealing with mildew—a nuisance, but hardly something affecting the fate of entire nations. "When you enter the land of Canaan, which I am giving you as your possession, and *I* put a spreading mildew in a house in that land, the owner of the house must go and tell the priest" (Leviticus 14:34–35).[2]

When they see a spreading mildew placed by God, Old-Testament homeowners must call for a priest. The priest will then follow certain procedures. But the passage poses a difficulty. How do folks distinguish God-sent mildew from the kind that just oozes onto the wall without divine assistance? The text doesn't say. Wonder why?

Next, we go to Exodus. There Moses is protesting to God that he's not eloquent enough to give Pharaoh the "Let My People Go" message. We tend to smile at this—the future author of *Genesis* and other best-sellers not eloquent? Perhaps he wrote better than he spoke. Some think he had a mild speech impediment. Possibly he was simply making excuses. In any case, "The LORD said to him, 'Who gave man his mouth? Who makes him deaf or mute? Who gives him sight or makes him blind? Is it not I, the LORD?'" (Exodus 4:11).

God makes people deaf, speechless, and blind? Genesis says so. However, since the writing of this verse, medical researchers have learned that blindness comes from chemical splashing-accidents and from genetic twists—and deafness (which affects speech) from prolonged fevers, bacterial meningitis, and loud noises happening too close.

Next, in Proverbs we meet a verse rarely posted in the coat-check rooms of Las Vegas hotels: "The lot is cast into the lap, but its every decision is from the LORD" (Proverbs 16:33). Casting lots makes decisions fair by letting chance settle things. Football teams flip quarters to see who kicks first. Hunting-lodge buddies draw straws to see who gets the hard bed. Ancient people drew different-color stones from the fold or "lap" of their cloaks for similar reasons. God picks the winner every time, says Proverbs. Every time? Well, he is sometimes frustrated in Nevada where we suspect that the Mafia occasionally loads the dice.

Next comes a passage in Amos: "When disaster comes to a city, has not the LORD caused it?" (Amos 3:6). Caused it? C'mon. Think of all the urban disasters you've seen covered on CNN: earthquakes, floods, street riots, AIDS epidemics, freeway pile-ups, leap-frogging apartment fires, bombing raids over Baghdad, terrorist explosions in major world cities—not to mention the fourteenth-century bubonic plague. Could the God we know and love possibly decree such horrors? Perhaps Amos misunderstood. After all, in 7:14 he admitted that, before God called him into the ministry, "I was neither a prophet nor a prophet's son."

By now we know that the Bible links the following to God's decrees: the crucifixion of Jesus, the fungus in your shower, sightless eyes, unhearing ears, crap game results, and urban (no mention of rural) calamities. Can we be reading this right? It sounds so callous. No doubt if we could read the above passages in the original Greek and Hebrew they would come across quite differently and be less troubling.

Speaking of troubling passages, here's another from Proverbs: "The king's heart is in the hand of the LORD; he directs it like a watercourse wherever he pleases" (Proverbs 21:1). Kings have ordered some rather cruel things over the centuries—undeserved hangings, oppressive taxations, the summoning of young women to the palace—the kinds of things Robin Hood got upset about. But this verse probably doesn't apply to us today seeing that democracy is in such vogue since the fall of the Soviet Union, and real kings are hard to find. Still, Lamentations does broaden the idea a bit: "Who can speak and have it happen if the Lord has not decreed it?" (Lamentations 3:37). Whew, this is a bit more sweeping. The verse embraces everyone—car salesmen making pitches, senators promising legislation, cops yelling traffic directions, and quarterbacks calling plays. It covers street people begging change, diplomats negotiating treaties, librarians going "Shhh!" and that nervous young man proposing marriage in the restaurant. It includes the Pentagon announcing new policies, and the baby-sitter announcing bedtime—every dictator ordering an execution, every teenager ordering a pizza. According to this verse, not even the guy telling his dog to get his slippers can have it happen if God doesn't will it. But ah! The verse reads, "Who can *speak* and have it happen . . . ?" Perhaps if all these people put their requests in *writing*.

Let's drop the irony. Unless the Bible is wrong, *nothing* happens outside of God's decree. Nothing good, nothing bad, nothing pleasant, nothing tragic. Not in Paul Ruffner's life, not in yours. We may not fathom God's reasons, we may not agree with his thinking, we may love him for it, we may hate him for it. But in simple language, God runs the world. "The LORD works out everything for his own ends—even the wicked . . ." "Our God is in heaven; he does whatever pleases him" (Proverbs 16:4; Psalm 115:3).

———

*But I still can't shake this robotish feeling—this image of God up in heaven pressing buttons on his remote. Why would a Christian ever study medicine, physics, or any other science if God just makes everything happen? How can people be human if God overrules what they think and do? Aren't you implying that at bottom no one really ever does anything but God? Regarding our trials, where does the Devil come in? Where do nasty, evil people fit in? Where do killer hurricanes and collapsing bridges—things science can explain—fit in? What you're saying seems to leave no room for anyone or anything else but God. God plans, God decrees, God acts, God, God, God.*

Weighty questions. We're going to need another chapter.

# Six

# HEAVEN'S DIRTY LAUNDRY?

*I*s everything only God, God, God? Is the Great Provider really just the Grand Manipulator? If we're reading the Bible correctly, if he always gets his way eventually, what does that say about him? His favorite planet has seen a lot of injustice over the years—this doesn't look good on his résumé. Where's all that compassion we saw only a few chapters ago? Was the gentleness of Jesus just a cover for a surly heavenly Father? If God's the boss, is Satan his employee? Does the Devil draw his salary from heaven? Is "the good Lord" really just a scary, evil dictator?

We'd better talk to someone a little more experienced on this than any of us. We'd better talk to Job.

## DO GOD AND SATAN WORK ALTERNATE SHIFTS?

You remember righteous Job. He had it all—money, land, status, family. One day in God's throne room, Satan broached his disgust over Job's pious reputation. "The man loves you because you bribe him," he argued. "But stretch out your hand and strike everything he has, and he will surely curse you to your face."

"He's yours," God answered, "only don't lay a finger on his person."

Soon came Job's blackest day. A servant ran up with bad news: Sabean brigands had plundered the donkeys and oxen and massacred the servants. The words were scarcely from his mouth when a second runner burst in. "The fire of God"—a Hebrew idiom for lightning—had killed all the sheep and shepherds (possibly by igniting brush fires).

More footsteps, another messenger, breathless: Chaldean raiding parties . . . camels taken . . . herdsmen slaughtered. But the worst was still to come, and the courier who brought word no doubt hesitated. "It's about your children." The details were almost secondary. All ten, said the courier, were to dinner at the eldest brother's when "a mighty wind swept in from the desert and struck the four corners of the house. It collapsed on them, and they are dead."

Job's reaction is moving—he tore his robe, shaved his head in sorrow, fell to his face, and worshiped. But Job's piety isn't our focus. We're asking about God—how does he relate to Satan when it comes to our trials? How does his role differ from that of evil people and of life's sad accidents that seem to happen naturally? What does Job's saga teach?

It teaches in a nutshell almost everything we need to know.

Ask yourself: who or what caused Job's trials?

At the most basic level, *natural forces* did. Desert winds blew and lightning struck. These phenomena weren't directly miraculous or surreal, as if God hurled thunderbolts straight from heaven or Satan puffed tempests right out of hell. Nature's laws weren't suspended—lightning and strong winds aren't unheard-of in that area of the world. In the hours preceding the tragedies meteorologists from Channel 6 News could have studied atmospheric conditions, predicted the storms, and explained them in scientific terms. According to the Bible, bad weather killed these people.

On this same basic level, *evil people* caused Job's trials. Greedy men willing to murder hatched a plan and carried it out. In a court of law, prosecuting attorneys would eat those Sabeans and Chaldeans for lunch. The defendants had motive: loot and plunder. They had opportunity: a deserted place. Nobody was coerced—this was greed pure and simple, perhaps with a dose of thrill-seeking thrown in. The verdict would be clear: guilty as sin. These desert-dwellers will one day answer to God for their crimes. According to the Bible, evil people slew Job's herdsmen.

Who or what caused Job's trials? At a deeper level, *Satan* caused them. "Everything he has is in your hands," God told him. Satan turns around, leaves God's presence, we scarcely blink, and carnage is everywhere. If ever the Devil's cauldron overflowed visibly into someone's world, it overflowed into Job's. Scripture doesn't say if Satan routinely has his finger on nature's trigger, but clearly he sponsored these storms. Scripture does say that all unbelievers are in Satan's hip pocket—"the whole world is under the control of the evil one" (1 John 5:19, see also 2 Corinthians 4:4 and 2 Timothy 2:26)—and clearly Satan prompted these roaming cutthroats. Although the storms were *natural* phenomena, and the pillagers acted in a way *natural* to violent men—yet according to the Bible, Satan engineered it all: the fire, the wind, the sword. He will pay for this in hell.

Who or what caused Job's trials? On the deepest level, *the decree of God* did. Satan asked permission to stir things up, but God signed the authorization papers. Job recognized this when he cried, "The LORD has taken away" and "Shall we accept good from God, and not trouble?" The book ends with the famous sufferer receiving comfort after "all the trouble the LORD had brought upon him" (Job 1:21; 2:10; 42:11)—this is not merely Job speaking; this is the biblical narrator. For his own good reasons, none of which God explains in the book, God decreed Job's trials. He was ultimately behind the suffering.

From one angle then, everything in Job's story *was* God, God, God. Nothing happened that God didn't decree. But see how this played out. Satan acted freely; no one forced his hand. His motive was raw mischief—he wanted to wreck Job's life and humiliate God. God's reaction to the devil was merely to lengthen his leash. If Hollywood were to do the movie version, it would have God replying to Satan: "Do what you've gotta do." The tone would be inaccurate and disrespectful, but not the basic idea that Satan contrived the scheme of his own accord, from the sewage in his own heart. It was similar with the Sabeans and Chaldeans. They didn't start their day with private devotions, seeking God's guidance, learning that he wanted Job's herds stolen and servants butchered, and riding off on a holy crusade. They were just a bunch of good ol' boys enjoying a drunken looting spree, savoring life's simple pleasures. No divine arm-twisting there. As for nature, it got up on the wrong side of the bed as it often does, helped along by Satan in a manner we aren't privy to. It got to howling and blustering—tossing some fire crackers, crumbling some buildings, frying man and beast. It didn't know the difference. As far as science is concerned, nature didn't color outside the lines that day. Following the laws of high-and-low pressure systems, electrical charges, and other scientific principles that nature itself didn't understand, nature just . . . shall we say it? . . . acted naturally.

So let's get our finger out of God's face. His decree made room for it, but he didn't *do* it. He became a stowaway on Satan's bus, erecting invisible fences around Satan's fury and bringing ultimate good out of Lucifer's very wickedness. He exploited the deliberate evil of some very bad characters and the impersonal evil of some very bad storms *without smothering anyone or anything.* He forced no one's hand, bypassed no one's will, and (to our knowledge) suspended no natural laws.

These are deep waters: God decreeing but not necessarily doing, God exploiting but not smothering. What gives? How does he pull it off? To understand his methods will help us understand his heart. Let's comb the Bible for clues.

## PERMISSION SLIPS

What's clear immediately is that God permits all sorts of things he doesn't approve of. He allows others to do what he would never do. He didn't steal Job's camels. He didn't guzzle vodka and crash into Paul Ruffner. He doesn't nod appreciatively at the peddling of heroin to ninth-graders. He didn't fire the ovens of Auschwitz. God is truly grieved at how we've ruined the world and abused each other. This grief is partly why he gave the Ten Commandments: Don't murder, he says—I hate unjust killing. Don't commit adultery—I despise seeing families ripped apart. Don't steal—society will crumble if you do. Habakkuk spoke accurately of God when saying, "Your eyes are too pure to look on evil; you cannot tolerate wrong" (Habakkuk 1:13).

This is movingly pictured in Judges 10:16 where God has been watching the Ammonite people oppress Israel. He's watching instead of helping because his people have sinned. The Jews wake up and realize this. They cry out in prayer and toss out their idols. Finally—here is the line—God "could bear Israel's misery no longer." This wasn't the first time his tenderness was roused by human anguish. Years earlier he told Moses: "I have indeed seen the misery of my people in Egypt. I have heard them crying out because of their slave drivers, and I am concerned about their suffering" (Exodus 3:7).

Doesn't sound much like a divine dungeon-master twisting thumb screws, does it? God permitted these things, but he didn't like them.

"Oh," someone says with relief, "so you're not turning God into a monster—*people* do the sinning while God merely allows them. Sinners are bad, God is good. We can all go home now. We all feel better."

But don't get too comfortable. Think what we're agreeing to. God *allowed* village massacres in Bosnia. He *stood back* during hate-lynchings in Mississippi. He *permits* war. He *tolerates* leukemia. How is this justifiable?

Suppose you were walking a city street at night and heard a woman's muffled screams down a dark alley. What should you do? Call the cops? But suppose you were a cop—off-duty but carrying your weapon. You slip down the alley. From the shadows you spy two street punks tearing at a woman's blouse, a knife to her throat. You've been trained for such situations. Now suppose you quietly back away, for whatever reason: fear, laziness, high blood pressure, lateness for an appointment. How would you sleep that night? What would anyone think who found out?

God comes across such situations and worse every hour, all around the world. We might say that he's been trained for them, that he's carrying his weapon. Yet he backs away. He allows them to happen. What do we make of that?

Some people make of it that there's nothing he can do. In their minds, he's *not* carrying a weapon—or he's given himself orders not to interfere in other people's business, at least until Judgment Day. This is the position of the best-selling *When Bad Things Happen to Good People*:

> God wants the righteous to live peaceful, happy lives, but sometimes even He can't bring that about. It is too difficult even for God to keep cruelty and chaos from claiming their innocent victims. . . . God has set Himself the limit that He will not intervene to take away our freedom, including our freedom to hurt ourselves and others around us.[1]

But this does no justice to the God of the Bible, the omnipotent One, of whom we read:

> The LORD foils the plans of the nations; he thwarts the purposes of the peoples. But the plans of the LORD stand firm forever, the purposes of his heart through all generations.... (Psalm 33:10–11)
>
> He does as he pleases with the powers of heaven and the peoples of the earth. No one can hold back his hand. . . . (Daniel 4:35)

The permitting, the allowing that God does in the Bible sounds far more deliberate than what people usually mean by those words. God gives the green light—not because he's helpless or has set himself restrictions against meddling with his creation—but because he's decisive. This is obvious in a passage like Ezekiel 20. There Jehovah is recounting Israel's sorry history of idol-worship that degenerated into human sacrifice. He says in verse 26: "*I let them* become defiled through their gifts—the sacrifice of every firstborn—that I might fill them with horror so they would know that I am the LORD."

"I let them." Centuries earlier God saw what was coming. He knew that Jewish infants would be slain in homage to the idol, Molech. He told Moses, "I know what they are disposed to do, even before I bring them into the land I promised them on oath" (Deuteronomy 31:21). Why did he permit it? He tells us: to expose the vileness closeted in their souls. He resolved to make them stare at their own heinousness and vomit. God *loathes* the murder of children—yet he left his weapon holstered. This is hard for us to grasp, but *exposing sin was more important to God than relieving human suffering, even unthinkable suffering.* So God decreed to allow it.

Other passages also make clear that when God allows something, he is acting deliberately—he is decreeing that event. For instance, in Numbers 35 he instructs Israelite courts how to treat anyone who "has killed someone *accidentally.*" The person responsible must have a place to flee for sanctuary until passions cool and a trial can be held. Any number of mishaps would require this: a stone mason trips on his scaffolding and his brick falls and cracks a head below; someone is chopping wood and the axehead flies off in a fatal direction—cases where the killer "did not intend" to harm anyone. Yet in Exodus 21:13, a parallel passage describing the same situation, God uses these words: "If he does not do it intentionally, but *God lets it happen*, he is to flee to a place I will designate." God doesn't just *watch* it happen—he *lets* it happen. What is accidental from our perspective was specifically allowed by God. He who holds all things together must sustain the very molecules of the brick and axehead as they fly toward their mark (Colossians 1:17). His allowing is not something offhanded or casual.

We all hesitate here. "This is fine for hypothetical ancient construction workers who knew the job risks. But what about my little girl who was run over by a trash truck?" Yes, and what about a Paul Ruffner? Here's where the Bible becomes practical. Are we tempted to reject its teaching on this subject? Do we find repulsive a God who gives the nod to our tragedies?

Think about the alternative.

Imagine a God who *didn't* deliberately permit the smallest details of your particular sorrows. What if your trials *weren't* screened by any divine plan? What if God insisted on a hands-off policy toward the tragedies swimming your way? Think what this would mean.

First, the world would be worse, much worse, absolutely intolerable—for everyone—every second. Try to conceive of Lucifer unrestrained. Left to his own, the Devil would make Jobs of us all. The Third Reich would have lasted forever. Your head would be mounted on Satan's wall above his fireplace. Human sacrifice would entertain basketball crowds at half-time. "Child Molesting Techniques" would be taught at community colleges. The only reason things aren't worse is that God curbs evil. "Satan has *asked* to sift you like wheat," Jesus told Peter—we can be certain the old snake didn't check in with God out of politeness (Luke 22:31). He *had* to get permission, which means that he operates under constraints. Evil can only raise its head where God deliberately backs away—always for reasons that are specific, wise, and good, but often hidden during this present life.

Second, if God's decrees did *not* deliberately allow your specific trials, what does this say about God? What does it say about the boat you find yourself in? It says that God is a poor protector of his people.

"Some protection his decrees have given!" groans a widow, a stroke victim, a diabetic who has just lost a foot.

But consider—it's one thing for God deliberately to let something happen, even something terrible, for reasons we may not understand. It would be another for the God who weeps over suffering to wish he could help but have one hand tied behind his back. Either God rules, or Satan sets the world's agenda and God is limited to reacting. In which case, the Almighty would become Satan's clean-up boy, sweeping up after the devil has trampled through and done his worst, finding a way to wring good out of the situation somehow. But it wasn't his best for you, wasn't Plan A, wasn't exactly what he had in mind. In other words, although God would manage to patch things up, your suffering itself would be meaningless. One Christian writer who believes that God has little to do with the specific circumstances that come your way expressed it like this:

> In 1982 someone laced capsules of the pain reliever Tylenol with cyanide and then put them back on store shelves in Chicago. Seven people died after swallowing poisoned pills. The families of those seven people no doubt agonized trying to find some shred of meaning in why God or fate or luck had picked on their loved ones, of all the people in Chicago. We can concoct some answer and perhaps take some small comfort in it, but sadly, *there was no meaning in those deaths. Each was a bizarre, horrible coincidence, nothing more.* Therein lies the tragedy.[2]

No, the real tragedy is that any Christian would settle for such darkness with the light of the Bible shining so clearly. If God didn't control evil, the result would be evil uncontrolled.

God permits what he hates to achieve what he loves.

## A GARDENER PLANTING THOUGHTS

We've been combing the Bible for how God can decree without doing, exploit without smothering, send trials without sinning. Answer number 1 was that he doesn't originate everything he permits. Answer number 2 is more intriguing—he plants thoughts into people's minds without violating their wills.

"He invades our mental privacy?" someone is sure to gasp. The very suggestion gives some people the willies. It sits especially poorly with Americans—we're fanatics about our constitutional right to privacy. But think about Satan. *He* taps into people's brains all the time. He's a regular soul hacker—like the techno-geeks on their modems at home, breaking security codes and logging onto sensitive government computer systems. Scripture calls him "the spirit who is now at work *in* those who are disobedient." It describes his access to the human soul: "When anyone hears the message about the kingdom and does not understand it, the evil one comes and snatches away what was sown in his heart" (Matthew 13:19).

People joke about this. "The devil made me do it," they laugh. They don't really mean it because they don't think he exists. If there is a devil, he's their ex-spouse. Meanwhile their minds are as soaked with his suggestions as a pickle in vinegar. They don't see him—he's a spirit. They don't hear him—he has tiptoed in sock-footed. If they do catch some small noise at their mind's door, they assume it's just opportunity knocking. But Christians know better; they understand the power of the invisible tempter.

If Satan can be stealthful for evil's sake, why not God for good?

In Ezekiel 38 God tiptoes into the mind of a most unlikely person—the mysterious Gog. Biblical scholars disagree on the exact meaning of the prophecy—who Gog is, where he comes from, and exactly what he does. But all agree that he'll in some way fight God's people shortly before the end of the world. "*I* will bring you against my land," says Jehovah. Why? So I can defeat him in battle and "show my greatness and my holiness."

What's fascinating is *how* God will bring him. "This is what the Sovereign LORD says: On that day *thoughts will come into your mind* and you will devise an evil scheme. You will say, 'I will invade a land of unwalled villages; I will attack a peaceful and unsuspecting people . . . I will plunder and loot . . .' " (Ezekiel 38:10).

"But you're accusing God of planting *evil* thoughts into people's minds."

No, no. James says that God never tempts anybody (James 1:13). To suggest otherwise is blasphemous. Rather, God sees the evil already there and *steers* it to serve his good purposes and not merely Satan's viperous ones. It's as if he says, "So you want to sin? Go ahead—but I'll make sure you sin in a way that ultimately furthers my ends even while you're shaking your fist in my face." This is why we can accept troubles as ultimately from God even when the most dreadful people deliver them.

"But can God do this without violating people's wills?"

Absolutely. He does it on the Bible's every third or fourth page. Here's a brief sampling.

Samson was a he-man with a she-weakness.[3] In Judges 14 he's stone-struck in love with a certain Philistine woman. Israelites aren't supposed to marry idol-worshipers, but the shape of her soul isn't Samson's primary interest. "Get her for me as a wife," he tells his parents. They protest, saying in essence, "What's a nice Jewish boy like you . . . ?" But the Bible takes us backstage: "His parents did not know that this was from the Lord, who was seeking an occasion to confront the Philistines."

"From the Lord"? The same Lord who commanded the Jews not to marry foreigners?[4] Yes. Not that Samson is doing right. Not that he won't answer for this. But if Samson wants to sin, God has determined to steer his attention to Phyllis Philistine instead of to Carla Canaanite because God wants to punish the Philistines. Punish them how? Through a very ticked-off Samson. In the days leading to the wedding Samson kills time by gambling at a riddle game with the groomsmen. They cheat, he loses. He must cough up thirty pairs of Levis jeans with matching denim jackets—that's how it reads in *The Living Bible*. Actually, he must cough up the ancient equivalent. Now where's a strapping, young, impoverished Israelite going to get thirty sets of clothes? Off the backs of thirty strapping, young, dead Philistines.

How did God arrange for Phyllis and not some attractive Jewish or Canaanite girl to catch Samson's eye? We don't know. Somehow he called attention to her, maybe by painting the perfect sunset on the first evening Samson met her. But Phyllis's charm and the evening's ambiance had to *score* within Samson. Somehow, God shot cupid's arrow—shot it such that Samson's already-present sinful weakness would yield in one particular direction.

Can God plant thoughts and leave human decisions intact? Wicked King Ahab of Israel is mustering his troops for war. Will he win or lose? A courageous prophet tells him what he doesn't want to hear: "The Lord has decreed disaster for you." Decreed, mind you—Ahab's death in battle is not a suggestion-box item that God is merely considering. The prophet vividly paints the heavenly council in which Jehovah plots Ahab's demise. The king is nervous. As a precaution, he forces an allied king to take the field decked in royal attire, while he himself dresses like a common soldier. But the ploy fails. How does Ahab die? "But someone drew his bow at random and hit the king of Israel between the sections of his armor. . . . Then at sunset he died" (2 Chronicles 18:33–34).

An enemy archer shot "at random." What could be less coerced? The Hebrew reads that he shot "in his innocence." Dozens, maybe scores of Jewish troops are within the marksman's range. He quickly takes his pick—eeny, meeny, miney, moe. Twang! What luck—he has just killed his nation's foremost enemy, achieved his army's top priority, yet doesn't even know it. But if ever an arrow had someone's name on it, this arrow did.

How did God attract the archer's bow in the king's direction? We don't know. Perhaps the man had been aiming twenty feet off when a sudden motion by Ahab caught his eye. Maybe he thought, "Now there's an ugly somebody I'd like to put down." What we do know is that this was no accident. God somehow planted a thought—somehow tapped the man's shoulder. The arrow did the rest.

Can God plant thoughts without violating people's wills? Take the Canaanites whose land the Hebrews invaded a few centuries earlier:

> Except for the Hivites living in Gibeon, not one city made a treaty of peace with the Israelites, who took them all in battle. For it was the LORD himself who hardened their hearts to wage war against Israel, so that he might destroy them totally, exterminating them without mercy." (Joshua 11:19–20)

God hardens hearts? How? Who knows. Maybe he had citizens of the land-of-milk-and-honey dream at night of how good it tasted on their breakfast cereal—"Lose it to those Israelites? No way!" Maybe he sent a bumper crop to make life on the homestead seem doubly sweet. But in some way, God influenced their thinking without making them zombies.

Or consider Prince Absalom, son of King David, now turned traitor and leading an army against the throne. (The full story is in chapters 15–17 of 2 Samuel.) As David and his men flee the capital city, Absalom enters it and considers his military options. He consults renowned counselor Ahithophel—a former favorite of David's but now a turncoat. Everyone always takes Ahithophel's advice as practically from God. The counselor lays out a wise plan that will crush David before you can say "Goliath is a thumb-sucker." But another advisor, secretly sympathetic to David, waxes eloquent proposing a hair-brained scheme that will give David time to escape. David is praying, God is answering. As young Absalom listens to the dueling advisors, the venerable Ahithophel starts sounding to him like an old geezer who is losing his marbles and should be set out to pasture. Absalom swallows the bad advice bones and all. David gets away, and within days Absalom's decision costs the rebel his life. God took away the prince's good sense, yet left the man's will intact.

So Absalom is killed for thinking as God wanted. Canaanites lose their country for serving God's purposes. Samson is later captured and blinded for being God's womanizer. Is this fair? Absolutely. It's fair because their motives were as warped and selfish as God's were holy. Two parties were behind all those scenes—God pursuing holy ends, people chasing sinful ones. As Joseph said to his brothers who sold him into slavery, "You intended to harm me, but God intended it for good . . ." (Genesis 50:20). Thus, God routinely—and rightfully—punishes wicked people who fulfill his decrees. He says of Judas: "The Son of Man will go as it has been decreed, but woe to that man who betrays him" (Luke 22:22).[5]

Have cruel or careless people broken your heart or stolen your dreams? By the time their sin splashed onto your life, it was the will of God for you—the God who loves you intensely and who will call them to account.

## TIMING IS EVERYTHING

We're looking into how God runs the world. Answer number 3 is that he arranges for *natural* events to occur at *specific times* to further his ends. In other words, he plans coincidences.

In Athens, the apostle Paul "reasoned . . . in the marketplace day by day with those who *happened* to be there" (Acts 17:17).[6] Some of those window-shoppers became believers. Yet the coincidence of their strolling the marketplace that week was no coincidence, for believers have been chosen "before the creation of the world" (Ephesians 1:4).

Five centuries earlier King Xerxes, an emperor of Persia, calls it a day and goes to bed. Did ever a man have such means to fall asleep when he wanted? There are servants to fan away the heat, musicians to strum away the boredom, a harem full of bed companions, endless wine to drink himself into oblivion. Why does he toss and turn on the pillow? Who knows? Hard day at the office? A tad extra spice in the dinner soup? Ingrown toenail? Athlete's foot? Yet, "that night the king could not sleep" (Esther 6:1). Instead of calling for his pipe, bowl, and fiddlers three he calls for some reading—the chronicles of his reign—guaranteed to make anyone nod off. As the reader drones on, an obscure passage sets Xerxes' mind to thinking in a certain direction. It precisely prepares him for an empire-altering request his wife Esther will make of him the next day. It tips his mental scales—he will grant the request. His granting it will end up saving the Jewish race from annihilation. A great people will be spared. Centuries later this people will produce a young boy who will grow up to die for the sins of the world. All because the king could not sleep.

Your life is no exception to God's delight in arranging coincidences. Consider your big Fourth-of-July picnic. You live near Philadelphia, so it's only right to eat a burger in Ben Franklin's honor. The sun is warm, the grill's working, the grass is mowed for softball, and everyone's bringing a Jell-O salad. But unknown to you, God wants it to rain. He wants your friends to go home. He wants your brother-in-law Ed to help you hurry the grill into the garage where you two will stand leaning against the car, listening to the downpour. There you'll get into a long conversation leading into spiritual things that will eventually lead to your brother-in-law's conversion. Your brother-in-law's been thinking about God lately but he's a private man, hesitant to broach personal subjects, and needs an ideal time and setting.

How does God pull this off? Miracle rain out of nowhere? Something that baffles AccuWeather and brings the X-File team in to investigate?

No. While it's still warm in your backyard, five miles above the air is starting to cool. A miracle? No, a polar jet stream—bringing colder air from the northwest. Dry and heavy, this air will drop, shoving the steamy air in your back yard upward. Rising, it will cool, and its water vapor become clouds. About three miles up, those clouds will make ice crystals. Watch out. Ice crystals get bloated from eating up nearby water molecules—too fat to keep floating. They start falling as snow, but it's summertime, and by the time they hit your infield it's raining.

"Bye, Smiths! Bye, Wilsons! It was fun while it lasted. Sure, Ed, I could use some help carrying this thing."

Yet not long ago the jet stream was two-hundred miles north. What shot it your way this particular weekend? Something that happened *three days ago*—a jet-stream disturbance over the Canadian Rockies—a disturbance just right to send things Philadelphia-ward. And to get this disturbance "just right"? A precise path of that jet stream over the mountains. And to achieve that precise path? A complicated sequence of atmospheric twists from the earth's rotation and the proper Pacific Ocean water-temperature a day earlier. Yet that temperature was being affected *back in April*—when the right amount of cloud-cover was letting in the right amount of sunlight. Six thousand miles away and *four years earlier*, a volcano spewed ashes into the atmosphere that affected last April's cloud-cover. And *eleven years before that* the sun was gearing up for its next sunspot cycle that eventually affected last April's Pacific temperature.

God's been thinking about your brother-in-law for a long time.

Of course, sure-fire rain doesn't guarantee that Ed will show up at the picnic. He had been looking forward to eighteen holes today. But his golfing buddy's wife caught an ad this morning about the "Red, White, & Blue Sale" at Harry's Lawn & Garden, and immediately swore that her husband had seen his last hot meal until he gets himself over there and finally buys that lovely Comfo-Life lawn furniture that promises EASY ASSEMBLY WITHIN MINUTES. So today God planted thoughts in a wife's mind and allowed advertisers to stretch the truth about assembly-required by about—oh, say, five and an half hours—in addition to lining up nature in advance. And God is doing the same with people all over the country who need a little rain, or sunshine, to further his work in their lives.

Totally natural. Mind-bogglingly complicated.

## ANY ROOM FOR MIRACLES?

And yes, God sometimes does perform actual miracles—answer number 4 to the question of how he operates. Thus, every so often our prayers for the sick are answered in a way that baffles doctors. Perhaps he also directly and supernaturally tweaks nature from time to time to steer it back on course, who can say? He did more that tweak it when Joshua's sun stood still and the Red Sea parted. Wouldn't a replay of that send the X-Files team scurrying! But miracles are not his day job, not his usual way of working.

Many Christians don't see God in their trials. If no miracles are happening—or at least the floods aren't receding or the cancer's not in remission—God must not be at work. "Those ten plagues on Egypt, now *that* was God up to something." Agreed, frogs and lice in Pharaoh's bed made for a great movie some years ago. But to see in heaven the movie of how God ran the world from behind the scenes—the infinite complexity of it all—the wrenching of good out of evil like blood from a turnip—the clandestine exploiting of Satan's worst escapades—the infiltration of grace and salvation behind even the barbed wire of Russian death camps—*that* will win an Oscar. Meanwhile, he wants us to trust him. As Jesus told skeptical Thomas after the resurrection, "Because you have seen me, you have believed; blessed are those who have not seen and yet have believed" (John 20:29).

So why do we still doubt? Our intellects are limited. We can't find a box big enough or wrapping paper wide enough to package neatly these truths. No one can grasp the Almighty. "Even angels long to look into these things" (1 Peter 1:12). But should that trouble a Christian? All Christians acknowledge the Trinity, yet no one can fathom it—three separate persons each being God, yet God being one. Our inability to comprehend something doesn't make it untrue. As Paul put it, "Oh, the depth . . . of the wisdom and knowledge of God! How unsearchable his judgments, and his paths beyond tracing out!" (Romans 11:33).

Why do we doubt? Faith is hard—God hides, says the Psalms. He plays his hand close to the vest; he never shows all his cards. "It is the glory of God to conceal a matter" (Proverbs 25:2). We can't see the good flowing from our heartaches. We may see some—perhaps we're a bit more patient since arthritis slowed us down—more sympathetic to single parents since our marriage collapsed. The faith of Paul Ruffner radiating from his wheelchair attracted several newcomers to Christianity. But the good we can tally, does it outweigh the bad that we see? No. Eden's lost innocence opened sluice gates of sorrow deep beyond telling. It will take heaven to dry it all up—to provide the total picture that will ease our hearts for ever.

Why do we doubt? At bottom, we're uncomfortable with these truths because we're sinful. By nature we all wish God were a few notches lower—a deity lofty enough to help in our trials, but not so . . . uncontrollable. C. S. Lewis pictured this wonderfully in his classic *The Lion, the Witch, and the Wardrobe*.[7] Two children are searching for their brother who is under the spell of the wicked White Witch. They hide in the home of Mr. and Mrs. Beaver. The beavers speak in hushed tones of a rumor—Aslan, the long-gone lion-king of Narnia, has been spotted and is again on the move. The lion is symbolic of Christ.

> "Is—is he a man?" asked Lucy.
>
> "Aslan a man!" said Mr. Beaver sternly. "Certainly not. I tell you he is the King of the wood and the son of the great Emperor-Beyond-the-Sea. Don't you know who is the King of Beasts? Aslan is a lion—*the* Lion, the great Lion."
>
> "Ooh!" said Susan, "I'd thought he was a man. Is he—quite safe? I shall feel rather nervous about meeting a lion."

"That you will, dearie, and no mistake," said Mrs. Beaver, "if there's anyone who can appear before Aslan without their knees knocking, they're either braver than most or else just silly."

"Then he isn't safe?" said Lucy.

"Safe?" said Mr. Beaver. "Don't you hear what Mrs. Beaver tells you? Who said anything about safe? 'Course he isn't safe. But he's good. He's the King, I tell you."

The sovereign God who holds your days in his hand is not safe. He's anything but. He's the King, I tell you.

But he's good.

# Section II

## WHAT IS HE UP TO?

# Seven

# A FEW REASONS WHY

We pretend to sit placidly as million-gallon truths are poured into our quart-size heads. We acknowledge that God is good and knows what's best, that he is able to steer calamities to serve his good purposes while remaining unscathed by evil, but still we struggle. It's hard to soak it in. If anything, God seems more awesome than ever! So high and mighty, his purposes so grandiose, of such epic proportions, that we wonder how—or even why—he would notice the cracked molar under our porcelain crown.

We're relieved to know heaven will one day dry up our tears, but what about now? To suffer is one thing, but to suffer and not press for meaning at all makes us itchy. We've touched on the "Who" behind suffering. But what's he up to? Perhaps we'd better itch the question, "Why?"

Are there reasons?

"Well, Joni, are there?" Karla Larson asked, as though the question itself rested on her shoulders like the weight of the world. Karla is a woman in her late thirties who is desperate to understand a few reasons why. Severe diabetes is the root of it all. Both legs amputated. A heart attack. A kidney transplant. Constant battles with collapsed veins. Severe edema and legally blind. When we first met at one of our JAF Family Retreats, I remarked, "Karla, I'm amazed you were able to make it," to which she replied with a grin, "I thought I'd better come before I lost any more body parts."

She hasn't lost her sense of humor. She recently mailed me one of her body parts. I opened the shoe box and discovered a used prosthetic foot with a note attached. "Since all of me can't be with all of you all the time, I thought part of me would just have to do!"

At this year's retreat she looked a little blue. With encroaching blindness and more surgical procedures looming, Karla was beginning to wonder whether or not it was worth fighting on. During a break after the morning session, we found a quiet corner by a large window. The words we shared were measured and heartfelt. Short and succinct. We agreed that suffering is a pain. We sighed about the temptation to give up. Finally, we got to the point. The one about "reasons why."

"Look at me," she said, dropping her gaze to her lap. Through her shorts, I could see the contour of the large plastic cups around her stumps. Karla wasn't wearing cosmetic legs, but the bare steel bar kind with a hinge at the knee. She held up her hand to show something new: a fat white gauze wrapped around the end of a knuckle. Her finger had been amputated. "I'm falling apart."

Children chattered outside the window. A phone rang at the receptionist's desk. Down the hallway, a group of teenagers burst into laughter over a joke.

After several moments, she continued, "I'm a Christian. I've suffered. Don't you think I've paid my dues?" she asked with pleading eyes. "I'm not depressed or anything, I just . . . don't see the point. I want to go home now. Heaven, I mean."

Normally, I wouldn't jump to answer questions like these. I'd just listen. But I know Karla. She passed the anger stage long ago, leaving behind bargaining, denial, and clenched-fist queries. Was she asking now out of a searching heart? I decided to gently step where angels fear to tread.

"Do you really want an answer?" I asked, sincerely.

She nodded.

"Well, you're here. You're not in heaven. This means God's got his reasons."

"What are they? What reasons are so good that they outweigh the pain of *this*—," she said, holding up her bandaged knuckle again.

"Grab your Bible," I said, gesturing to the one squeezed between her leg and the side of her wheelchair, "and read for me Philippians 1:21."

Karla fumbled through the pages with her bandaged hand. (I told her I wished I could help but my hands were no better; in fact, worse.)

She found the page and read aloud, "'For to me, to live is Christ and to die is gain.'" She brightened, "Hey, there it is! See? To die would be gain. Even an apostle agrees with me."

I smirked. "Read on."

"Okay, okay . . . 'If I am to go on living in the body, this will mean fruitful labor for me. Yet what shall I choose? I do not know! I am torn between the two: I desire to depart and be with Christ, which is better by far; but it is more necessary for you that I remain in the body'" (Philippians 1:22–24).

Watching a half-blind, legless, ailing woman trace the words on the page with a bandaged hand and give them voice made my throat clutch. "It's okay to be torn between the two," I said softly. "To go home to heaven is better by far." Karla gave a puzzled look as if I were granting her permission to end it all with sleeping pills. "But," I said quickly and emphatically, "—but it is more *necessary* that you remain here."

"Why?" she scrunched her face.

"Look, read it again, it says, 'It is more necessary *for you* that I remain.' You may think it's far better to depart and be with Christ, but as long as you remain in the body, your family and friends have something to learn. Something of eternal importance."

Karla turned her face toward the window, her faraway look revealing she was deep in thought. Maybe she was thinking about Christie, her transplant nurse, cool-headed in the operating room but cold-hearted about spiritual things. Maybe she was musing over other nurses at the clinic who spend their coffee break whining about new regulations. Perhaps her friends at church whose major problems were menopause and mid-life crises. Coworkers from her old office. Neighbors down the street. Bag boys and grocery clerks who always greeted her at the supermarket.

She turned back and asked, "It's more necessary for *them* that I remain?"

## THE POWER OF EXAMPLE

Go back with me to the bomb blast that gutted the Oklahoma City office building leaving 168 people dead and missing. A pastor-friend invited me to come and visit the families at the First Christian Church, where they were huddling and waiting for news of their loved ones. Before I was permitted to enter the family center, I had to be cleared and credentialed by the American Red Cross.

When I wheeled into the Red Cross center, an officious woman wearing a white lab coat exclaimed, "My God, are we glad to see *you!*"

I looked over my shoulder. Did she mean me? Did she recognize me from an interview? Later, when I learned she was in charge of the counseling services and didn't have a clue as to who I was, I asked why she welcomed me with opened arms.

"Honey, I wish we had more people like you in wheelchairs volunteering during a crisis. When victims come in here for help and see someone like you, handling your own personal crisis, it gives them hope. You are a powerful example to them, a promise that they too will survive their tragedy."

Oklahoma City is surviving its crisis. But so many in our culture of comfort are not. Slump-shouldered and near defeat, they need the power of example. They need to see someone experiencing greater conflict than they *make it.* "We do not want you to become lazy, *but to imitate those* who through faith and patience inherit what has been promised" (Hebrews 6:12).

If people are floundering in the mire of their problems, if they are infected by a spirit of complaint, or if they are (God forbid) lazy like the battle-weary believers mentioned in Hebrews, they need to be reminded that the power of God works—really works, not in theory, but in reality—in someone else's life. It's a good "reason why" behind our suffering. Karla Larson is a powerful example.

"Do you realize God needs you?" I asked her.

"He doesn't need anybody."

"That's true," I concurred, "but he likes to use you anyway, especially when it comes to other believers. Look up another verse. Colossians 1:24."

"What is this, Theology 101?"

"For you, yes!" I poked back. "Besides, I don't know these things by heart."

"Okay, here it is," Karla said, finding the passage. "'Now I rejoice in what was suffered for you, and I fill up in my flesh what is still lacking in regard to Christ's afflictions, for the sake of his body, which is the church.'"

She reread it silently then looked up. "Huh?"

"Nothing is lacking when it comes to what Christ did on the cross. It is finished, just as he said. But something *is* lacking when it comes to showcasing the salvation story to others. Jesus isn't around in the flesh, but you and I are. When we suffer and handle it with grace, we're like walking billboards advertising the positive way God works in the life of someone who suffers. It's for the benefit of believers. But it's more than a matter of example or even inspiration," I stammered, groping for words. "It's *you*. Because we are one in the body of Christ, we are linked together. Your victories become mine" (see 1 Corinthians 12:26).

I watched the idea sink into Karla's head. I realized I was one of those benefiting. Sure, I'm a quadriplegic, but I don't consider my problems as severe as hers. Karla, with all her angioplasties, manhandles more serious dilemmas than I. She shows me how to handle a bothersome ulcer on my foot that won't heal. Backaches for which aspirins do zilch. If a woman who has to borrow a kidney can do it with God's help, then so can I.

Karla patted the place where her prosthesis was joined to her stump and sighed, "You're right. I wouldn't be leaning as hard on God were it not for *this*. And there's always Christie. And my other friends who don't know God. I should think of them."

I beamed with pride at her, as though she had just received a Ph.D. in practical theology. "And if God can sustain you in the shape you're in, then we *all* ought to be boasting in our weaknesses! When people who face lesser conflicts—like sow bugs in the shower—when they see someone handle greater conflicts, it speaks volumes. They learn something powerful about God from observing you."

It's like this homespun poem I received the other day:

I saw the woman in the chair; she was in church again today.
Someone said they've sold their house; they're going to move
    away.
No! I cried, they cannot go; they cannot move away.

I didn't get to know her; there's something I need to say:
Please tell me your secret; I want to sit at your feet,
I need to know how you handle the pain that is your daily meat.
How do you keep on smiling when each day your health
    grows worse?
How do you keep depending on God when you're living with
    a curse?
Every time I see her; her smile comes from deep within.
I know her fellowship with God isn't scarred by the chair she's
    in.
She admits her health is failing; she knows she's fading away.
How can she remain so calm when I'd be running away?
My friend, can you tell me how you can trust the Lord
How can you stay so gentle and sweet when He seems to
    wield a sword?
You are to me a promise that even in the midst of pain
God is near and faithful if I will turn to Him again.

Liz Hupp

No man is an island. We are all connected. "For none of us lives to himself alone and none of us dies to himself alone" (Romans 14:7). The purpose of life is to live for others. Jesus showed us that. Especially "others" 1 Corinthians 1:27 talks about: "For God chose the foolish things of the world to shame the wise; God chose the weak things of the world to shame the strong. He chose the lowly things of this world and the despised things—and the things that are not—to nullify the things that are, so that no one may boast before him."

Karla shames the worldly wise who scoff at God. She shames the stiff-necked who trust in their strength. She casts shadows on them, and they know it. They can't hold a candle to her gritty, gutsy faith. But that's good. How else would their boasting be nullified? How else would they be stripped of confidence in their slim waistlines, tight abdominals, flashy photogenic smiles, big brains, bucks, and brass plaques on their office walls?

Karla may lose another finger—and if she does, the watching world will be forced to swallow its pride and drop its jaw in disbelief at her tenacious trust in God. Either she is mad or there is a living God behind all of her pain who is more than a theological axiom. Her life is a living proof that he works. Christianity asserts some pretty broad and sweeping claims; the stronger the claims, the stronger its substantiation must be. God eagerly invites unbelievers (and a few vacillating believers) to examine the foundations of Karla's faith. Her witness is as bold as the claims upon which it rests and this makes people think twice about him.

> Praise be to the God and Father of our Lord Jesus Christ, the Father of compassion and the God of all comfort, who comforts us in all our troubles, so that we can comfort those in any trouble with the comfort we ourselves have received from God. "For just as the sufferings of Christ flow over into our lives, so also through Christ our comfort overflows. If *we* are distressed, it is for *your* comfort and salvation; if *we* are comforted, it is for *your* comfort which produces in you patient endurance of the same sufferings we suffer. (2 Corinthians 1:3–6)

If Karla is distressed, it's for the comfort of others. If she is suffering, it has a bearing on the salvation of her transplant nurse. It is for the endurance of her friends in mid-life crisis or menopause.

"I'm beginning to see it." Karla straightened and said, "If my body is going to fall apart piece-by-piece, then God must be allowing it not just for my good—"

"But also the good of those around you," I finished her sentence.

Karla Larson may go completely blind. She eventually may be unable to physically do anything. When it happens—and it might—she still won't have to worry about feeling useless, that she has no purpose for living or no reason for going on. She will continue to *be* God's witness (Acts 1:8).

This "reason why" is echoed in this note I received from a young woman named Tina who takes care of her grandmother:

Dear Joni,

> Yesterday Grandma was struggling with feeling useless. She wondered what good she was, what purpose she could possibly

fulfill, what meaning life could have when she lives mostly between a bed and a couch. I saw how easily we equate our purpose/meaning/usefulness with things we physically *do,* and how little emphasis we place on things of the spirit and acts of encouragement which require little or nothing of us physically.

I told Grandma this, but then suddenly realized that I was not focusing on glorifying God in my inner life—my purpose had become "taking care of Grandma" and not listening to the Lord, focusing in prayer, and thus practicing genuine concern for others. These are things that must happen *inside* me.

Love, Tina

## FOR THE SAKE OF OTHERS

Conversation flowed between Karla and me. Smiles were warm. Tears were real. The thoughts that surfaced out of the Bible were soul-strengthening. We glanced at our watches and realized the next retreat session was about to begin.

After we prayed, she turned her wheels to go. "I'm going to think about what we covered," she said over her shoulder as she went ahead. I watched as a few of Karla's friends who had brought her to our retreat gathered around her. One of them gave her a bottle of water, a straw, and a hug. It *is* better, it is necessary for them that Karla remains.

Something nagged, though. Does this make hurting people nothing more than audio-visual aids in the hands of a utilitarian God? Object lessons from which others can learn? Are suffering people who keep emptying themselves mere role models of inspiration? What does Karla stand to gain?

I hearkened back to the example of Paul. After he acknowledged it was more necessary that he remain in order to strengthen and encourage others, he added: "I know that I will remain, and I will continue with all of you for your progress and joy in the faith, so that through my being with you again your joy in Christ Jesus will overflow on account of me" (Philippians 1:25).

I like that part "on account of me." What others gain from observing Karla gets credited to her eternal account. It's the old principle of

John 15:5, 8: "I am the vine; you are the branches. If a man remains in me and I in him, he will bear much fruit."

The Almighty Lord of the Universe notices when Karla sows seeds in the lives of others. He keeps tabs every time she waters the seed with her prayers. If something good stirs in a soul, even in the souls of those she doesn't know, God chalks it up to her account. He records it on Karla's balance sheet when he observes faith flowering and fruit ripening in the life of someone in whom she has invested her example.

If they profit, she gains. If they are rewarded, she reaps. If they are lifted up, she is raised with them. She shares in the blue ribbon for the fruit borne in their lives. This is why the apostle Paul spoke of those in whom he invested his life as "his joy and crown" (Philippians 4:1). Other people are *our* crown!

I want to jump in Karla's corner of the ring. I'm not asking for her suffering; I'm wanting her attitude. She reminds me how we are all richer when we recognize our empty-handed poverty. We are all stronger when we face up to our frailty. We all gloriously gain when we kiss shattered dreams good-bye.

We sacrifice comfort but fall back on the cushion of God's arms. We forfeit earthly pleasure but rise to euphoria that is out of this world. We empty ourselves and get fat and sassy on the grace of God. It's a pattern given to us by Christ himself:

> Your attitude should be the same as that of Christ Jesus: Who, being in very nature God, did not consider equality with God something to be grasped, but made himself nothing, taking the very nature of a servant . . . he humbled himself and became obedient to death—even death on a cross! *Therefore God exalted him to the highest place.*" (Philippians 2:5–9)

Notice the "therefore" part. Like a math formula. Like an inverse proportion. Rather, like an equation blowing all proportions. God raises us up not to just any old high place, not just to the spectator's gallery, but as a co-heir with Christ, we get seated alongside him. "We are heirs of God and co-heirs with Christ, if indeed we share in his sufferings in order that we may also share in his glory" (Romans 8:17). Astounding! We suffer with Christ—that we may share in Christ's *highest glory.*

Believers who face the greatest conflict yet hold on to God with all their hearts, at times clinging to hope like the string of a kite—these are the ones who have the greatest confidence in sharing Christ's glory.

All the power, honor, glory, blessing, and riches showered upon Christ on his crowning day, all of it, overflowing all the universe, we will share in. What is it worth? "I consider that our present sufferings are not worth comparing with the glory that will be revealed in us" (Romans 8:18).

God offered Adam and Eve a path that led straight from Eden to an eternal Paradise. But since our first parents opted for a detour, since suffering is now part of what it means to be a *Homo sapiens,* God is going to use it. Not half-heartedly, but in delight. For as dark and pernicious as it is, God will squash suffering like a grapefruit in the face of the Devil, turning it inside out into something sweet. If suffering can't be avoided, God's going to redeem it to usher us into the highest echelons of heaven.

It's hard to think of heaven when you're hurting—its blessings for others and benefits for you. All the more reason to "let us not become weary in doing good, for at the proper time we will reap a harvest if we do not give up. Therefore, as we have opportunity, *let us do good to all people"* (Galatians 6:9–10).

It's a thought with which to fan ourselves every time we feel like fainting.

## BUT WHAT IF?

What if Karla's example did no good to anyone? What if she were unable to come to a family retreat or lived completely alone? Godly lives should be observed. But what about the widow who seldom ventures outside her apartment? The foreign student who spends lonely weekends on an empty campus? The prisoner in isolation? The older man in the nursing home who lives in the last room at the end of the hallway? What if he hardly connects with the staff? Perhaps a few nurses are encouraged by his life of quiet trust, but what if no one else notices?

Loneliness mixed with affliction is a dangerous potion. You lie awake, persistently needled by pain. Physical pain, yes, but also mental. The mountains you face are unknown to others. "Suffering for nothing" is a poisonous thought. Whether we're actually alone or lonely, if we get the feeling that no one notices our sorrows, it can drive us to despair.

I'm thinking of John McAllister. The six-foot-three-inch oak of a man withered and weakened from the degenerative disease. The man whose eyes twinkle from their sunken sockets. My friend who lived through the attack of ants. Remember him? John no longer rubs elbows with people. In the beginning stages of his disease, he could drive himself to church, to the mall, and to a residential facility where he led a Bible study for young people with cerebral palsy. Neighbors at the mall would wave hi. Folks would stop him in the parking lot. Gas station attendants looked for his happy hello and wave of the hand. But years have passed and the novelty of his wheelchair has worn off. People don't drop by much anymore. Gaunt and unable to speak, his days are spent sitting up in bed in the middle of the living room. Birds outside the window are his main companions.

Is John McAllister *really* alone?

Something dynamic and electrifying is abuzz in John's room, filling the air, agitating the atmosphere around and above his home. Angels, along with powers and principalities in the heavenly realms, are watching, listening, and *learning.* People may not be noticing John McAllister, but the spiritual world is. Angels—even demons—are intensely interested in the thoughts and affections of every human being.

"His purpose was that through the church [that is, through Christian] all the rulers and powers in the heavenly world will now know God's wisdom, which has so many forms" (Ephesians 3:10).

I can hear you thinking, *Angels eyeballing and eavesdropping on me? Angels sitting in the passenger seat of my car and getting an earful of my outburst when that red Chevrolet cut me off? Demons wringing their hands in glee, hoping I'll curse at my kids when they cross me? Principalities and powers watching on tiptoe to see whether I turn to God or turn away?*

This isn't science fiction. Luke 15:10 is nonfiction: "I tell you, there is rejoicing in the presence of the angels of God over one sinner who repents."

God's angels actually get emotionally charged up when people choose to trust in God. Read Ephesians 3:10 again. God's purpose is to teach millions of unseen beings about himself; and we are—John McAllister is—a blackboard upon which God is drawing lessons about himself for the benefit of angels and demons. God gets glory every time the spirit world learns how powerful his everlasting arms are in upholding the weak. They learn it is God who permeates every fiber of John's being with perseverance. My friend's life is not a waste. Although not many people seem to care, someone—a great many someones—care more than John can imagine.

John's life does something else. It disgusts Satan. The trust he shows God drives the Devil up a wall. Even though his body is emaciated and his eyes are virtually robbed of sight, he's like an old warrior hearing a far-off bugle from a battlefield. "I'll never curse God, no matter how much he takes away from me."

John is a little like Job, whom Satan threw in God's face, jeering, "Job doesn't love you, he loves your blessings. You're not great enough, God, to get someone to follow you on your own merits."

But Job said, "Though he slay me, yet will I hope in him" (Job 13:15). A statement like that speaks highly of Job (it speaks highly of John McAllister). But it speaks more highly of God. Nothing wounds the Devil more—and John has a part in rubbing salt in those wounds. The life of the most insignificant man is a battlefield on which the mightiest forces of the universe converge in warfare—this elevates the status of the lowliest and least person on earth!

I picture that day when John will depart earth and head for heaven. When his spirit rises out of his shell of a body, the entire universe of angelic hosts will stand erect, holding their breath in respect. They will salute in amazement, watching his spirit ascend as a sweet-smelling savor to God. And then—watch out!—the party will really break loose.

Each day we go on living *means* something. God is up to something good when it comes to our trials. There are reasons. For us, for others, for the glory of God, and for the heavenly hosts.

## FOR THE GLORY OF GOD

But suffering accomplishes even more than this. It sets the stage for offering something exceedingly precious to God: "Through Jesus, therefore, let us continually offer to God a sacrifice of praise—the fruit of lips that confess his name. And do not forget to do good and to share with others, *for with such sacrifices God is pleased"* (Hebrews 13:15–16).

David, the psalmist, did it all the time. He sighs in Psalm 43:5, "Why are you downcast, O my soul? Why so disturbed within me?" But before his soul can drag him under, David jerks it upright: "Put your hope in God, for I will yet praise him, my Savior and my God."

God is pleased with praise, but he swells with joy when the praise he breathes has the aroma of a sweet-smelling sacrifice.

Nothing delights him more. How so? Let's say a woman with arthritis in her hands embroidered a set of pillowcases for you. The gift would probably mean more to you than if sewn by a woman with nimble fingers. Why? Because the arthritic woman expended extraordinary effort. Her gift involved cost and sacrifice. You'd weigh the extra hours she invested, the frequent breaks she took to rub her knuckles, the pain she endured with each tiny stitch. Most likely, you would be moved to tears. Her suffering "glorified" her gift, making it more valuable in your eyes.

If *we* respond this way to sacrifices, how much more is *God* enthused? A sacrifice of praise makes praise more glorious.

Ken and I worship in a small church where we have to shuffle a couple of folding chairs to make room for my wheelchair in the left aisle. The Pomeroy family usually sits a few rows up on the right. Mother, father, two boys, and youngest daughter, Veronica, who likes to wear pretty hats over her blonde hair. Veronica coughs a lot in church. I used to think she was a child plagued by frequent colds. I later learned she has cystic fibrosis, a severe lung disease that constantly clogs her breathing passages with phlegm. The prognosis for CF is never good. Veronica doesn't let it get her down. She's only eleven years old, yet she rallied her classmates this past Christmas to collect hundreds of toys for orphaned children in Bosnia.

I enjoy glancing over at Veronica during worship service. Especially when we sing hymns.

Breathe on me, Breath of God,
   Fill me with life anew,
That I may love what Thou dost love,
   And do what Thou wouldst do.

She coughs in between the lines and I wonder what God must be thinking as he receives her praise. A genuine sacrifice of praise, it is, as she wheezes through the hymn. Veronica, with her limited lung capacity, inspires me to fill my chest and harmonize with all my heart.

A sacrifice brightens God's glory. It demonstrates the enormously high value we attach to him. Such praise costs us our logic, pride, and preferences. But it's worth it. "Worthy is the Lamb, who was slain, to receive power and wealth and wisdom and strength and honor and glory and praise!" (Revelation 5:12–13).

## IN THE MEANTIME

I just learned that Karla Larson had another setback. She mentioned it in the P.S. of a note she sent after the retreat:

> Dear Joni,
>
> After speaking with you, I feel I can "run the race" and "fight the good fight" again. My reasons for not wanting any more medical procedures were based on fear. I now realize that my decisions not only concern me, but affect family, friends, and others who watch. I am alive because of God's grace, mercy, and faithfulness to me. So when the need for the next angioplasty or whatever arises, I'm ready to go for it.
>
> Love, Karla
>
> P.S. I just learned I have uterine cancer.

I slid the note aside and drew a deep breath. *Thanks, Karla, for the reminder. I'm ready to keep running the race too.* Her example is growing in importance and power, and if her family and friends forget that, or if I do, there are always angels and principalities looking on. There is always God.

*There is God.*

He is not passive. He is not a casual onlooker.

Karla may have a better handle on a few of the good "reasons why," but as she and her friends at church grow closer, as they help each other, one more "reason why" will become clear. It will become clear to them all.

The "reason why" has to do with God himself.

## LET'S RELIEVE THE SUFFERING

God's heart intent is to alleviate suffering. He is bending over backward to make it happen. God is moving heaven and earth to dry the tear, lighten the load, ease the burden, take away the pain, stop the wars, halt the violence, cure the disease, heal the heartbroken, mend the marriage.

God is straining to feed the homeless, clothe the naked, visit the prisoner, adopt the orphan, comfort the grieving, console the dying, defend the children, bandage the battered, give to the poor, care for the widow, uproot injustice, clean up pollution, prevent abortion, right the wrong, protect the animals, rectify racism, support the elderly, sustain the downcast, stamp out crime, stomp out pornography, help the disabled, prevent abuse, cease corruption, muffle the cursing, get rid of gambling, turn stone hearts to flesh and dead men into living ones.

He rallies us to his noble cause, but we fall behind. If God is weeping, it is because he has made his heart intent regarding suffering abundantly clear, but few—even of his own people—are moved into action. We aren't listening.

> For day after day [my people] seek me out; they seem eager to know my ways, as if they were a nation that does what is right and has not forsaken the commands of its God. They ask me for just decisions and seem eager for God to come near them. "Why have we fasted," they say, "and you have not seen it? Why have we humbled ourselves, and you have not noticed?" "Is not this the kind of fasting I have chosen [says the Lord]: to loose the chains of injustice and untie the cords of the yoke, to set the oppressed free and break every yoke? Is it not to share your food with the hungry and to provide the poor wanderer with shelter—when you see the naked, to clothe him, and not to turn away from your own flesh and blood?" (Isaiah 58:2–3, 6–7)

God longs to push back the pain through those who serve as his body, his hands and feet on earth. "He is the head of the body, the church" (Colossians 1:18). And "From him the whole body . . . builds itself up in love, as each part does its work" (Ephesians 4:15–16).

The body is supposed to do its work. God's work. "We take our lead from Christ, who is the source of everything we do" (Ephesians 4:15, from Eugene Peterson's THE MESSAGE). We take directions from our Head—everything from giving the gospel to giving shelter to the poor wanderer. The directions couldn't be spelled out more clearly. In some places, God appeals to our philanthropic senses, urging us to "be an instrument for noble purposes" (2 Timothy 2:21). In other places, he has to rap on our desks and repeat it as though we were second-graders: "Religion that God our Father accepts as pure and faultless is this: to look after orphans and widows in their distress and to keep oneself from being polluted by the world" (James 1:27).

But we hem and haw. This is ironic since so many of us fault *him* for allowing suffering to be the world's status quo. (The quo wouldn't be so status if we got off our duffs and followed his lead). But we shuffle along, so slow to move. Often we are disobedient, listening to pride or prejudice while refusing to do anything. Suffering then breeds and spreads like an insidious virus. It could be held at bay, halted, and eradicated in many instances, but misery foments because most often we do nothing to stop it. His hands and feet fail to alleviate suffering because we have "lost connection with the Head" (Colossians 2:19).

So what does this have to do with Karla and her friends at church?

"God has combined the members of the body and has given greater honor to the parts that lacked it, so that there should be no division in the body, but that its parts should have equal concern for each other. If one part suffers, every part suffers with it; if one part is honored, every part rejoices with it" (1 Corinthians 12:24–26).

The hands and feet of God are strengthened when the body includes someone who is suffering. The nerve endings stand at attention and the adrenaline flows. Muscles are spring-loaded for action. Eyes are focused on the need and ears are attentive to the call. Feet begin moving forward. The body starts working when it goes the extra mile. It becomes united in purpose, "having no division" . . . and sharing "equal concern for each other." There's no time for a church to be splintered into factions when someone in the congregation is suffering.

This is why God knows it is more necessary that Karla remains. She helps the body. It's happening already. Her Sunday school class is now on the lookout for ways to minister to other people. They are paying the way this summer for others to attend our retreats for families with disabled children.

The Word of God virtually shouts, "Those [who] seem to be weaker are indispensable" (1 Corinthians 12: 22). This is why Jesus keeps driving home the point about giving special honor to the weak, the poor, and the lame in our fellowship. Heaven knows that without the Karla Larsons in the pews, the Church would be enfeebled. After all, "Has not God chosen those who are poor in the eyes of the world to be rich in faith?" (James 2:5).

As the Church exercises its muscles in sacrificial service, it rises to its calling, it steps into the grand purpose for which it was designed. As it does, God smiles. Suffering is being squelched. Pain is being purged. And the darkness that chokes hearts and blinds eyes is being pushed back.

It's a good, a very good answer to her question, "Why?"

But there are even better reasons.

# Eight

# THE BEST ANSWER
# WE HAVE

Once on a tour through the south of England, my friend Judy pointed out an obelisk in the crossroads of a tiny English village. On it were the names of eighteen young men who perished in World War I.

"All of them from this little place?" I asked in disbelief. There were only a handful of cottages, a few shops, a barn or two, and a church. She explained that British army recruiters promised young men that if they signed up together, they could serve together. In the wholesale carnage of World War I, it meant they all died together. Nearly a million Britons were among the nine million slaughtered.

The village was never the same. Shops were draped in black and curtains were drawn. But families clung to one another, the church was filled, parents huddled together, tears were dried, needs were met, grief was eased, and that little town gained a heart and soul more noble, more courageous than the greatest capitals on the continent.

Despite all the horror and heartache, some good came out of it all. Yes, there were sacrifices of praise; yes, principalities and powers looked on in amazement; yes, many suffered for the benefit of others; yes, unbelievers were shamed and their boasting was nullified; yes, people with lesser conflict learned from those on the front lines; yes, the body of Christ in that village grew and built itself up in love.

Corporately, people may have gained. But consider the individual. The British mother who, behind the locked doors of her cottage, wailed privately into her pillow, making it wet with tears and grief. Crying over the loss of not one son, but two. Maybe three. Or a husband.

Wholesale benefits to suffering and how it affects heaven and angels, the church, and the watching world are an unsurpassed reality. But the individual heart requires comfort closer to home, something in tune with the interior of the soul. For suffering is so terribly and horribly personal.

God knows this. That is why, as the grieving mothers and broken-hearted widows in that English village opened their Bibles in search of comfort, they were never assaulted by any passage depicting Jesus laughing uproariously.

They opened their Bibles and found a man of sorrows, acquainted with grief:

> During the days of Jesus' life on earth, he offered up prayers and petitions with loud cries and tears to the one who could save him from death and he was heard because of his reverent submission. Although he was a son, he learned obedience from what he suffered and, once made perfect, he became the source of eternal salvation for all who obey him. (Hebrews 5:7–9)

This is good news for the suffering soul. The Son of God did not exempt himself from affliction but lived through it and learned from it. Once that process was complete, he became the source of help for all who obey him. Should we suffer? "A student is not above his teacher, nor a servant above his master," says the One who learned obedience from what he suffered. "It is enough for the student to be like his teacher, and the servant like his master" (Matthew 10:24–25).

We open our Bibles and find that God has his reasons for allowing suffering, not just in the larger realm, but in the life of the individual. Learning some of those reasons can make all the difference in the world.

## THE SCULPTURE

In the English village was a statue, a sculpture of a soldier. As our van crept by, it symbolized for me the bravery of those daring young men on the battlefields of northern France. No less brave are the people who survived World War I, the scourge of influenza in 1918, World War

II, the Armenian earthquake, the great monsoons of Bangladesh, and any number of catastrophes in between.

Suffering has inspired and forged more sculptures than one can count. And not just the bronze kind that rest on pedestals in village squares.

Suffering fashions us into a "holy and blameless" image of Christ (Ephesians 1:4), much like a figure sculpted out of marble. An artist in Florence, Italy once asked the great Renaissance sculptor Michelangelo what he saw when he approached a huge block of marble. "I see a beautiful form trapped inside," he replied, "and it is simply my responsibility to take my mallet and chisel and chip away until the figure is set free."

The beautiful form, the visible expression of "Christ in you, the hope of glory" is inside Christians like a possibility, a potential. The idea is there, and God uses affliction like a hammer and chisel, chipping and cutting to reveal his image in you. God chooses as his model his Son, Jesus Christ, "For those God foreknew he also predestined to be conformed to the likeness of his Son" (Romans 8:29).

What does the sculpture look like? "We have this treasure in jars of clay to show that this all-surpassing power is from God and not from us. We are hard pressed on every side, but not crushed. . . . We always carry around in our body the death of Jesus, so that the life of Jesus may also be revealed in our body" (2 Corinthians 4:7, 8–10). It's an image of all-surpassing power.

God continues to chisel, chipping more away. "To keep me from becoming conceited . . . there was given me a thorn in my flesh" (2 Corinthians 12:7). God works deeper, carefully fashioning every hidden crevice, even our temperament: "Your attitude should be the same as that of Christ Jesus: Who . . . made himself nothing. . . . He humbled himself and became obedient to death—even death on a cross!" (Philippians 2:5–8).

Will this sculpture last the weathering of more storms and trials? "We rejoice in our sufferings because we know that suffering produces perseverance; perseverance, character; and character, hope" (Romans 5:3). It's an image of rock-solid hope.

God continues to hammer: "Before I was afflicted I went astray, but now I obey your word. . . . It was good for me to be afflicted so that I might learn your decrees" (Psalm 119:67, 71). Before my paralysis, my hands reached for a lot of wrong things, and my feet took me into some bad places. After my paralysis, tempting choices were scaled down considerably.

God uses suffering to purge sin from our lives, strengthen our commitment to him, force us to depend on grace, bind us together with other believers, produce discernment, foster sensitivity, discipline our minds, spend our time wisely, stretch our hope, cause us to know Christ better, make us long for truth, lead us to repentance of sin, teach us to give thanks in times of sorrow, increase faith, and strengthen character. It is a *beautiful* image!

And it's an image like no other. When Christ is unveiled in me, it's a unique sculpture. It's what patience, self-control, endurance, gentleness, kindness, as well as a healthy hatred of sin, looks like on "Joni." That's different than the way sensitivity and self-control look on my husband or anyone else. My particular affliction is divinely hand-tailored expressly for me. Nobody has to suffer "transversal spinal lesion at the fourth–fifth cervical" exactly as I did to be conformed to his image.

Yielding to the chisel is "learning obedience from what we suffer." Our circumstances don't change; *we* change. The "who" of who we are is transformed, like a form unfolding, into his likeness with ever-increasing glory. "And we, who with unveiled faces all reflect the Lord's glory, are being transformed into his likeness with ever-increasing glory, which comes from the Lord, who is the Spirit" (2 Corinthians 3:16–18).

I cannot afford to focus on the hammer and chisel. I cannot look around me and bemoan what God is chipping away.

My heart breaks to think of the many people—Christians especially—who live their entire lives this way. They are eaten up by suffering. For years, I was. My wheelchair insisted, whined, and screamed for my undivided attention. Demoralized, I gave in. I allowed my wheelchair to define who I was. All it accomplished was a dry and brittle soul. I didn't become a bad person, I just lacked passion for life. With no spiritual energy, I spent my days in tired defeat, the day-to-day routine sucking me down. Relief was not sought in prayer or the Bible but in TV sitcoms and weekends at the mall.

Bitter resignation is no better. "Oh, well, this is my lot in life," we groan. Suffering becomes a predictable environment with familiar, albeit painful, boundaries. But not for long. Capitulating to suffering weakens the soul. Or stirs up anger. I know a sixty-three-year-old man who may soon lose his leg to diabetes. "Well, if it happens," he huffs, "I'll just park myself in front of the television. I'll go to my bedroom and never come out." This man is fuming about the future—and he hasn't even lost his leg yet.

Pride is worse. I recall, as a child, crying from a bruised knee and bearing the brunt of my Uncle Henry's words, "Chin up, you have nothing to cry about. A little hurt always helps!" The words matched his rough-rider image of Teddy Roosevelt with puffed-out chest and clenched smile. I sniffed back tears and promised myself I'd never cry again around my uncle. Others must have felt the same. "Stay out of Uncle Henry's way," was the word. Stoicism shrivels the soul.

Believing in suffering is a dead end.

Believing in the Sculptor is living hope.

Turn your focus on him, trusting that he will never cut or gouge too deeply. Are you frightened that God will make it worse? Give you another child with a birth defect? Force you into a nursing home with Alzheimer's disease? Leave you penniless? God is not a casual or capricious Sculptor. "'For I know the plans I have for you,' declares the Lord, 'plans to prosper you and not to harm you, plans to give you hope and a future'" (Jeremiah 29:11). He promises to be precise with the chisel. As Eugene Peterson's paraphrase of 1 Corinthians 10:13 says, "No test or temptation that comes your way is beyond the course of what others have had to face. All you need to remember is that God will never let you down; he'll never let you be pushed past your limit; he'll always be there to help you come through it."

The hurting and hammering process won't end until we become completely holy (and there's no chance of that happening this side of eternity). This is why I accept my paralysis as a chronic condition. When I broke my neck, it wasn't a jigsaw puzzle I had to solve fast, nor was it a quick jolt to get me back on track. My diving accident was the beginning of a long, arduous process of becoming like Christ. Sure, there are times I wish it were easier: "Three times I pleaded with the Lord to take [the suffering] away from me. But he said to me, 'My grace is sufficient for you, for my power is made perfect in weakness.' Therefore I will boast all the more gladly about my weaknesses, so that Christ's power may rest on me" (2 Corinthians 12:8–9).

I'm not perfect yet. I have a long way to go until my sculpture is polished and complete. God's grace—the desire and the power to do his will—is enough. "Therefore, strengthen your feeble arms and weak knees. Make level paths for your feet, so that the lame may not be disabled, but healed" (Hebrews 12:12). Health and wholeness, maturity and completeness will be mine one day!

So when I get bone weary of the process, I remember James 1:2–4, "When all kinds of trials crowd into your lives, my brothers, don't resent them as intruders, but welcome them as friends! Realize that they come to test your faith and to produce in you the quality of endurance. But let the process go on until that endurance is fully developed" (PHILLIPS).[1]

Endurance fully developed. It's one of the "reasons why" and yet it makes me wince. *But please, God, destroy anything in me that you are pleased to carve away. In your hands, what falls away is unimportant. If I am to delight in intimacy with you, I must "be ye holy as you are holy." It's needed. Especially since I'm headed for heaven, the holy habitation of holy inhabitants.*

"Dear friends, do not be surprised at the painful trial you are suffering, as though something strange were happening to you. But rejoice that you participate in the sufferings of Christ, so that you may be overjoyed when his glory is revealed" (1 Peter 4:12).

If I love God, suffering does not ultimately matter. Christ in me is what matters. Pain does not cease to be pain, but I can "rejoice in suffering" (Romans 5:5) because the power of God in my life is greater than suffering's vice-grip can ever be. I want to see the sculpture finished.

> When God wants to drill a man, and thrill a man and skill a
>     man,
> When God wants to mold a man to play the noblest part,
> When He yearns with all His heart to create so great and bold
>     a man

That all the world should be amazed,
Watch His methods, watch His ways:
How He ruthlessly perfects whom He royally elects;
How He hammers him and hurts him,
And with mighty blows converts him into shapes and forms of
    clay
Which only God can understand,
While man's tortured heart is crying and he lifts beseeching
    hands;
Yet God bends but never breaks when man's good He
    undertakes;
How He uses whom He chooses,
And with mighty power infuses him,
With every act induces him to try His splendor out,
God knows what He's about.

Author Unknown

I want "to be for the praise of his glory" (Ephesians 1:12). I want to be conformed to his image. The Sculptor desires it too, for "he who began a good work in you will carry it on to completion until the day of Christ Jesus" (Philippians 1:6).

All these are reasons behind our suffering. They answer in part the question "Why?"

But only in part.

Somewhere after my first decade in my wheelchair, I was gratified by what I was beginning to see. I was thankful for what I was learning. The image of Christ was slowly emerging as I reflected his kindness and compassion, as well as a sensitivity to evil. I marked that first decade as a milestone, a passage. I sensed that God wanted to show me more, lead me on, raise me higher, "refine the sculpture," as it were. To "leave the elementary teachings about Christ and go on to maturity" (Hebrews 6:1). I glanced in my rearview mirror and made a checklist:

> All things are working together for my good. For God's glory.
> Doesn't mean being a best-selling author or speaker. Simply
> means being like Christ. Check.

Hardships have forced me to make decisions about God. Made muscular my faith. I can believe in him more now than before the wheelchair. Check.

Suffering has done a job on my character. Not so sloppy about relationships. Stick to promises. Am more patient, at least somewhat. People matter more. Check.

Being paralyzed has really made heaven come alive. Not in a cop-out way, but in a way that makes me want to live better here because more is coming there. Check.

No doubt about it. My thoughts have been jerked right side up. Can't reach for the common temptations most people do. Having no hands helps with that. Check.

Suffering has made me a little more sensitive to others who are hurting. Couldn't have cared less about quads like me before my accident. Different story now. Check.

A checklist like this sounds dry and technical, but years ago, it helped answer—at least in part—that sticky question, "Why does God pile on hardships so high?" Why? Well—hey!—God is more concerned with conforming me to the likeness of his Son than leaving me in my comfort zones. God is more interested in inward qualities than outward circumstances. Things like refining my faith and humbling my heart, cleaning up my thought life and strengthening my character. Not a bad answer.

But not always the best one.

Sometimes good answers aren't enough.

## THE ONLY ANSWER THAT SATISFIES

"Hey, Connie," I said to my friend over the phone, "I'm flying into Baltimore for a speaking engagement in a couple of weeks and I would love to get together with some old Young Life club friends." I couldn't think of a better way to spend time off in my hometown than to dress up for a fancy luncheon with my high school girlfriends and swap stories, pass photos, dig up funny memories, and carve out an hour for prayer and hymn-singing. We hadn't been together since graduation in '67, and I was on pins and needles to see them.

I wheeled through Connie's front door three weeks later, geared up for a soulful afternoon.

"What did you do to your hair?"

"Hey, I brought a couple of old songbooks."

It was a traffic jam of hugs and hellos in the entry way of her house until Connie called us into the dining room. Linen, china, bowls of fruit, and fresh flowers greeted us.

"Okay, I have only three requests," I announced after grace was sung and platters started around the table. "Set aside time for prayer, singing, and each give an update on what's been happening."

Millie, at the far end with her arm in a cast, started. Yes, we'd all sign her cast before leaving, and, yes, I promised I wouldn't drool when I autographed it with my mouth. No, we didn't realize it had been on for months. Oh really? The prognosis is that bleak? The news of chronic infection subdued us.

Next, was Jacque, my fun-loving friend with whom I shared boyfriends, milkshakes, and laps around the hockey field. "You all know about my husband. It didn't work out between us. My son's having a rough time getting off drugs," she spoke to her plate, pushing food with her fork. The table was quiet except for the clinking of silverware.

The mother of my high school boyfriend, Mrs. Filbert, told how her son's wife had fled the marriage, leaving her to tend to her grand-children while he worked. Now that the grandkids were older, she was devoting her time to her husband stricken with Parkinson's. I heard words, but I saw memories of long ago Friday evenings when I would play the piano in her stately home. A safe, orderly, beautiful home, which kept heartache beyond the threshold. "Some people say I shouldn't give up speaking at Christian Women's Clubs," she said, her eyes becoming wet. "But I'm convinced the Lord has me where he wants me."

At the far end sat Diana, taking it all in. She hadn't said much. When we greeted each other, she seemed unusually quiet. It was her turn to speak. Diana's glum look fit her words as she shared a story of rebellion and drug abuse in her family. Dishes stopped clattering. Ever since high school, Diana had been a spiritual stalwart. Closer to God than any of us. But today, the immovable and unshakable Rock of Gibraltar stared into her lap. "I wasn't going to come to this luncheon. We brought my son home late last night from the rehab unit. It was pretty bad. I don't know. . . . I just don't know."

Silence settled over us. One person felt uneasy with the quiet—Jacque, the one who also had a son with drug problems. "Well, you gotta keep hoping, keep praying. Somehow, you gotta know it's going to work out. Keep believing. Who knows? Maybe this happened because—" Jacque checked off a few inward qualities God was probably fashioning as a result of outward circumstances. Ironclad faith. Robust character. Buoyant hope. Sensitivity to others. But a heavier silence. Diana already knew all that.

She could tie any of us up in a tangle of theological thread from her years of Bible study, not to mention a Masters in counseling. She knew the doctrinal ropes; she had spoon-fed me "suffering develops patience" and "suffering refines faith" when I kept bugging her as to "why?" Diana was doing that thirty years ago.

Slowly, out of the silence, a song began. First faintly, then swelling as all joined in:

> There is a balm in Gilead
>   To make the wounded whole;
> There is a balm in Gilead
>   to heal the sin sick soul.[2]

The old favorite from Young Life Club days came rising out of our memories as though we were saddle-shoed teenagers again, sitting cross-legged on the church-hall floor.

It was an old spiritual inspired by the prophet Jeremiah who, amidst the horror of the Babylonian invasion, asked, "Is there no healing for our wounds? Is there no answer for our weeping?" Back in high school, we sang about God, the balm in Gilead, to soothe a wounded heart from a sophomore crush. But now the lyrics glowed with a smooth patina from years tarnished by divorce, paralysis, disease, and drugs.

We sang the last note, then Connie sighed, "Dessert, anyone?" Mrs. Filbert got up and began clearing the table. Chairs shuffled, dishes clinked, and the room filled with pleasant chatter. As coffee was served, I sat back and realized I had just passed—we all passed through—a new milestone.

When your heart is being wrung out like a sponge, an orderly list of "sixteen good biblical reasons as to why this is happening" can sting like salt in a wound. You don't stop the bleeding that way. A checklist may be okay when you're looking at your suffering in a rearview mirror, but when you're hurting in the present tense, "Let me explain why this is happening" isn't always livable.

Answers, no matter how good they are, cannot be the *coup de grace*. Purified faith is never an end in itself; it culminates in God. Stronger character is character made muscular not for its sake, but God's. A livelier hope is more spirited because of its focus on the Lord. To forget this is to tarnish faith, weaken character, and deflate hope. "If you have these qualities existing and growing in you then it means that *knowing our Lord Jesus Christ* has not made your lives either complacent or unproductive" (2 Peter 1:8 PHILLIPS).

We must never distance the Bible's answers from God. The problem of suffering is not about some *thing,* but *Someone.* It follows that the answer must not be some thing, but Someone. "Knowing our Lord Jesus Christ" is keeping your eye on the Sculptor—not on the suffering, or even suffering's benefits.

Besides, answers are for the head. They don't always reach the problem where it hurts—in the gut and the heart. When a person is sorely suffering, like my friend Diana, people are like hurting children looking up into the faces of their parents, crying and asking, "Daddy, why?" Those children don't want explanations, answers, or "reasons why"; they want their daddy to pick them up, pat them on the backs, and reassure them that everything is going to be okay.[3]

Our heartfelt plea is for assurance—Fatherly assurance—that there is an order to reality that far transcends our problems, that somehow *everything will be okay.* We amble on along our philosophical path, then—Bam!—get hit with suffering. No longer is our fundamental view of life providing a sense of meaning or a sense of security in our world. Suffering has not only rocked the boat, it's capsized it. We need assurance that the world is not splitting apart at the seams. We need to know we aren't going to fizzle into a zillion atomic particles and go spinning off in space. We need to be reassured that the world, the universe, is not in nightmarish chaos, but orderly and stable. God must be at the center of things. He must be in the center of our suffering. What's more, he must be Daddy. Personal and compassionate. This is our cry.

God, like a father, doesn't just give advice. He gives himself. He becomes the husband to the grieving widow (Isaiah 54:5). He becomes the comforter to the barren woman (Isaiah 54:1). He becomes the father of the orphaned (Psalm 10:14). He becomes the bridegroom to the single person (Isaiah 62:5). He is the healer to the sick (Exodus 15:26). He is the wonderful counselor to the confused and depressed (Isaiah 9:6).

This is what you do when someone you love is in anguish; you respond to the plea of their heart by giving them your heart. If you are the One at the center of the universe, holding it together, if everything moves, breathes, and has it's being in you, you can do no more than give yourself (Acts 17:28).

It's the only answer that ultimately matters.

And we've only just begun.

# Nine

# MAKING SENSE
# OF SUFFERING

Reasons reach the head, but relationships reach the soul. It's the friendship of God reaching out to us through our trials that draws the bottom line of suffering.

Try this story. You are walking down a street, minding your own business, when you are accosted and forced to carry a huge and heavy basket on your back. You're ordered to walk three blocks, turn left, go two blocks, turn right, then proceed straight on. Staggering under the weight, you stumble on, bewildered and angry. The weight of the basket is crushing. Your back is breaking. The whole thing is meaningless and haphazard. You resent how the heavy burden consumes you, becoming the focal point of your entire existence.

When you are halfway down the third block, reeling under the burden, you finally bellow, "What gives!"

The truth is then revealed. The burden you are carrying is your child, injured and unconscious. "What?" On top of that, you discover you are not trudging through a meaningless rat-maze but the most direct route to a hospital emergency room.

Immediately you straighten. You inhale new vigor. Your knees quit buckling. Adrenaline and fresh energy quicken your pace, and you move forward with a new attitude. Why the change? The suffering you're going through involves a relationship. Not just any relationship, but one with your child. It is the love you have for your child that quickens your step and buoys up your heart. Your relationship gives your burden *meaning*. Even your twisted path makes sense. You know where you are going. Your journey has a positive end—the hospital—and this instills *hope*.

Suffering has no meaning in itself. Left to its own, it is a frustrating and bewildering burden. But given the context of *relationship,* suffering suddenly has meaning.

## FINDING RELATIONSHIP IN SUFFERING

In the film *Sleeper,* Woody Allen plays a character who wakes up in another century, having been frozen in a scientific experiment. He is given a stack of photographs from our century to identify, which prompts a series of hilarious one-liners. Billy Graham's picture comes up. Allen pauses, then says, "Billy Graham . . . claimed to have a personal relationship with God." The audience, of course, cracks up. That is how absurd the idea sounds to some. Indeed, it is an astonishing claim.[1]

What's more astonishing is that God doesn't crack up. There's nothing absurd, from his point of view, about a personal relationship with humans. He's a host issuing party invitations left and right. He's a shepherd leaving the ninety-nine in the field, seeking the one lost lamb. He's a king lavishing a party on beggars. He's got a place reserved. He's interested in relating.

I want to know God like this! Shove me under the waterfall of the Trinity's joy, which splashes and spills over heaven's walls. If he's always in a good mood, I want to catch it. If I'm lost, I want him to find me. Part the heavens, Lord, come down, kick aside the money tables, trash the "Don't Touch" rules and embrace me.

It should be that passionate. But we, creatures of systems and procedures, get stuck. Maybe in a style of worship, whether liturgical or "guided-by-the-Spirit." Maybe in a favorite way of studying the Bible or a certain method of prayer: confession first, repentance second, then praise and thanksgiving, intercession next, then praise again. We make these things the focus.

Study methods and worship techniques are helpful in getting introduced to God (we have to start somewhere), but they easily become flat and mechanical when cultivating a personal relationship. Even Jesus was astounded that people could devote their entire lives to studying

Scripture and yet fail to know the One to whom Scripture was pointing (John 5:39–40). Focusing on regiment and routines will do for
business executives, army sergeants, and Pharisees, but not God. You
might scratch the surface with him, but it's more—much more—than
"Do A, B, or C and you will know God better." He is not a missing
piece of our life which, once found, can be bolted into place so our
spiritual lives run efficiently and smoothly.

Personal relationships don't work that way. Certainly not when it
comes to God. If we want to grow closer to someone—God or anybody—it means pressing hearts together. Talking, discussing likes and
dislikes. Finding joy in each other. Checking in with each other, as with
your spouse. "Anything I can do for you? Do you need something?"
Rolling up your sleeves and muscling a job-well-done together. A
strong relationship is the weaving together of many shared experiences.

Such things make for intimacy. Yet intimacy can't be regimented.
Disciplining myself to spend regular time with someone can be regu-
lated but not the intimacy itself. Intimacy happens as two souls rub
together. It's what we long for more than anything else. To know and be
known. Even in the best relationships, we are still left aching for someone to comprehend our world and enter our struggle—to embrace us
with a passion that seizes and melts us into a union that will never be
broken. God answers that ancient longing. A yearning that echoes with
the message that we were made for him. Strike the tuning fork of God's
perfect pitch and something resonates in us, not on key, but in the same
range. We're like the harlots, the homeless, and the handicapped of Jesus'
day who knew that he could fill the gaping hole in their souls. They
followed him everywhere. Shared experiences ease the ache.

One experience in particular does it. You wouldn't choose it. It's
not tidy. You can't deal with it methodically. It's ugly, messy, painful,
and risky because it can draw you closer to God or drive you away.
But once you muddle through, you wouldn't trade the sweetness of
your intimacy with God for anything. It knits your heart together with
his like nothing else.

This particular experience binds you to God like it binds you to
people. Veterans from World War II know this. So do survivors of cancer,

a plane crash, or the polio epidemic of the fifties. Roommates in a hospital ward feel it.

It's shared suffering. When you're in the trenches, handing bullets to your buddy and fighting a common enemy, hearts can't help but be pressed together. Your knowledge of each other is unique and intimate to you. To you both.

I have a friend named Skip who was spinal cord injured the same day and year as I. Whenever our paths cross, we size up each other's wheelchairs and—instant camaraderie! I'm closer to my neighbors since the Northridge earthquake of 1994; my husband Ken ran outside after the initial jolt and, in the dark, nearly collided with Brian and Mr. Hollander. They froze, feeling the street beneath them shake like a jackhammer. "Here's someone who's been there. Who knows exactly how I feel . . . what I've experienced. We share something unique to us."

The *esprit de corps* among fellow sufferers is deep.

Suffering shared with God is deeper.

## I WANT TO KNOW CHRIST

"When do I get to have my wheelchair, Daddy?" Five-year-old Matthew looked up into the face of his father, his liquid brown eyes doleful and pleading. Matthew and his brother, Stephen, had spent a week with their parents volunteering at one of our JAF Retreats. They made buddies with scores of boys and girls who used crutches, walkers, and wheelchairs. I laughed when Jim, their father, relayed to me Matthew's request. This little boy doesn't need a wheelchair. He has no use for one. But try telling him that!

A wheelchair, for Matthew, would top his Christmas wish list. A wheelchair means a joy ride. It also means an initiation into a wonderful club: a special group of kids who enjoy a special relationship with Joni. This five-year-old hasn't a clue about the pain and paralysis, the heartaches and hurdles. He discounts all of that, disregarding the dark side. All he desires is a chance to be among my best friends, a chance to identify with me, be like me, a chance to know me. If it means having a wheelchair, great. He'll welcome it.

It takes a child like Matthew to illuminate the true emotion behind the apostle Paul's words, "I consider everything a loss compared to the surpassing greatness of knowing Christ Jesus my Lord, for whose sake I have lost all things. I consider them rubbish that I may gain Christ and be found in him" (Philippians 3:8–10). Matthew wanted to join a club, but the fellowship of Christ's sufferings is not an inner circle of elite believers. The word *fellowship* in the original text was *koinonia*—the experience of sharing something in common.

The apostle Paul had this in mind when he wrote, "I want *to know* Christ and the power of his resurrection and the fellowship of sharing in his sufferings, becoming like him in his death" (Philippians 3:10). You can almost hear the excitement in Paul's voice, his eyes—like five-year-old Matthew's—doleful and pleading. Paul disregards the dark side, the heartaches and the hurdles. If it means suffering, fine. He'll take it. He'll take on anything for the sake of knowing Christ. Pain and death, when they entered the world by the fall of humans, wasn't what God cherished for man; but when Adam chose suffering over the joys of union with God, the Lord turned suffering into a way man could know God better. Paul understood this. *I want to know Christ!*

The words "to know" mean a warm, intimate, and deep union. As in the book of Genesis where it says Adam *knew* his wife, Eve (Genesis 4:1 KJV). It's a spiritual picture of a physical joining-together. Paul didn't want simply to know Jesus in his head; he wanted to experience him in his heart, his whole being. Not only to catch God's good mood and delight in the cascade of his joy, but to feel God embracing him with a passion, seizing and melting him into a union never to be broken.

When you melt into God like that, it's more than knowing about him, it's knowing *him*. The inside stuff. How the Father loves the Son. How the son pleases the Father, not himself. How the Spirit reveals the Son, never himself. How the Son reveals the Father, never pointing to himself. The Father begets the Son, the Son honors the Father, the Spirit reveres them both. It's a kind of divine "dying to self."

Paul knew if his heart were to be knit to God's, it would mean suffering. Never pointing to himself but honoring and revering the Other. To get in the trenches with God where they could fight a common enemy. Where their hearts could be pressed together.

This is real *esprit de corps*. To know God in the trenches is to know why we trust him. Why shouldn't you trust the one covering your back in the crossfire? To know God is to be free of the incessant need to understand exactly what he is doing before you place confidence in him. Members with such *esprit de corps* are the happiest people in the world.

Such people know the real enemy. They know God will never run out of bullets—there will always be enough grace. They know God will never fail them. They know his mercy when they falter. His protection. His peace in the midst of the battle. His compassion for the hurting.

They are convinced God is *with* them in the trenches.

## I WANT TO KNOW … THE FELLOWSHIP OF SHARING IN HIS SUFFERINGS

This is the best part: He delights in identifying with us in our suffering.

When the apostle Paul was on the road to Damascus, the risen Lord didn't say, "Saul, why are you persecuting my people?" God said, "Why are you persecuting *me*?" (see Acts 9:4). He considers our sufferings his sufferings. He feels the sting in his chest when you hurt. He takes it personally. "If the world hates you, keep in mind that it hated me first," he said in John 15:18. This is intimacy described from Jesus' perspective.

Jesus is a Savior who can "sympathize with our weaknesses … one who has been tempted in every way, just as we are—yet was without sin" (Hebrews 4:15). My blind friend Peter shares how humiliated he was when, as a teenager, he fell after striking his head on a low branch. Sprawled on the ground in front of his friends, he felt hurt and embarrassed. His confidence in God was shaken: *You don't understand what it's like to be blind, God. To not know where the next blow might come from!* But Jesus does. "The men who were guarding Jesus began mocking and beating him. They blindfolded him and demanded, 'Prophesy! Who hit you?'" (Luke 22:63–64).

Another friend, Gloria, fell into deep anguish over the dismal prognosis of her daughter's illness. Little Laura had already suffered enough from the degenerative nerve disorder she had been born with, and now the doctors' forecast included more suffering and impending death. One night after leaving her daughter's bedside, she spat, "God, it's not right. You've never had to watch one of your children die!" As soon as the words escaped, she clasped her hand over her mouth. He did watch his child die. His one and only Son.

Early on when I realized Jesus is a Savior who could sympathize with our weakness, I was passionately telling everybody how "Christ was paralyzed on the cross." How he understood how I felt. A stressed-out firefighter happened to cross the wake of my enthusiasm. In the diner where we met, I offered, "He's been there. He understands." Outside, taxis honked and trucks rumbled by, but we were oblivious. The fireman's gaze held mine—me, cheerful and sincere; he, disbelieving and with scorn lining his tired mouth. "So he understands. Big deal. What good does that do me?" he bristled as he raised his arms from under the table. His rolled-up sleeves revealed the smooth ends of two stumps where hands should be. "Burned off in a blaze. Lost my job."

I was taken aback. I was fresh out of the hospital and certainly no theology student or expert on the Bible. Cheer drained from my face. I answered as honestly as I knew how. "I don't know all the answers. And I'm not sure if I did that it would help. But I do know the One who has the answers." A long pause. His gaze lowered. "—and knowing him makes all the difference." I had never spoken with such confidence, but I sensed the *esprit de corps* with this man with no hands. I then shocked myself by saying for the first time since my accident, "I'd rather be in this chair knowing him than on my feet without him."

The fireman didn't need a briefcase full of words. He needed the Word. The Word made flesh—gouged, with nail-pierced wrists, hands nearly ripped off. Spat upon, beaten bloody, with flies buzzing and hatred hammering. These aren't merely facts about Jesus. This isn't love as an abstract idea. This is love poured out like wine as strong as fire. In that diner, the fireman stopped thinking of God as a meditating mystic on a faraway mountain. No longer was he an abstract deity. Nothing neat and tidy about him. God got messy when he smeared his blood on a cross to save people from hellfire. This held a strange appeal for this man who had injured himself rescuing others from the flames.

Programs, systems, and methods sit well in the ivory towers of monasteries or in the wooden arms of icons. Head knowledge comes from the pages of a theology text. But the invitation to know God—

really know him—is always an invitation to suffer. Not to suffer alone, but to suffer with him. "If anyone would come after me, he must deny himself and take up his cross and follow me. For whoever wants to save his life will lose it, but whoever loses life for me and for the gospel will save it" (Mark 8:34–35).

The fireman was gripped. God didn't merely expose the fireman's sin, he entered it. He came into it. Like entering a burning building to hand a baby out the window just in the nick of time. But Jesus lost more than his hands; he lost his life. Thankfully, he was not scorched by death. He burst back to life. What power! If I'm to be held steady in the midst of my suffering, I want to be held not by a doctrine or a cause but by the most powerful Person in the universe.

Amazing love, how can it be? That God should plunge the knife in his heart for me—all the while, me, dry and indifferent, cool and detached. That he, the God of life, should conquer death by embracing it. That he should destroy the power of sin by letting it destroy him. This is "the foolishness of God . . . wiser than man's wisdom, and the weakness of God . . . stronger than man's strength" (1 Corinthians 1:25).

Little wonder the apostle Paul was aching to experience him "and the power of his resurrection."

## I WANT TO KNOW . . . THE POWER OF HIS RESURRECTION

Julia Beach stood behind the crumpled form of her husband, Bob. She, graying, slight-built and short, he, massive, muscular and with a patch over his eye from a hunting accident. She sighed, confessing, "Before I open my eyes in the morning, I am sometimes hit with the thought, *Dear Jesus, I can't face another day.* I'm overwhelmed by discouragement before I even throw the covers back." I wondered how they manage from day to day. Mrs. Beach needs power from out of this world.

You can't rise above your circumstances without power. Can't push through your pain without a force on your side. Can't even grasp a brighter perspective, a happier hope without strength from somewhere.

But why does Paul say "the power of his *resurrection*"?

And how does it help Julia?

First, she's helped just by knowing Jesus empathizes. For Jesus to be resurrected, he first had to die. To die, he first had to become human (without ever surrendering his deity). So the resurrected Jesus once walked in Julia's shoes and felt the pain of this earthly life. Even though he's now in heaven, he has a "divinely" good memory that recalls his days upon earth. He knows what Mrs. Beach goes through. Is Julia Beach broken? He is broken with her. Do neighbors no longer come by to help? Jesus couldn't get his three best friends to spend an hour in prayer with him. If she feels like the world has passed her by, he too was ignored. Is she sinking into sorrow? He sunk low as "a man of sorrows, and acquainted with grief" (Isaiah 53:3 KJV). Does he descend into her hell? Yes, for Julia may cry, "The darkness is all around me," but "even the darkness is not dark to him" (Psalm 139:12). You can endure most anything, even hours sitting vigil by a sickbed, if you know God is sitting next to you.

Secondly, the "power of his resurrection" helps Mrs. Beach because she's earmarked as a recipient of the Spirit whom the resurrected Jesus won the right to pour out on her. This means she has immediate access to incredible power.

But wait. There's no gain without pain; remember, Jesus had to conquer sin and death in order to pour out that power. Access to this power will cost us something, like "an eye gouged" or "if your right hand causes you to sin, cut it off and throw it away. It is better for you to lose one part of your body than for your whole body to go into hell" (Matthew 5:29–30). Jesus becomes one with us in our suffering; we, in turn, become one with him in his. He takes on our flesh; we take on his holiness.

> Our fathers disciplined us for a little while as they thought best; but God disciplines us for our good, *that we may share in his holiness.* No discipline seems pleasant at the time, but painful. Later on, however, it produces a harvest of righteousness and peace for those who have been trained by it.
>
> Hebrews 12:10–11

If Jesus died *for* sin, we die *to* sin. This doesn't mean we must die as Christ did, paying sin's penalty, but if we are to experience life-changing, suffering-shaking power in our lives, we "always [bear] in the body the dying of Jesus" (2 Corinthians 4:10).

At first, this might not sit well with Mrs. Beach. It sounds cold and hard. "Gouge an eye? My husband's already lost one. What more could you possibly want from us, God?" What God wants is for this frail, tired woman to die to her doubts, fears, anxieties, and abilities. God knows they are a burden too heavy for her to bear.

Dying to self. It's just a small taste of the pangs and affliction Christ experienced, but taste it, we must. If we're going to cash in on his joy, peace, and heavenly home, if we are going to partake of all of Christ's benefits, then it means, "sharing in the fellowship of his sufferings, becoming like him in his death." Death is the gateway to life.

And the gateway to power.

But how do we walk through the gate?

## THE CROSS

By itself, suffering does no good. But when we see it as the thing *between* God and us, it has meaning. Wedged in the crux—the cross— suffering becomes a transaction. The cross is the place of transaction. "The cross is . . . the power of God" (1 Corinthians 1:18). It is the place where power happens *between* God and us.

It's where *relationship* is given birth and depth. The cross was, first, a transaction between the Father and the Son. Because of what transpired there—the work of salvation—the cross has meaning. Not only between the Father and the Son, but between the Son and us. For our salvation, yes, but also for our suffering. The cross is the center of our relationship with Jesus. Something literal happened there 2,000 years ago. It is where we were given spiritual birth.

Something symbolic is happening still: the cross is where we die. We go there daily. But it isn't easy. Normally, we will follow Christ anywhere—to a party, as it were, where he changes water to wine, to a sunlit beach where he preaches from a boat, to a breezy hillside where he feeds thousands, and even to the temple where he topples the tables of the moneychangers. But to the cross? We dig in our heels. The invitation is so frighteningly individual. It's an invitation to go alone. The

Lord does not give a general appeal but a specific one, personal to you. The transaction exists between the Almighty of the universe and you.

We know it as a place of death. "Put to death, therefore, whatever belongs to your earthly nature . . ." (Colossians 3:5). Who wants to do that? Crucify his own pride? Kill his own daydreams and fantasies? Dig a grave for his pet worries?

We simply cannot bring ourselves to go to the cross. Nothing attracts us to it.

Thus we live independently of the cross. Or try to. As time passes, the memory of our desperate state when we first believed fades. The cross was something that happened to us "back then." We forget how hungry for God we once were. We grow self-sufficient. We go through the motions—turning the other cheek and going the extra mile—but the effort is just that, an effort. We would hardly admit it, but we know full well how autonomous of God we operate.

This is where God steps in.

He permits suffering. He allows Peter's blindness, Laura's degenerative disease, Mr. Beach's hunting accident, my paralysis. Suffering reduces us to nothing and as Søren Kierkegaard noted, "God creates everything out of nothing. And everything which God is to use, he first reduces to nothing." To be reduced to nothing is to be dragged to the foot of the cross. It's a severe mercy. Our dark side abhors it; our enlightened side recognizes it as home base.

A miraculous exchange happens at the cross. When suffering forces us to our knees at the foot of Calvary, we die to self. We cannot kneel there for long without releasing our pride and anger, unclasping our dreams and desires—this is what "coming to the cross" is all about. In exchange, God imparts power and implants new and lasting hope. We rise, renewed. His yoke becomes easy; his burden light. But just when we begin to get a tad self-sufficient, suffering presses harder. And so, we seek the cross again, mortifying the martyr in us, destroying the self-display. The transaction then is able to continue. God reveals more of his love, more of his power and peace as we hold fast the cross of suffering.

Stray away from it and . . . no power.

When I was a child on our family's farm, one of my favorite places was the pond down in the pasture by the barn. Tadpoles and crayfish occupied me for hours. I'd rest on my haunches and wonder where the pond water came from. I'd walk around its edge but could never see any stream splashing into it. No trickling rivulet over a rock. No pipes feeding it from the spring house.

My dad patiently tried to explain that the pond was fed by a spring, from water deep in the earth. That spring, he told me, bubbled up and filled the pond. If Dad would have dug the pond area larger, the spring would have continued to fill it. To me it was a mystery, but I was sufficiently satisfied to go on playing with frogs and crayfish.

It's no longer a mystery now that I've felt the crunch of decades of paralysis. The encroachments of my limitations often feel like the cutting edge of a spade, digging up twisted vines of self-centeredness and the dirt of sin and rebellion. Uprooting rights. Clearing out the debris of habitual sins. Shoveling away pride. To believe in God in the midst of suffering is to empty myself; and to empty myself is to increase the capacity—the pond area—for God. *The greatest good suffering can do for me is to increase my capacity for God.* Then he, like a spring, is free to flow through me. "He who believes in Me, as the Scripture said, 'From His innermost being shall flow rivers of living water'" (see John 7:38).

Not a rivulet, but a powerful river of peace.

## THE LOVE OF GOD CONSTRAINS US

Suffering makes for this marvelous transaction, this *between* God and us. And when something marvelous happens between God and us, his cross no longer seems just a symbol of death. Another miraculous exchange occurs: the cross becomes a symbol of life. Victorious life. We no longer go to the cross kicking and screaming, we race to it for dear life. "The love of Christ compels us" to yield further to love's demands; thus we "throw off everything that hinders and the sin that so easily entangles" (2 Corinthians 5:14; Hebrews 12:1).

We no longer go to the cross to get something, even something so sweet as "peace like a river." We don't "go" to the cross at all. We are drawn to it. Compelled.

The love of Christ places inexorable and insistent demands on my heart, wooing, enticing, luring, and drawing me like a magnet into the inside stuff about God. My heart is aroused by Psalm 25:14; if "the Lord confides in those who fear him," then any amount of suffering is worth gaining the confidentiality of the Almighty. Backaches. Lung infections. Long stints in bed feeling claustrophobic. Sitting down in a world that stands up. "No, in all these things we are more than conquerors . . . for I am convinced that neither death nor life, neither angels nor demons, neither the present nor the future, nor any powers, neither height nor depth, nor anything else in all creation, *will be able to separate us* from the love of God that is in Christ Jesus our Lord" (Romans 8:37–39).

God wants no separations. He permits suffering *between* Jesus and me so that nothing will be between Jesus and me.

Deeper and more delightful, onward and upward we journey toward the cross, confessing and trusting, yielding and obeying. Poets and sages, Christian mystics and martyrs have ached to find words that would convey the sweetness, the pleasure, the rapture of such intimate communion with God. I wish there were a word for this joy-peace-pleasure-rest-freedom all rolled into one. I only know earth offers no such satisfaction. It's the answer to Jesus' prayer to our Father: "I in them and you in me" (John 17:22–23).

> Never further than Thy cross,
> Never higher than Thy feet;
> Here earth's precious things seem dross;
> Here earth's bitter things grow sweet.
>
> Here, O Christ, our sins we see,
> Learn Thy love while gazing thus;
> Sin, which laid the cross on Thee,
> Love, which bore the cross for us.
>
> Here we learn to serve and give,
> And, rejoicing, self deny;
> Here we gather love to live;
> Here we gather faith to die.

Pressing onward as we can,
Still to this our hearts must tend;
Where our earliest hopes began,
There our last aspirings end.

Till amid the hosts of light,
We in Thee redeemed, complete,
Through Thy cross made pure and white,
Cast our crowns before Thy feet.

Elizabeth Rundle Charles (1828–1896)[2]

Resurrection power is found at the cross, the place where we die to fierce unrest and low ambition. Resurrection power is cleansing power. Purifying power. It's the ability to sweep clean every skeleton in your closet and shake loose every monkey off your back. Strength to break the ball and chain around your soul and swing wide the prison door to the fresh air of freedom. Power to say no to doubts and fears and power to say yes to God's enabling. It's what 2 Timothy 2:11–12 is all about: "If we *die* with him, we shall also *live* with him; if we *suffer* with him, we shall also *reign* with him."

Maybe this answers that ancient longing I spoke of earlier. The yearning that echoes the message that we were made for him. If we strike the tuning fork of God's perfect pitch, we will hear . . . perfection. Perhaps our desire to know him and the power of his resurrection is really an intense desire for holiness.

To be all that he created us to be.

## COME TO THE CROSS AND FIND YOURSELF

Shawna Leavell could be a model in Paris, gliding down the runways at the finest fashion shows. Tall, lithe, with a blonde mane that breezes behind her as her long legs stride. When she was little, we'd camp up in the Sierras. I'd sit at the bottom of a cliff and enjoy vicarious rock climbing through her. Or trout fishing. "What a helpful kid," I'd say to her mother as Shawna toasted me marshmallows or pushed me along the road of Coldwater Campground. Years later, art school and wardrobe work in the movie industry pushed her into a different life. An unsafe life.

Living alone in downtown Los Angeles, she walked the edge of darkness and depression. On a lonely Friday night, after a couple of glasses of gin, she stumbled out of the house, clouded and numb. In a fog, she climbed into her car, drove down the street and got on the Hollywood freeway. Up the exit. Shawna was speeding north straight into southbound traffic. Oncoming cars veered, flashing their high beams and honking. She doesn't remember the head-on collision. She doesn't recall the police cars, helicopters and bullhorns, and evening news reports on the television. One man dead. Another seriously injured. A wife left without a husband and three children without their father.

Days later, a policeman was still posted outside of Shawna's hospital room where she lay bruised in a body cast. When I wheeled up to her bedside, she moaned through swollen lips. "I am . . . so sorry." Gone was the happy, free-spirited little camper with the sunny hair. She would never be the same.

The proof is in her letters from prison. It took over two years for her final sentencing, but in the custody of her mother, she diligently prepared for prison by attending Pastor Jack Hayford's church five nights a week and then Sundays at her mother's church. Bible institute. Prayer meetings. Witnessing. And always, whenever we were together, tender tears of repentance. When she was finally led away in chains, she welcomed justice. She embraced the chance to tell other women in prison that a sinful, self-serving life kills.

Shawna wasn't expecting the prison to be so overcrowded that she would be forced to endure a stint on death row, isolated and without her Bible. "I needed that. It tested my foundation." I heard this week she was finally moved to a cell with seven other women. Shawna stands out. They are tough; she's tender since the accident. They are black; she is very white. They never went camping with their mothers, rode horses, or went to art school. But differences attract attention. Many of the women are approaching Shawna for prayer and advice. One of them scoffed, "You think you're so high and mighty, better than us," to which Shawna replied, "Oh no, you're wrong. I'm the worst. I had every chance. I was given every opportunity. And I blew it. But Christ has forgiven me, the worst of sinners. And he can forgive you, too."

When Shawna is released from prison, she hopes to approach the family of the victims and play a part in redeeming their spilled blood. She, after all, spilled it. She will be forever reminded by the rods in her back and the pain in her ankle that sin destroys. But suffering—especially suffering as a consequence of sin—"is better than a life of rebellion," to use her words.

Shawna may have thought that, at the core, she was the fun-loving bohemian at home on Rodeo Drive or the high Sierras. Perhaps she thought her identity was wrapped up in the art world or in the movie world. But suffering forced her to be utterly alone with herself. Suffering is what most tested her as a person, examining her, sifting and asking, "Who are you?" When Shawna tried to answer, she was overwhelmed. Her darker side may have been hidden before, she may have manipulated circumstances before that fateful night, she may have succeeded in not appearing petty or vindictive, but the accident changed all that. Suffering interrogated her, asking, "You think you're so good!"

Shawna's true identity was scraped off the concrete of the Hollywood freeway. A sinner deserving death. And it's a good thing. If sin had kept its free hand in her life, it would have destroyed the very depth of her personality.

> Sin destroys the one reality on which our true character, identity, and happiness depend: our fundamental orientation to God. We are created to will what God wills, to know what he knows, to love what he loves. Sin is the will to do what God does not will, to know what he does not know, to love what he does not love . . . in all these things sin proves itself to be a supreme injustice not only against God but, above all, against ourselves.[3]

"It was needed," she writes, "in order for me to die to the pull of sin."

"Therefore, since Christ suffered in his body, arm yourselves also with the same attitude, because he who has suffered in his body is done with sin. As a result, he does not live the rest of his earthly life for evil human desires, but rather for the will of God" (1 Peter 4:1–2).

The test of suffering is never ameliorated. We cannot escape its interrogation. It will always reveal the core of who we are. If we love ourselves selfishly, suffering will carbonate into sin. Evil in us will fizz to the surface and spread poison. Hardships will make us hateful and, in order to avoid suffering, we will inflict pain on ourselves and flail out at others. When that happens, suffering makes us worse than we were. Affliction doesn't teach us about ourselves from a textbook, it uses the stuff inside of us.

It's humiliating to be sandblasted to the core. The mask of pride ripped away. The veneer of pettiness peeled off. But there's something refreshing about knowing yourself at the core. The vulnerability. The transparency. The "nothing" *between* God and us.

And thankfully, God doesn't leave us stripped bare.

The beauty of being exposed and empty is that God can then cover you. Like a surface that must be scrubbed clean before you can bond anything to it, the bonding of intimacy between God and us won't adhere until the film of dirt goes, the ambitions, the vanity, everything that sets itself up against others and God.

It's not just that sin is removed; the saint is built up: "For those God foreknew he also predestined to be conformed to the likeness of his Son" (Romans 8:29). Remember when we said that God delights in his own reflection? That the mirror image of himself is his Son? Think of his joy when he sees Christ in you. Nothing enthralls him more. When the soul empties itself of pride and pettiness, Christ fills it up. It's just another way of saying Colossians 3:3, "For you died, and your life is now hidden with Christ in God." You die. He lives.

Nothing could be more gloriously bittersweet. Not sweet, but bittersweet.

Have you ever noticed that there is a kind of suffering and a kind of dying that we secretly long for, that is indescribably delicious in a mystical way? This is not ordinary suffering (unless we are masochists). But we want to die when we have a mystical experience. I only felt it twice: once when swimming in the ocean in a great storm and once when first hearing Beethoven's Ninth Symphony. The French call sexual intercourse *le petit mal,* the little death. It is an end, a consummation, like death, yet a consummation devoutly to be wished. The mystics speak of their deep desire to die in God, to become nothing in God. . . . What does it mean that we long to die, to suffer total self-loss? And what does it mean that joy is close to tears and that the most wonderful things are not sweet but bittersweet?[4]

Tears never tasted so good until I entered the fellowship of Christ's sufferings. Until then, I never wept bitterly over lost souls and a hurting world. The ache in my heart never felt so fiery and passionate. Sorrow and joy never seemed so sweetly mingled. Hope never seemed so solid. Being alone never seemed so satisfying.

My mother has always been surrounded by family, friends, neighbors, but now that she's eighty-three, has lost her husband, and has sold the family home, she spends a great deal of time by herself. Loss has emptied her, but God has filled her. I used to worry about her being alone until she said recently, "Joni, God has changed me. I don't mind being by myself. I like myself and so I enjoy being with me." Mom likes what she sees: not herself, but Christ in her, the hope of glory.

Affliction is the gristmill where pride is reduced to powder, leaving our souls naked, bare, and bonded to Christ. And it feels beautiful.

## POWER IN SUFFERING

It happens by sharing in the fellowship of Christ's sufferings.

It's poignant that when the Son of Man walked on earth, he had the comfort of his Father, but none from his friends. No fellowship of suffering on this planet for him. He only had the blind insensitivity of his disciples. No moral support. No joy in carrying his cross—he bore it "for the joy that was set before him." He went without comfort so that you might be comforted. He went without joy so that you might have it. He willingly chose isolation so that you and I might never be alone. Most wonderfully, he bore God's wrath so that you wouldn't. God has no anger for you; only forgiveness, mercy, and grace.

If "God's kindness leads you toward repentance" (Romans 2:4), then there's only one response to love like this: beat the breast and "submit yourselves, then, to God . . . come near to God . . . wash your hands, you sinners, and purify your hearts . . . grieve, mourn and wail" (James 4:7–9).

Sound morbid? Maybe. But this is where *real* power kicks in—not primarily to overcome suffering. That's putting the cart before the horse. Resurrection power is meant to uproot sin out of our lives. Then we, with holy hearts, experience a greater degree of his love. It is in Christ's love that we become more than conquerors. Intimacy with Jesus gives us the brighter perspective, the happier hope. When it comes to pushing through pain, Jesus is the force on our side. "Apart from me, you can do nothing" he reminds us (John 15:5).

Remember Julia Beach? We left her lying in bed, wondering how she will find the strength to face another day. Today, before she opens her eyes and throws back the covers, she will pray, "I can do everything through him who gives me strength" (Philippians 4:13). She will leave behind the fears and overwhelming feelings, the sin. Divine energy will surge through her the moment she begins moving into the morning's challenges. As the hours wear on, it'll be a struggle. She will have to go to God many times out of desperate need, but she'll have strength— Jesus' strength. "I have been crucified . . . and I no longer live, but Christ lives in me" (Galatians 2:20), or to use Mrs. Beach's words, "Dear Jesus, I am overwhelmed, I don't have the strength . . . but you do. As I put one foot in front of the other today, I trust you'll give me your power."

And he will. "That power is like the working of his mighty strength, which he exerted in Christ when he raised him from the dead and seated him at his right hand in the heavenly realms" (Ephesians 1:19).

If God can raise Jesus from the dead, he can raise Mrs. Beach above her circumstances.

# Section III

## HOW CAN I HANG ON?

# Ten

# CRY OF THE SOUL

I don't get it. I just don't . . . get God."

It's a common comment when I'm with Greg Ericks, my coworker, heading to a meeting, a long freeway ahead and time to talk. Sometimes we're quiet and I just watch him from my wheelchair behind the driver's seat. Not many men have a profile as handsome as Greg. Tall, Dutch, blonde, and bright-eyed. Dresses nice too. Plaid shirts, jeans, and tweed jackets are his style, betraying that he'd be more comfortable camped by a trout stream in Montana than leading workshops.

The profile I see today is not picture-perfect for *Gentleman's Quarterly*. Greg is divorced, and every once in awhile the half-healed wound seeps. Like this afternoon. He has one hand on the wheel while stretching with the other to feed his son, Ryan, banana and crackers. Ryan—his beautiful ten-year-old, whose happy-hearted smile makes you forget he's retarded, incontinent, and, except for his giggles or occasional shrieks, can't put two words together in a sentence. Ryan is as handsome as his father. And despite the many seizures, just as pleasant to be around. I watch them and try to picture Ryan's mother on the scene, holding him on her lap, banana neatly sliced and peeled in a Tupperware. Banana mush drips from Ryan's chin.

Greg is diabetic, I remember as, with his free hand, he tosses the banana peel and reaches for his insulin kit. Prick finger. Watch freeway. Swig sugary apple juice. Eye on Ryan. "Hey, big boy," he puckers. Ryan dazzles us with his grin. Greg's as driven as he drives, his hamster-wheel-days made dizzy, one problem to solve after the next. Then there's his twelve-year-old daughter, Kelsey. Blossoming, budding, and forcing her dad to be the best he can be.

Sundays are the hardest. Like last Sunday afternoon when he and the kids bumped into their mother in a drug store. Kelsey, Ryan, and Mommy became a bundle of hugs. Greg wished he could be part of the bundle, but it was the usual awkwardness. Niceties were exchanged, then it was time to move on. Screams and tears from Ryan as they part company. More screams from him when Greg drops Kelsey off. Screams again as Greg leaves Ryan at the door of his foster group home. The day closes out with a speeding ticket, going fifty in a thirty-five-mile-per-hour zone. He stares vacantly at the policeman. Greg doesn't care.

We drive for a long time in silence. Finally he sighs, "Ryan, with those traces of scars on his face from falling down—" he leans over and touches his son who is the angel asleep in the front seat. "I love the way he runs, stumbles, and trips his way to me whenever I come to pick him up. Still, the fury occasionally simmers. I don't get why God does this . . . allows this. All of this," his voice trails. "I just don't get it."

*I don't get it either,* I want to say. The long stretch of darkening freeway has set the straight-ahead tone for "I don't get it" conversation, reducing the world to good and bad, black and white, "why" and "why not?" I don't get why Greg and his ex-wife can't be a real family. Greg loves his children. When I met their mother months earlier, she was equally loving and caring. I want to grab them both and say, "Things aren't that bad—love and goodness should triumph here." But it's a world of irreconcilable differences. An ex-world. Like some weird divorce between God and his Creation that should have never happened.

As we turn into our hotel, I catch Greg's profile highlighted by headlights. I shake my head. It's Sunday night. After Greg drops me and my friends off, he heads with Ryan to his group home. If Ryan stays asleep as he carries him to the front door, it will be a good night.

If not, it will be worse than bad.

Most of the world lives this way. I don't mean that most people are divorced or the single parents of handicapped children; I mean that the troublesome situations most people find themselves in don't go away. They don't get better. Greg and his former wife probably won't remarry. It's doubtful Ryan will experience a miracle of healing. When it's day-in and day-out, lifting one foot in front of the other, suffering doesn't have to be as severe as divorce or a serious disability; it could be the weariness of constantly refereeing rowdy teenagers. It could be slaving all afternoon in the kitchen and not hearing a hint of "Good dinner, Mom!"

Most of the time we can manage. Like jugglers spinning plates on long sticks. And if rowdy teenagers or drop-dead dinnertimes discourage us, we squeeze in a heart-to-heart talk with a close friend before rushing to spin the next plate. We keep a journal, venting our frustrations on paper. We soak in the tub, sweat on the treadmill, splurge on a new dress, or get away to the mountains for a weekend. Prayer groups and Bible studies help. God won't load us up with more plates than we can handle, and with his enabling we will be able to keep them spinning. But sometimes we're pressed hard to believe it. Something, we assume, has to give.

This is what happened to Greg Ericks and his wife. Too many hurts unresolved. Too many failures at communicating. When Ryan arrived on the scene, he unwittingly stoked the fire. A severe disability threw fuel on an already volatile situation. The flames licked higher, the pressure mounted, and the unbearable anguish began to choke faith out of Greg and his wife.

When pain lumbers through the front door, squats down in the middle of your life, and makes itself at home day after day, year after year, we can choke. We can crack. We erupt in anger.

## GOOD ANGER

Spurned husbands aren't the only ones who let off steam. Plenty of believers long before Greg Ericks have bordered on losing faith. Listen to the writer of Psalm 88:

> You have put me in the lowest pit,
>     in the darkest depths.
> Your wrath lies heavily upon me;
>     you have overwhelmed me with all your waves.
> You have taken from me my closest friends
>     and have made me repulsive to them.
> I am confined and cannot escape;
>     my eyes are dim with grief. . . .

> Why, O LORD, do you reject me
>> and hide your face from me?
> From my youth I have been afflicted and close to death;
>> I have suffered your terrors and am in despair.
> Your wrath has swept over me;
>> your terrors have destroyed me.
> All day long they surround me like a flood;
>> they have completely engulfed me.
> You have taken my companions and loved ones from me;
>> the darkness is my closest friend.
>
>                                              (Psalm 88:6–9;14–18)

Period. End of sentence. The author of Psalm 88 abruptly stops on a note of resentment. No set-up for a hopeful ending. No hand-is-quicker-than-the-eye move from moaning to happy-hearted praise. Not even a sniff of joy in the entire eighteen verses. God seems snide and cruel, smashing underfoot helpless humans as though they were cigarette butts. The words are ugly. Then again, so is life.

God is big enough to take on anger like this. It doesn't fluster him.

First, he knows stuff happens. He himself said, "In this world you will have trouble." Secondly, he doesn't tiptoe around it, embarrassed and at wit's end to explain our woes. He doesn't cover up the gore and guts of a person's rage like a Mafia hit man who trashes his blood-stained gloves so he doesn't get nailed. Remember God's rage nailed God to a cross. He wrote the book on suffering. And he invited people like the one who wrote Psalm 88 to be his co-authors. In so doing, he invited angry people to air their complaints.

He invites Greg Ericks to do the same.

"God, I don't get it, I don't get *you!* Okay, okay, I'll take responsibility for my marriage problems, but this thing with Ryan, his seizures—God, what are you *doing?* Every time Ryan has a seizure and falls down, every time he bangs his head, cuts his lip . . . how can you allow this? Don't you *care* about my little boy?"

Strong words. We're usually scared to death to talk to God this way. Too often we repress our deep emotions about suffering. We choose the polite route, bottling up our unspeakable feelings toward God and hiding behind a religious pretense as we "give it all over to the Lord" too quickly. All we've done is shove the problem to the back burner. There, it simmers. This is *real* trouble. We can't smell problems burning when they're repressed. And so, we naively think things will work out. But they don't. Hope is aroused, then deferred. It revives, then gets snuffed again. "Hope deferred makes the heart sick." The fire goes out. Our hearts become cold.

Anger keeps pushing the problem to the front burner. Fiery feelings make the problem a hot potato, propelling us into action and triggering activity. We are not allowed to wallow in our failures. Hot-hearted rage spurs an immediate and decisive choice and forces us to face our need.

Anger—even the sort of heated emotions Greg experiences—may not be all that bad. When Ephesians 4:26 states, "In your anger do not sin," it's clear that hostility is not always synonymous with sin. Not all anger is wrong.

Cancer, bankruptcy, divorce, or the birth of little boys with multiple handicaps push people to extremes. Affliction either warms you up toward spiritual things or turns you cold. Jesus said in Revelation 3:15–16, "I know your deeds, that you are neither cold nor hot. I wish you were either one or the other! So, because you are lukewarm—neither hot nor cold—I am about to spit you out of my mouth." Hate is sometimes closer to love than indifference. And lukewarmness is the only road that never gets to God. There's nothing mediocre about feelings of fury. Better that Greg is mad. Much better than ho-hum half-heartedness. Jesus says so.

Strong emotions open the door to asking the really hard questions: Does life make sense? Is God good? More to the point, our deep emotions reveal the spiritual direction in which we are moving. Are we moving toward the Almighty or are we moving away from him? Anger properly makes *Someone* the issue of our suffering rather than some *thing.* And that's moving in the right direction.[1]

The thing I love about Greg—the thing I believe God loves about Greg—is that he is taking his complaints to God. He is moving toward the Lord, venting disappointment, expressing hurt, and, when it comes to Ryan's violent seizures, questioning the goodness of the Almighty. Plus, Greg hasn't quit the family. He hasn't given up on his ex-wife, abandoned Ryan, or turned his back on Kelsey. Neither is he sowing seeds of discord nor inciting rebellion among his friends against God. He's not talking about God behind God's back. He's angry enough to engage him head-on.

This makes Greg's rage a good rage. The strain in his neck muscles reveals how earnest he really is. When I listened to him in the van, I could hear, embedded between the lines, an honest hunger. A "wanting to stay connected." After all, the people you really get angry with are the ones you trust most deeply. "I am mad as a hornet, God, and I don't understand what you are doing one bit!" sounds like the dark side of trust, but it's trust, nonetheless.

## GOD'S ACTION IN ANGER

Anger has a dark side too. It has incredible potential to destroy.

It digresses into a black energy that demands immediate release and relief. It despises being vulnerable and helpless. It relishes staying in control. It loathes dependence on God and so gains macabre pleasure in spreading the poison of mistrust. Ironically, this sort of anger—unrighteous anger—turns on us. It is a liar, offering us satisfaction, when in truth it guts us and leaves us empty.

Who can endure such emptiness? I'm reminded of this whenever I see the famous painting "The Scream" by Norwegian artist Edvard Munch. It's a horrific portrayal of despair, a painting of a gaunt and ghoulish figure, twisted and tormented, with eyes wide and mouth open. The figure is wailing, and horror is magnified by the fact that you cannot hear its cry. He is a painted figure and his is a silent scream. A pure and distilled scream of despair.

Unrighteous anger—anger that leads us away from God—sucks the last vestige of hope from our hearts. We stop caring, stop feeling. We commit a silent suicide of the soul, and sullen despair moves in like a terrible damp fog, deadening our heart to the hope that we will ever be rescued, redeemed, and happy again.

God will not stand for this. He is intolerant of despair. He is, I am sure, no fan of "The Scream" and will not allow us to exist like ghouls.

He will not permit our puny shields of unrighteous anger to stall him. And so he encroaches, presumes, invades, and infringes. He tears aside the curtains of despondency and throws open locked doors. He hits the light switch in our dark hearts. He pierces our complacency and boldly intrudes into our self-pity, brashly calling it what it is and challenging us to leave it behind.

He does it, occasionally, by heaping on trouble.

I'll never forget when God crashed through my despair. Somewhere after the first year of lying paralyzed in my hospital bed, somewhere after my bleak prognosis drained every ounce of hope—even anger, both righteous and unrighteous—out of me, despair moved in. I refused to get up for physical therapy. I turned my head away when friends came to visit.

Hazel, a black nurse's aide from Mississippi, noticed I was slipping away. She knew I had taken a liking to her. She would amble into my room, pull up a chair, and take her cigarette breaks by my bedside. "Wanna tell me about it, girl?" she'd ask, lighting up. No reply. She'd smile, slowly blowing a stream of smoke in the other direction. I'd grunt. "You feel like bawling, you just tell me. I've got a kerchief here handy," she'd say, patting her pocket.

"Um." I was numb. I didn't want to talk.

I didn't want to eat. Once when Hazel was feeding me dinner, half-chewed food dribbled out of the side of my mouth. "What in the world are you doing!" she shouted. My body reacted with a violent spasm. Hazel slammed down the fork and peas scattered. She forcefully wiped my mouth with a napkin, crumpled it, and threw it down on the tray. "You get yourself together, girl. Ain't nothing wrong with you that a good look around this hospital won't cure."

My cheeks flushed with embarrassment. I fought back tears.

"Now are you gonna eat this or what?"

Hazel had roused deep feelings of resentment. My eyes narrowed. "Yes," I spat back. The food was tasteless and hard. I chewed mechanically, forcing myself to swallow against a knotted stomach. Not a word was spoken between us. After she left, I struggled harder to contain the tears. I could not allow myself to cry because there would be no one to blow my nose or change my damp pillow. All I could do was choke out a whisper, "I can't . . . I can't live like this. Please help me."

Suddenly I realized, *I'm feeling something.* Like a hibernating animal waking up, I felt something stir. No more emotional numbness. Instead, a magnetic pull toward hope. In the darkness, I found myself saying out loud, "God, if I can't die, please show me how to live." It was short, to the point, but it left the door open for him to respond. Little did I realize he would: "The LORD is close to the brokenhearted and saves those who are crushed in spirit" (Psalm 34:18).

I sensed a stronger interest in the Bible. When I lay face down on the stryker frame, I was able to flip the pages of a Bible with my mouth stick. I didn't know where to turn, but the psalms intrigued me. I was not so much interested in the despair of Psalm 88 but in the other 149 psalms that hinted more of hope:

> Will the Lord reject forever?
>   Will he never show his favor again?
> Has his unfailing love vanished forever?
>   Has his promise failed for all time?
> Has God forgotten to be merciful?
>   Has he in anger withheld his compassion?
>
> (Psalm 77:7–9)

Seven rapid-fire questions packed with explosive power. The psalmist's despair turns godly when it turns God-ward. Something awesome *has* to happen when we choose the direct line to the Lord. "The irony of questioning God is that it honors him: it turns our hearts away from ungodly despair toward a passionate desire to comprehend him."[2]

The psalmist's questions serve as a reality check, exposing the fantasy of a blissful world. Questions that cut to the core destroy any illusion that the world can ever really keep its promises. They shake us awake, reminding us not to get too comfortable in a world destined for decay. Heart-wrenching questions expose false hopes. And hopes that are false should be blown to smithereens.

Lastly, these questions are not just penned by a sobbing psalmist; these utterances are the Word of God. Something suffering-shaking happens when we hand-pick a psalm to voice our heart-wrenching questions "For the word of God is living and active" (Hebrews 4:12). We are speaking God's language, echoing his own words back to him. When we wrap our anguish around a biblical psalm, we're searching for him. And when we seek, we will find (Matthew 7:7–8).

Gut-wrenching questions honor God. Despair directed at God is a way of *encountering* him, opening ourselves up to the One and only Someone who can actually do something about our plight. And whether we, like Greg, collide with the Almighty or simply bump up against him, we cannot be the same. We never are when we experience God.

The damp fog of my despair did not dissipate overnight, but I knew beyond a shadow of a doubt I had turned a corner. I was moving in the direction of God. My questions also created a paradox: in the midst of God's absence, I felt his presence. I found him after I let go of what I thought he should be. My despair ended up being my ally because through it, he took hold of me.

## DESPAIR TURNED GOD-WARD

This does not mean our questions get answers. And it certainly doesn't mean cancer gets cured, wars cease, and drunk drivers stay at home. Most likely our hard questions will never get answered, which results in suffering multiplied by two: our hardship doesn't go away plus we don't have a clue as to why.

But remember, "reasons why" don't ultimately satisfy anyway. Those who suffer are like that hurting child who asks his daddy, "Why?" The child opens himself up to the one and only someone who can actually *do* something about his plight. He knows his pain will be eased by his father's embrace. He knows his pain stirs the heart of his father like nothing else.

My friend Jim knows all about this. He often has to leave his three little boys when he flies away on business. On a recent trip, as the family drove together to the airport, his seven-year-old gladly took last-minute instructions on "how to help Mommy" while Daddy was away. The five-year-old bravely tucked in his chin and promised he would do his chores. As they turned into the airport, the two-year-old, all smiles and jabber up until then, spotted an airplane on the runway. Suddenly, wailing and sobbing!

"It tore my heart out," Jim exclaimed. "I almost canceled the trip right then. I just kept hugging that little boy."

As I saw his eyes well up with tears, I thought, *If that boy's cries tug at Jim's heart, how much more must our tears move our heavenly Father.* Nothing grips God's heart like the tortured cry of one of his children.

Watch what takes place in Psalm 18 after David says, "I cried to my God for help." David's plea reaches God's throne. God is roused . . .

> From his temple he heard my voice;
> my cry came before him, into his ears.
> The earth trembled and quaked,
> and the foundations of the mountains shook. . . .
> He parted the heavens and came down. . . .
> He mounted the cherubim and flew;
> he soared on the wings of the wind. . . .
> He reached down . . . and took hold of me.

Our questions and cries powerfully move the Almighty. He parts heaven and shakes earth to respond. He reaches down. He takes hold. Jesus is God's embrace, his way of reaching down and taking hold. Jesus is where we encounter him.

When we seek, God promises our anguished hearts will find Jesus. And it's a good thing. When it comes to heartfelt questions and despair, Jesus experienced both like no human ever has. He did not linger in the damp fog of Gethsemane, succumbing to despair. He moved in the direction of his Father and proceeded to the cross. There, he aimed his cries God-ward, not choosing his own words to wrap around his wretchedness, but—you guessed it—the words of a psalm. "My God, my God, why have you forsaken me?" he groaned, quoting Psalm 22:1. Jesus prayed this in a situation far worse than we'll ever know. No one was more God-forsaken than Christ (being God-forsaken is what Jesus' death for our sins was all about).

But it doesn't stop there. Can God the Father turn a deaf ear to the plea of his own Son? (If Jim can't, you can bet God can't. And if he can, we're in *big* trouble.) The answer resounds from an empty tomb three days later: No, may it never be! And because the Father raised Jesus from the dead, there is hope for us all. Jesus felt God's slap so that we could feel God's caress—oh, we may *feel* forsaken in the midst of our suffering, but the fact remains, we're *not*. "My God, why have you forsaken me" was the cry of Christ on behalf of all humanity so that, in contrast, he could tenderly say to us, "Never will I forsake you" (see Hebrews 13:5). Despair may be bound to God, but so is all hope.

Despair that rises in a direct and vertical line to God opens us up to change, real hope, and the possibility of seeing God as he really is, not as we want him to be. Once we give an inch, God will take a mile. He'll take a million miles. He'll soar on the wings of the wind from heaven to here to show you who he is, to embrace you with his love.

## WHAT DO WE DO WITH OUR EMOTIONS?

Deep, passionate emotions force us to face questions we would rather ignore. For many of us, this is precisely why it is easier not to feel, to blanket our emotions with everything from distractions to drugs. But when we fail to feel, we are left barren and distant from God as well as others. We don't prefer hopelessness. Yet the alternative—anger—seems so destructive.

What do we do with our anger? Do we call it wrong? Turn from it? Squelch it?

No. We do much more. "Emotions are the language of the soul. They are the cry that gives the heart a voice. To understand our deepest passions and convictions, we must learn to listen to the cry of the soul."[3]

The Psalms show the heart not only how to speak, but to listen. If emotions are the language of the soul, then the Book of Psalms gives us the grammar and syntax, teaching us how to wrestle, inviting us to question, and vent anger in such a way as to move up and out of despair. The Psalms wrap nouns and verbs around our pain better than any other book.

Long enough, God—
you've ignored me long enough.
I've looked at the back of your head
long enough. Long enough

I've carried this ton of trouble,
lived with a stomach full of pain.
Long enough my arrogant enemies
have looked down their noses at me.

(Psalm 13:1–2, THE MESSAGE)

The Psalms tell us what to do with our anger. The prescription is
succinctly written in Psalm 37:7–8, 11, "*Be still* before the Lord and *wait*
patiently for him ... refrain from anger and turn from wrath; do not
fret—it leads only to evil ... [those who lack anger] will inherit the
land and enjoy great peace." Merely replacing a destructive feeling with
a constructive one is a surface solution, like white-washing greasy walls
or putting Band-Aids over gaping wounds. A deeper transformation is
needed. And so God asks us to wait. "In your anger do not sin; when you
are on your beds, search your hearts and be silent" (Psalm 4:4).

Good advice! The old Puritans had a word for it: "Sit with yourself," they would say. Or sit with your rage. Waiting is not denial nor is
it a distraction. It is refraining from evil, turning from wrath, counting
to ten, as it were, to let the steam escape. It is not "doing nothing"; it
is a definitive and spiritual exercise. Choosing to wait on God takes
you beyond the immediate problems, the painful circumstances, and
gently eases you into the presence of the Lord.

I am still confident of this:
    I will see the goodness of the LORD
    in the land of the living.
Wait for the LORD;
    be strong and take heart
    and wait for the LORD.

(Psalm 27:13–14)

Did you read that promise? We can be confident that while we are
still alive and kicking and in the midst of deep suffering, we *will see* the
goodness of the Lord. Awesome!

After I was released from the hospital, I discovered the value of
waiting on the Lord. Psalm 46:10 advised me, "Be still, and know that
I am God." In stillness and silence, I recalled the destructive rage of my

anger. I pondered times when I would have punched God had I been able to reach him. While waiting, the thought surfaced that I already had punched him. In fact, I had dealt him a death blow when he was on the cross.

In humiliation, I discovered a more accurate focus for my anger. Satan. Satan was the one who started this whole mess. Disease and death, deformities and catastrophes of nature. He was the one who, because of pride, brought on himself—us included—every horror of the curse.

Dr. Allender and Dr. Longman, in their book *The Cry of the Soul,* state,

> Pondering the character of God does not pacify anger; it deepens it. Our struggle is never that we are too angry, but that we are never angry enough. Our anger is always pitifully small when it is focused against a person or object; it is meant to be turned against all evil and all sin—beginning first with our own failure of love.[4]

Anger like this gave birth to Mothers Against Drunk Driving. Help For Victims of Violent Crimes. Just Say No. Child Help. Battered Wives Anonymous. These are just a sampling of how people used their anger to inspire entire movements that have pushed back darkness and brought light and awareness to our society.

I'll never forget several years ago visiting Auschwitz and Birkenau, the dreadful Nazi death camps of World War II where millions of Jews, Poles, and others were exterminated. I sat by the train station where men, women, and children, crammed into box cars, had been emptied out onto the ice and dirt to face growling dogs and guards. Children were gun-butted one way, their mothers herded the other. Men were separated into groups of the old and the young. But virtually all of them ended up in one place—the incinerator, which is now crumbled and overgrown at the far end of the railroad tracks.

My husband picked up a piece of rusted barbed wire. We stared at it, quietly considering the evil that fueled the gas chambers. When we lowered our heads to pray, all I could think of was my disgust for the Devil and his hoards, as well as the words from Psalm 139:21–22:

Do I not hate those who hate you, O LORD,
　　and abhor those who rise up against you?
I have nothing but hatred for them;
　　I count them my enemies.

Thank God, he invades our despair and elbows us out of our complacency. And what of those who remain arrogant and unwilling to focus their anger against its rightful target? Will they taste the wrath and judgment of God?

> God promised to make the arrogant drink a foaming cup of his wrath, a reflection of God's furious hatred of sin. But the one who drank this bitter, foaming cup of wrath was Jesus. It is beyond our comprehension—the perfect Adam, adored and loved by the Father, was also despised by the Father ... consequently, we are promised that we will never bear the staggering weight of his fury. It has already been poured out on the perfect human being—the glorious Son.[5]

It's enough to make even the most arrogant individual start moving in the right spiritual direction.

Thank God for certain kinds of anger.

Which reminds me. I saw Greg Ericks the other day. His soul seemed ... settled. Greg told me he and his former wife are working together on a new diet for Ryan. A high fat, cholesterol-laden diet including extra dollops of butter and whipped cream. Hopefully, Ryan will fall in among the success stories of other children whose seizures have been dramatically curtailed. But it's not an easy routine. Ryan's mother and Greg are working on a schedule, taking shifts in the hospital, carpooling him back and forth from the clinic, shopping for special foods and preparing specific meals. I'm praying. I'm hoping. And I'm pulling for the Ericks family.

But if the sometimes-strange will of God does not include reprieve for Ryan and his seizures, if the specialized diet does not work, Greg will carry on. If he and Ryan's mother do not get back together, life will move forward. Greg's tumultuous emotions will give energy and shape to helping other families like his. He will continue to work hard to see that other parents of children like Ryan are forewarned. He'll fashion support networks and respite care, even full-scale retreats for moms and dads. He'll campaign to open the doors of churches to children who struggle with limitations. He'll bang doors, pray kneeling, raise money, dial phones, counsel couples, and keep moving.

And at night—especially Sunday nights—after he returns home late from dropping off Ryan, he'll head for the fridge, click on the TV, watch some junk, and then hit the sack. Maybe he'll slump on the edge of his mattress and listen for a moment to the silence of his apartment. He'll flick on the lamp and reach for his Bible before retiring.

If I were to guess, he will turn to the Psalms.

## THE PSALMS: A FABRIC OF FEELINGS

Emotions are one of the least reliable yet most influential forces in our lives. One day we are hopeful; the next, we hate. Despair at one time; delight, the other. Emotions are the surging, restless tides that keep ebbing and flowing, drawing us up, then pushing us down. The Psalms are a gyroscope, keeping moving things level, like a ship held steady in turbulent seas. This is why the Psalms often repeat the admonition to "look to the LORD and his strength; seek his face always. Remember the wonders he has done, his miracles, and the judgments he pronounced" (Psalm 105:4–5). To remember the strength of the Lord is to set the gyroscope spinning.

To remember is to stabilize.

It's another way of saying: Never doubt in the darkness what you once believed in the light. When hardship settles in to stay, dark and brooding skepticism surges over us in a tide of doubt and fear. The only sure dike against a flood of feelings is *memory*. We must recall sunnier times when we drove deep the pilings of God's goodness and felt our moorings of trust hold ground. Times when we lived on his blessings, knew his favor, were grateful for his gifts, and felt the flesh and blood of his everlasting arms underneath us. This is what all forty-five verses of Psalm 105 call us to do:

He allowed no one to oppress [his anointed]. . . .
The LORD made his people very fruitful. . . .

He brought out Israel, laden with silver and gold. . . .
He spread out a cloud as a covering,
    and a fire to give light at night. . . .
    [he] satisfied them with the bread of heaven.
He opened the rock, and water gushed out. . . .
For he remembered his holy promise
    given to his servant Abraham . . .
Praise the Lord.

(Psalm 105:14, 24, 37, 39, 40–42, 45)

Remember, remember, and remember again.

The Psalms also point us to the future, encouraging us to hold on, hold on, for heaven is just around the corner. Passionate feelings—especially those kindled in suffering—remind us that we will never truly be at peace until heaven breaks on the horizon. Fanny Crosby knew this. She suffered much as a blind person living in the nineteenth century, and found solace in the book of Psalms. Alone and vulnerable, she took special comfort in Psalm 27:4–5:

One thing I ask of the LORD,
    this is what I seek:
That I may dwell in the house of the LORD
    all the days of my life,
to gaze upon the beauty of the LORD
    and to seek him in his temple.
For in the day of trouble
    he will keep me safe in his dwelling;
he will hide me in the shelter of his tabernacle
    and set me high upon a rock.

Miss Crosby realized her affliction exposed her to powerful emotions that, if untempered, could sway her faith. When she leaned on the Psalms, she found them to be a wellspring of inspiration, and they provided the basis for many of her 6,000 hymns. Psalm 27 was, in fact, the inspiration for:

He hideth my soul in the cleft of the rock
    That shadows a dry, thirsty land;

He hideth my life in the depths of His love,
    And covers me there with His hand
    And covers me there with His hand.

When clothed in His brightness transported I rise,
    To meet Him in clouds of the sky,
His perfect salvation, His wonderful love,
    I'll shout with the millions on high.[6]

Between the past and the future, the Psalms provide comfort in our present circumstances. As we travel the path of suffering and journey through "the valley of the shadow of death," which one of us—even in mild suffering, perhaps sitting in a dentist's chair waiting for the Novocain to take affect—hasn't turned to this old favorite, softly reciting lines memorized to quiet our nerves and force peace into our hearts?

The Lord is my shepherd, I shall not be in want.
    He makes me lie down in green pastures,
he leads me beside quiet waters,
    he restores my soul.
He guides me in paths of righteousness
    for his name's sake.
Even though I walk
    through the valley of the shadow of death,
I will fear no evil,
    for you are with me;
your rod and your staff,
    they comfort me.

(Psalm 23:1–4)

The Psalms even serve as a confessional. Suffering will occasionally have us trespassing the "Danger Ahead" barrier and treading on the thin ice of seething spite against God, angrily taunting him. But then we realize that, were it not for Christ, we'd fall from grace and drown. We stop. Clamp our hands over our mouths. Drop to our knees. The Psalms then give voice to our repentance:

Have mercy on me, O God,
    according to your unfailing love;
according to your great compassion
    blot out my transgressions.
Wash away all my iniquity
    and cleanse me from my sin.

For I know my transgressions,
    and my sin is always before me.
Against you, you only, have I sinned
    and done what is evil in your sight,
so that you are proved right when you speak
    and justified when you judge. . . .
Surely you desire truth in the inner parts.

(Psalm 51:1–4, 6)

## A WINDOW INTO OUR SOUL

In 1951 a child was born to a drunken mother.[7] The woman's husband was not the father. Could the father be a man at the Naval Officer's Club? Or someone else near the military base? The child never knew for sure. All she knew was her mother's temper, the empty bottles, and the man they lived with whom she called Daddy.

Safe haven was often found at Uncle Bob's and Aunt Edith's. Theirs was a real home where little Glenda could play "hospital" with neighbor friends and scar up the driveway with hopscotch chalk. A home where she could spend long, unmolested moments and stare into a mirror at the gaping space where two front teeth should be. Teeth scattered somewhere on the floor back at her house after the savage beating.

When Glenda was five she made her last visit to Uncle Bob's. Harsh words were exchanged between her uncle and her father. It was forever back to his four-room house built near the docks for shipyard workers. A little house heated by an oil-burning stove in the living room. Her mother, who always seemed to be recovering from a drinking binge, gave orders that Glenda's sister, then fifteen, should move to the front room to sleep with her. Glenda, the littlest, was to sleep in the back room with her daddy. Mother made the decisions. Everyone followed.

The child heard the patter of rain at night. It made her sad. She could hear the muffle of drunken snores through the wall. But she would freeze when she heard the sigh of her father lying next to her, a man whose needs had not been met for years, sleeping with a little girl, not his own, fighting off anger from long days of hard work and an alcoholic wife. The floor boards around the oil stove creaked. So did the boards beneath the child's bed.

In that little room, Glenda's innocence was mauled over and over again. The knowledge that there was nowhere to go, no one to tell, horrified her. She wanted to run, but he held her down; she wanted to scream, but he told her to be quiet. So over the years, in that desolate bed, with tears running back into her ears and her father asleep at her side, the little girl stared at the ceiling and prayed. Surely, God would answer her prayers if only she would be good. She tried to be ever so good.

Yet everything was terribly bad.

The best change came when she turned twelve years old. Her father moved into the front room, her mother returned to the living room couch, and Glenda slept alone. Perhaps puberty and the fear of another unwanted baby in the house prompted the switch. Glenda did not understand at the time, but God was at work.

It was hard to see, though. The years faded away, but the bruises were always fresh. High school friends stayed cool and aloof. Little wonder. Glenda never invited classmates over to her house. She was embarrassed by the drunkenness, the cursing, and the filth. For at least a year, Glenda would hide in corners of restrooms, or her backyard, and sit, rocking back and forth with a pack of razor blades. Nothing happened, although she derived morbid pleasure in the possibilities.

"I do not remember," Glenda says, "ever feeling that I deserved a different home or different parents or a different life. Yes, I longed for them, especially for a mother who would love me. But I never believed that I had a right to them. I recognized early that there are few disappointments for the little girl who expects nothing."

Years marched on. Nursing school provided Glenda's first reprieve. A solace. A shelter. Still, loneliness knocked constantly on the door of her dorm. One Friday night as she was walking through the hospital lobby on her way back to her room, a brochure on a table caught her eye. Good thing. The front read, "God's Four Steps to Salvation." It was the night she had intended to collapse into bed, open the Ziploc bag of pills she'd been saving, and disappear permanently. She closed her bedroom door behind her. Instead of reaching for the bag, she opened the tract. Before the night was through, Glenda had slid to the floor by her bed to pray. She knelt down in grave clothes, then stood up in robes of righteousness. Christ's righteousness.

Saturday dawned, a bright, cold day. Glenda took the bus into town to buy a Bible. God's words danced on the pages, every verse jumping alive with meaning. She had a relationship—a real, live relationship with God. Breathing. Pulsating. Exploding with joy. But one thing clouded it. Over the months, even years, after she was married with children of her own, as Glenda drew closer to God, her past appeared blacker.

New feelings of resentment surfaced. *How could my parents have done those horrible things to me?* she thought. *I was just a little girl. Why didn't they let me be a little girl? I was beaten, stripped, molested, cursed, screamed at, kicked, and hated when all I ever wanted was love. I would have done anything for their love. And now I hate them. I can't help it.*

Her anger was revealing something foul inside her heart. Psalm 119:165 spoke softly . . .

Great peace have they who love thy law:
and nothing shall offend them. (KJV)

*Incredulous! God could really take away my offense?* Glenda wondered. *My murderous hatred?* "Nothing shall offend" the verse answered. The two lines weren't long enough to be considered a spear or a javelin. Not even an arrow piercing her heart. The short verse was a tiny dart, but God's aim was impeccable—it pinpricked the hot balloon of anger Glenda had been inflating all those years.

"Oh God," Glenda prayed, "if it displeases you for me to be

offended, then somehow take it from me. I'm burning up with hatred and I can't survive this way. Tear out the resentment. I long to be yours completely. I want to forgive those who have offended me just as you forgave me all my offenses. Now help me, Father, for Jesus' sake."

Some would think Glenda's offense should be aimed against God rather than her parents. Stripped? Molested? Cursed? A child doesn't have the strength to push away a lewd man ruled by urges. But God does. A little girl cannot outrun a drunken parent swinging a belt. A child cannot hold up a shield big or thick enough to ward off words that cut deep into her psyche. Where was God? Why not take offense at him?

What answers could possibly atone for such horrific treatment? "It would be better for [a man] to be thrown into the sea with a millstone tied around his neck than for him to cause one of these little ones to sin," says God himself (Luke 17:2). Fine: wicked men will one day face the anger of a righteous Judge, but what about now?

We want answers now. But even if we know why, will it satisfy? We might ask, "Where was God? Was it his fault?" and be assured that although he is sovereign, it was not his fault. Or, "Was it an assault from the Enemy?" and find that, yes, it possibly was. Or we may press further, "Is it the consequence of living in a fallen, wicked world, and not the direct personal assault of either the Devil or God?" and learn that, more than likely, it is. Back to square one: do such answers satisfy? Probably not.

Glenda, with God's help, found the only answer that satisfied—an answer that reached into the heart where it hurt. Her anger helped show her need. Her anger helped move her in the right direction.

She realized her seething hatred was just as heinous, just as nauseating as the sins committed against her. She was no better than her parents. As surely as her father thrust himself on her, she had in her imagination, thrust a knife, with hot fury, into his chest. Glenda could have easily been the one flinging curses and spitting hatred, torturing and nailing God to his cross. In fact, in acknowledging her sin, she was. The memory of spit on her seven-year-old face must have paled in comparison to the spit on her Savior. Glenda discovered, as few believers do, the depth of God's love in that "while we were yet sinners, Christ died for us" (Romans 5:8).

"In order to suffer without dwelling on our own affliction," Thomas Merton once contemplated, "we must think about a greater affliction, and turn to Christ on the cross. In order to suffer without hate, we must drive out bitterness from our heart by loving Jesus. In order to suffer without hope of compensation, we should find all our peace in the conviction of our union with Jesus. These things are not a matter of ascetic technique but of simple faith."[8]

God suffering on a cross. There is no answer to the question "Why?" apart from Jesus. That God is part of the problem of suffering may not complicate matters after all. How, or to what extent, he created the problem, is not the question.

He is the answer and we need him.

# Eleven

# GAINING
# CONTENTMENT

A contented man is the one who enjoys the scenery along the detours."[1]

A quote like this deserves a story . . .

Your heart is racing as you sketch out plans for a move. A move to Rome, Italy. You study the language, food, and art, and buy history books of the Basilica and Sistine Chapel. You flip through home buyers' guides and picture breakfast on a balcony overlooking a sunny bay. Your hopes are soaring. It'll be the adventure of a lifetime.

Winging your way to Rome, the plans change. Your 747 lands in Holland. You stumble out of the Amsterdam airport bewildered, clasping Italian brochures and asking, "Where am I? What's going on?" The landscape is flat; the weather cold and damp. You gag on Dutch Brussels sprouts and learn how to say "tot ziens" rather than "arrivederci." Even though disappointment stings, you may as well get used to wearing wooden shoes. Holland is now your home. Shelve your shattered hopes and get on with living. Once in awhile you miss Italy, but you learn to survive in Holland. It's not unbearable, just different.[2]

That's life. You're flying along at a good clip, then plans change. A heart attack sidelines your brother or AIDS infects your son. God may part the heavens with a miracle, but more than likely, you will have to accept the obvious. You will bear the pain and hang on. You will spend weekends helping your brother's family. You will push aside prejudice and change the sheets on your son's bed. Or you will change the diapers of your twelve-year-old who is mentally handicapped. You will hold on to marriage vows despite a cold shoulder and an empty bed. Stick to a budget and forestall vacation. Clamp the lid on raging hormones and make a date with the TV and dinner-for-one.

You resign yourself to the way things are.

Once in awhile you wonder what it would be like—or was like—to live without the dull ache of constant pain. But most of the time, you block it out. You cope with a new language, different ways of doing things—not the ways you prefer—and you learn to survive in a world you'd never choose.

I can't live, really *live* that way. I don't believe you can either. Maybe pets who are trained for the leash can and horses who are schooled for the bit, but not humans. Animals submit—horses yield to the heavy harness and resign themselves to the plow. But we are not animals. God weeps when he sees us put the blinders on, like horses with spirits broken. He weeps because he never intended for us to live lives of solemn resignation. For one reason, stoics unwittingly place themselves at the center of everything. For another, our souls are too significant. Even in the desperation of silence, inside the shell of a hardened heart, passion pulsates like a dying ember. A warm breeze revives a distant memory. A song stirs a faraway hope. A hand on the shoulder awakens desire. We long to be fully human. We ache, we taste bitterness and gall. We taste tears. Animals don't cry; or if they do, they don't wonder, "Is there more to life than survival?"

Maybe we can survive, but it can't stop there.

"Will I ever be happy, really happy again?"

Yes and no. You can be "sorrowful, yet always rejoicing; poor, yet making many rich; having nothing, and yet possessing everything" (2 Corinthians 6:10). In other words, you may end up enjoying Holland. Perhaps more than Italy.

## WHEN YOU CAN'T ESCAPE

*Will I ever be happy in this place?* It's all I could think of after I got out of the hospital and wheeled through the front door of my home. Doorways were too narrow. Sinks were too high. Three little steps were a roadblock preventing access to the living room. I sat at the dining room table, my knees hitting the edge. A plate of food was placed in front of me, but my hands remained limp in my lap. Someone else—at least for the first few months—fed me. I felt confined and trapped. Our cozy home had become an adverse and foreign environment.

My confinement forced me to look at another captive.

The apostle Paul had seen the inside of more than one small room from which there was no escape. For over two years, Paul had been shifted from "pillar to post" as one Roman leader after another disclaimed any responsibility for him. Nobody—neither Felix nor Festus—wanted to touch him with a ten-foot pole. So he was shipped to Rome.

Once there, Paul, shadowed by a guard, continued to be under house arrest. He thanked the believers in Philippi for their concern and reassured them with his words in the fourth chapter of his epistle: "I have learned to be content whatever the circumstances. I know what it is to be in need, and I know what it is to have plenty" (Philippians 4:11).

Paul was talking about an internal quietness of heart, supernaturally given, that gladly submits to God in all circumstances. When I say "quietness of heart" I'm not ruling out the physical stuff like prison bars, wheelchairs, unjust treatment, and disease. What I *am* ruling out is the internal stuff—peevish thoughts, plotting ways of escape, and vexing and fretting that only lead to a flurry of frantic activity. Contentment is a sedate spirit that is able to keep quiet as it bears up under suffering. Paul understood how to live this way.

He *learned* it. It meant acquiring skills. Understanding something and then practicing it. What did he understand? "I have *learned the secret of being content* in any and every situation, whether well fed or hungry, whether living in plenty or in want" (Philippians 4:12).

What was the secret Paul learned? In his seventeenth-century classic *The Rare Jewel of Christian Contentment,* Jeremiah Burroughs notes that the New Testament word rendered as "contentment" in our English Bibles carries the idea of sufficiency. Paul uses the same Greek root in 2 Corinthians 12:9: "My grace is sufficient for you, for my power is made perfect in weakness." Paul's secret was simply learning to lean on the Lord of grace for help. "Let us then approach the throne of grace with confidence, so that we may receive mercy and *find grace to help us in our time of need*" (Hebrews 4:16).

Paul had to master this. It meant making tough choices—deciding this, not that; going in this direction, not that one. Why does the secret involve such hard work? Because "approaching the throne of grace with confidence" is not our natural bent. "Finding grace to help in time of need" doesn't come automatically. Just take a look at a few of Paul's well-chosen words in Philippians: "I press on . . . I strive . . . I stand firm."

In a small way, I understand making choices like these. I got tired of being fed at our dinner table. But when I tried to feed myself with paralyzed arms, I wanted to give up. A bent spoon was inserted into a pocket on my leather arm splint. With weak shoulder muscles, I had to scoop food on the spoon, then balance and lift it to my mouth. It was humiliating to wear a bib, smear applesauce all over my clothes, and have it land more times on my lap than in my mouth.

I could have surrendered—it would have been easy and many wouldn't have blamed me for quitting. But I had to make a choice. A series of choices. Was I going to let embarrassment over my food-smeared face dissuade me? Was I going to let disappointing failures overwhelm me? I decided the awkwardness of feeding myself out-weighed the fleeting satisfaction of self-pity. It pushed me to pray, *Oh, God, help me with this spoon!* My secret was learning to lean on the Lord for help. Today I manage a spoon with my arm splint quite well.

I didn't get back use of my arms or hands.

But I did learn to be content.

Christ is not a magic wand that can be waved over our heartaches and headaches to make them disappear. "In [him] are hidden all the treasures of wisdom and knowledge" (Colossians 2:3). Wisdom and knowledge—including knowing how to be content—are *hidden* in him, like a treasure that needs to be searched for. To search for something concealed requires hard work: "You will seek me and find me when you seek me with all your heart" (Jeremiah 29:13).

God doesn't leave us on our own. "I have learned the secret of being content. . . . I can do everything *through him who gives me strength*" (Philippians 4:13). As we wrap our hands around a task and, in faith, begin to exert force, eureka! Divine energy surges through us. God's strength works in us at the moment we exercise faith for the task. "I have strength for all things in Christ Who empowers me—I am ready for anything and equal to anything through Him Who infuses inner strength into me [that is, I am self-sufficient in Christ's sufficiency]" (Philippians 4:13 AMPLIFIED).

You make the choices and God gives you the strength. He gives you the strength to hold your tongue when you feel you have cause for complaining—even when your husband hasn't attended his fair share of PTA meetings. He imparts the strength to look out for another's interest before your own—even when it's the coworker in your office who uses you as a stepladder to the top. He infuses the strength to choose a bright attitude when you wake up in the morning—even though it's another day of the same old routine as you care for your disabled child.

You still have an irresponsible husband, a greedy coworker, and a handicapped kid, but you have quietness of heart.

## GAINING THROUGH LOSING

Remember when I said suffering is having what you don't want and wanting what you don't have? Subtract your wants and you'll have contentment.

It's a way of equalizing your desires and circumstances. The apostle Paul was an expert at this arithmetic. For example, he was glad his Philippian friends were sending him gifts. "I rejoice greatly" he says, but quickly adds, "I am not saying this because I am in need . . ."

Not in need? In a jail? "I am amply supplied," he assures his friends (Philippians 4:18). Good grief, Paul, why then are you rejoicing greatly? "I am not looking for a gift," he explains, "but I am looking for what may be *credited to your account*" (v. 17). Paul subtracted his desires and, in so doing, increased his joy—his joy over supplying the needs of others.

Paul wasn't living in denial in that dank dungeon; he simply adjusted his longings in light of Christ's sufficiency. Christ was more than enough whether Paul was "well fed or hungry, whether living in plenty or in want" (Philippians 4:12).

The world is clueless to this sort of math. The world will try to improve its circumstances to match its desires—increase its health, money, beauty, and power. It's wiser to subdue your heart to match your circumstances. Christians may not be able to rule their life situations, but they can rule their hearts: "The brother in humble circumstances ought to take pride in his high position. But the one who is rich should take pride in his low position, because he will pass away like a wild flower," says James 1:9. Burroughs wrote, "Here lies the bottom and root of all contentment: When there is an evenness and proportion between our hearts and our circumstances."[3]

Cecile Van Antwerp has lived in a wheelchair many more years than I, plus she resides in a nursing home. When I went to visit her, I was struck by the small size of her living alcove—just enough room for a bed and chest of drawers in the corner by a window. Yet with photos, a flower arrangement, a colorful afghan, and a plaque on the wall above her headboard, she has made it her home. She has scaled down her heart's desires and fashioned a small, cozy nest out of a tight, cramped space. She's contented.

How do we become skilled in such arithmetic? How do we get this kind of "subtraction"? By feeding the mind and heart on those things that bring contentment rather than arouse desire. I'm not talking about rule-keeping. Rules only lead to the arousal of cravings. (You can't help but dabble in desire as soon as you see, "Don't Touch This" and "Don't Do That.") I am talking about common sense.

Or call it behavior modification. Don't want to get hurt? Then stay away from things that cause hurt. You'll never catch me lingering in the lingerie department where they display tall, elegant mannequins wearing beautiful silk negligees. I don't care if it's a Styrofoam model—it's standing up, and I'm not. And it's gracefully wearing things that hang like a sack on me! Being paralyzed, it's not practical to wear lacy garter belts or brocade bedroom slippers. Gazing at these gorgeous garments makes me think restlessly, *Boy, I'd love to wear that!* and so I only remain on third-floor lingerie long enough to purchase a few necessities and then I'm out of there.

It's the same with sixties psychedelic music. Those weird, crazy sounds were background music to my suicidal despair, when I would wrench my head back and forth on my pillow, hoping to break my neck at a higher level. Now I turn the dial whenever I hear screeching guitars or a hard, angry beat. I cannot listen. I'm not living in denial or refusing to face up to reality; I merely have a healthy respect for the powerful effect of music—I am as paralyzed now as I was then, and I'm asking for trouble if I expose my mind to music that conjures dark thoughts.

Food is another thing. Because I can't exercise like most people, I have to watch my calories more closely. In the evening when I leave the office, I occasionally catch the enticing aroma of char-broiled steak wafting from *The Wood Ranch Barbecue Pit* across the freeway. It's murder. I'm a pushover for their fried Maui onion rings. I avoid that restaurant when I'm starving, just as I bypass the French pastry aisle at the supermarket.

Gaining contentment does not mean losing sorrow or saying good-bye to discomfort. Contentment means sacrificing itchy cravings to gain a settled soul. You give up one thing for another. It's hard. Hard, but sweet. You are "sorrowful, yet always rejoicing." You "have nothing, yet possess everything." First Timothy 6:6 says, "Godliness with contentment is great gain" and the gain always comes through loss.

No wonder contentment requires enormous strength!
Jeremiah Burroughs writes,

> [A Christian] is the most contented man in the world and yet the most unsatisfied man in the world; these two together must needs be mysterious. . . . He is contented if he has but a crust, but bread and water . . . yet if God should give unto him Kingdoms and Empires, all the world to rule . . . he should not be satisfied with that. A soul that is capable of God can be filled with nothing else but God.[4]

## ANOTHER EQUATION

"I complained about having no shoes until I met a man with no feet."

Trite but true. Involve yourself with those in more humble circumstances. It fosters contentment in you and revives it in others. A double blessing.

I'd have sworn I was satisfied, sitting at a coffee bar in the mall with my out-of-town guest, Mary Jean. She, like me, almost never takes a break. She travels long hours and works hard in Christian ministry.

When Mary Jean flew out for a relaxing visit, I assumed it would be good for us both to do something normal—what better than to kick back and meander a mall? We got as far as ordering Café Lattes outside of Nordstrom's. We sat, sipping drinks, cooing at babies parked in strollers, and admiring spring dresses on passers-by. We chatted about fat grams and the First Lady's newest hairstyle. The conversation inevitably drifted to Christian ministry.

I told Mary Jean about my friend Bonnie Young who lives at Magnolia Gardens Nursing Home at the other end of the valley. "Bonnie's neuro-muscular disease has advanced to the point where she lies in bed all day," I told her. "It'd be good if we could spend some time praying for her today. I heard she is very depressed."

We sat in silence.

Suddenly, we exclaimed together, "What are we doing here?!"

We gathered our stuff and scurried to a phone. Yes, Bonnie was able to receive visitors. No, we wouldn't be intruding—she doesn't have many friends drop by. We sang hymns driving down the freeway until we pulled into the shaded driveway of the nursing home. We hurried down the dimly lit hallways, greeting the wheelchair users lined up against the walls. Bonnie's room was the last on the right.

Her eyes lit up when she saw us. She couldn't communicate much through her stiffened smile. Breath and words did not come easily. We sang to Bonnie and occasionally sat quietly, enjoying birds chirping outside the window. At the close of our visit, I asked if she would like to slowly repeat with us the Lord's Prayer. Expressionless, she nodded. While a bedpan clattered on the floor down the hallway and someone kept babbling by the nurses' station, we united our hearts and spoke to our Father.

Mary Jean enjoyed her visit, including a jaunt to the beach and an evening out at a fancy restaurant. But the highlight was the marvelous chance to visit a friend in more humble circumstances than us. There will always be a sale at Nordstrom's but not always an opportunity to foster contentment by involving ourselves with a friend in need. "In humility consider others better than yourselves. Each of you should look not only to your own interests, but also to the interests of others" (Philippians 2:3–4).

It's not a matter of comparing another's tragic plight to your circumstances in order to jack up a grateful spirit. It's not "pitying the poor unfortunate." It's all about perspective. Like the letter I received from one of the mothers at a JAF Family Retreat . . .

Dear Joni,

I am writing to let you know about four-year-old Zachariah who now has a growth on his aortic valve. Because Zach is ventilator dependent, the cardiologist is worried about doing surgery.

It is very painful as a mother to watch her son suffer knowing he doesn't understand why. It is not the worst situation nor is it the best. But in God's great wisdom and love for us, it is his will and I humbly submit, knowing his faithfulness reaches to the skies. Zach is a child and this is his 26th hospitalization and 15th surgery. Through times of pain, surgery, questions, decisions and tears, I know that I know that I *know* he will see us through this, too. Not barely, not hanging on by a thread, but gloriously and peacefully.

I stand in awe of everything he has done in my life. He took me out of a deep, dark pit of incest, prostitution, depression, self-hate, and so on and he set my feet on a solid rock. He put a new song in my heart and like Psalm 40 says, "Many shall see it and shall fear and shall trust in the Lord." I am not great, but I serve a great God. When I think of where he brought me from, I know I am not worthy. But still when I am faithless, he is faithful.

Love, Jeri

## CONTENTMENT AND JOY

Zachariah's mother is full of joy. Amazing!

The apostle Paul affirms this, "Therefore I will boast *all the more gladly* about my weaknesses, so that Christ's power may rest on me" (2 Corinthians 12:9). The world has a philosophy that says, "What can't be cured must be endured." Christians have a philosophy that says, "What can't be cured can be enjoyed."

"The answer is not to get rid of unhappiness," Elisabeth Elliot suggests, "but to find a new definition for it. Define happiness in things like duty, honor and sacrifice, faithfulness, commitment and service." Honor gives value to a bad marriage. Sacrifice is the true expression of love to ungrateful children. Faithfulness in guarding the reputation of a coworker is worth far more than a promotion. Commitment and service to others brings joy unspeakable to the afflicted person who focuses off himself.

Contentment and joy go hand in hand.

Consider again the apostle Paul. When he wrote the Philippian letter, he was under guard, waiting for his case to be processed before the imperial court. There were long delays. Come what may, he was not only ready, he was . . . full of joy! In his letter he says:

> The things that have happened to me have fallen out to the advantage of the Gospel . . . in every way, whether in pretense or in truth, Christ is being proclaimed and in this I *rejoice*. . . . Yes, and I shall continue to *rejoice*, for I know that . . . this will turn out to my salvation. . . . Now as always Christ will be magnified in my person, whether by life or by death. . . . For the rest, my brothers, *rejoice* in the Lord. . . . *Rejoice* in the Lord always. Again I will say *rejoice*. . . . Now I *rejoice* in the Lord greatly.

From beginning to end, the letter sparkles with joy.

Paul's prison experience was rich in joy and contentment because he had learned from previous times in prison. Years earlier, Paul and Silas were cast into the inner cell of a different prison. Yet deep in the darkness of midnight, during the loneliest hour, they were found singing praises to God. No half-hearted humming. In spite of thick walls and heavy doors, other prisoners actually heard them singing praises (Acts 16:25).

Paul's arithmetic for contentment was to subtract his earthly wants so that something of greater value could be attained: Christ's cause advanced throughout the world. This gave him enormous joy. Joy based on his conviction that suffering Christians are used more powerfully in God's kingdom. And when he was thrown into prison the next time— and for the last time—he was rejoicing greatly.

How odd. Yet how like God. It's the way Jesus lived when he was on earth. The Son of Man "despised and rejected by men, a man of sorrows, and familiar with suffering" was also the Son of God who was the Lord of joy (Isaiah 53:3). "Let us fix our eyes on Jesus, the author and perfecter of our faith, who for the joy set before him endured the cross, scorning its shame, and sat down at the right hand of the throne of God. Consider him who endured such opposition from sinful men, so that you will not grow weary and lose heart" (Hebrews 12:2–3).

## CONSIDER HIM

If you only try to stave off discontentment, you will fail miserably. Unless you add the massive promise of superior happiness in God, you can subtract all the desires you please and you'll still be restless.

When it comes to contentment, God *must* be our aim. Whether it's wayward thoughts, bad-mouthing our circumstances, or comparing ourselves with others whose lot in life is easier, the battle involves more than eschewing evil; it involves pursuing God. Hebrews 11:25 says,

> It was by faith that Moses . . . chose to share ill-treatment with God's people instead of enjoying the fleeting pleasures of sin. He thought that it was better to suffer for the promised Christ than to own all the treasures of Egypt, for he was looking forward to the great reward that God would give him. (LIVING BIBLE)

I am still learning this. What my body can't have, my mind will shift into overdrive to deliver. But fantasies only frustrate. I must fight to stay satisfied with God, and so I glut myself on the promises of Christ. Dr. John Piper has written superbly on this subject in *The Pleasures of God*.

> We must swallow up the little flicker of [earthly] pleasure in the conflagration of holy satisfaction. When we make a covenant with our eyes, as Job did, our aim is not merely to avoid something erotic, but to gain something excellent. . . . We do not yield to the offer of sandwich meat when we can smell the steak sizzling on the grill.[5]

In the quest for contentment, we should not give up so easily and get detoured by earthly pleasures when there is the promise of maximum, full-forced joy in the Lord. After all, "In Thy presence is fullness of joy; at thy right hand there are pleasures evermore" (Psalm 16:11 KJV). Contentment has the upper hand in your heart when you are satiated in Christ. When, with Paul, you see him as sufficient. As enough. "Whom have I in heaven but you? And being with you, I desire nothing on earth" (see Psalm 73:25).

It is what Jesus means when he says, "I am the bread of life. He who comes to me will never go hungry . . ." (John 6:35).

Contentment is being full.

Never wanting more.

We need not ever be hungry for "Man does not live on bread alone but on every word that comes from the mouth of the LORD" (Deuteronomy 8:3). The role of the Word of God is to feed faith's appetite for Christ.

## SUBTRACT ONE MORE THING

The Lord once preached a superb sermon on the promises of superior happiness in God. He whets our appetite for God as he lists through his Beatitudes in Matthew 5:3–12.

When I was a kid, the Beatitudes baffled me. I wanted to get excited about God and be blessed and happy as much as anyone, but Jesus seemed to make it a "minus" rather than a "plus." He employed more of the same gaining-through-losing arithmetic.

If I wanted the kingdom, I'd have to know persecution. Subtraction.

If I longed to be comforted, I'd have to mourn. More subtraction.

Inherit the earth? Be meek. Subtract again.

The Beatitude especially linked to contentment is verse 3, "Blessed are the poor in spirit, for theirs is the kingdom of heaven."

Do you want to know contentment pure and deep? Become poor in spirit like this: "Search me, O God, and know my heart; test me and know my anxious thoughts. See if there is any offensive way in me, and lead me in the way everlasting" (Psalm 139:23–24). See yourself as spiritually impoverished, and you'll find satisfaction in God.

"Godly sorrow brings repentance that leads to salvation and leaves no regret" (2 Corinthians 7:10). Why no regrets? The one who recognizes his low estate before a good God has low expectations, much like the prodigal son who said to his father, "I am no longer worthy to be called your son; make me like one of your hired men" (see Luke 15:21). I would say it this way, "I would rather be in this chair knowing him, than on my feet without him." No regrets. Even the apostle Paul, the most contented yet most maligned Christian who ever lived, saw himself as the least of the apostles, the least of all saints, and the chief of sinners.

When you realize you are among the least, the littlest, the last, and the lost, God becomes everything. To be caught up in his superior happiness, is to see his love infused in and entertained around everything. Absolutely everything.

You find your heart drawn nearer to God by the smallest of enjoyments. "When your husbands are at sea," says Jeremiah Burroughs, "and they send you a token of their love, it is worth more than forty times what you already have in your houses. Every good thing the people of God enjoy, they enjoy it . . . as a token of God's love . . . and this must needs be very sweet to them."[6]

To the contented person, the God-given token can be an hour of listening to Bach by the fireside. Sitting under a tree on a blustery day. Pulling over on the road to take in a kaleidoscope sunset. You find yourself peeling an onion only to stop and marvel at the beauty of its concentric rings, all perfect and delicate. You see a kitten wrestling with a sock and giggle over God's sense of humor. Our duties are sweet when seen as service to him. Ruth Graham boasts of a sign in her kitchen that reads, "Divine service conducted here three times daily." When everything becomes a token of God's love, you feel as though you possess everything; yet you have nothing!

First Corinthians 3:21–23 says it best: "So then . . . all things are yours . . . the world or life or death or the present or the future—all are yours, and you are of Christ, and Christ is of God." This is the way I feel at Wednesday night prayer meeting in our little church, which is no more than two trailers hooked together. We're not fancy. Not big. But when the eight of us sing hymns before prayer time—and we're not great singers—the joy brings tears to my eyes.

It is a taste of heaven.

All contentment is a foretaste of eternity where "God himself will be with them and be their God. He will wipe every tear from their eyes. There will be no more death or mourning or crying or pain, for the old order of things has passed away" (Revelation 21:3–4). Contentment in heaven will go far beyond satisfaction. It is satisfaction overflowing. Rest in motion. It is, as G. K. Chesterton says, peace dancing.

Do you enjoy your friends now? You'll have more in heaven. Do you like sailing? One day you'll glide through the universe. Do you enjoy movies? One day you will delight in the real "videos" of history. Do you get a charge out of intellectual discussions? Soon you shall converse with the angels, the saints of the ages, and with God.

Contentment is a deposit, a guaranteeing of what is to come, "the first installment of future bliss" or, as THE MESSAGE puts it, "He puts a little of heaven in our hearts so that we'll never settle for less" (2 Corinthians 5:5).

## WHAT IF I DON'T SUFFER?

"Joni, you make it sound like I'm missing out."

Joyce is a top executive with an international publishing company who jet-sets in a multi-million dollar world. She's single and loves it. Unlimited opportunities to travel. Flexibility in her schedule at home. A condominium tastefully decorated. Church committees seeking her support. The friends with whom she spends time, like her, are cosmopolitan in their choice of books, plays, and art.

"I don't suffer," she said one day while we were having tea. "My life is remarkably pain free. My family isn't facing any major crisis, and my worst problem is fighting off an occasional flu." She set down her teacup and thoughtfully added, "Does this mean I can't be as close to God as those who go through a lot of hardship?"

This is a head-scratcher. The Bible tells us that all who live godly lives will suffer. Believers *should* encounter persecution. The promise is "In this world you will have trouble" (John 16:33). Jesus was hated by his own for the light that he shed on their evil deeds. Yet some people—like Joyce—seem to have found peace with their families, friends, and employers. We are supposed to deny ourselves and take up our crosses daily. It would seem odd that one could carry the weight of a cross and not feel its pain.

Nevertheless, there are those who seem to have an easier lot in life.

So Joyce's question is a good one. Are only scarred survivors of the mission field close, *really* close, to God?

It reminds me of the prodigal son's older brother in Luke 15. Hardship never seemed to touch the man's life. After his younger brother headed for "Hollywood," the older son kept faithfully managing the farm and paying the bills. He kept his nose clean and never suffered consequences of disobedience. Then one day, when his younger brother showed up, the father went hog-wild. Steaks on the barbecue. Crepe paper on the tent posts. It wasn't the cost of confetti and fatted calves that irked the older brother, but the gushing favor his father showered on his sibling. Just when the older brother thought he was missing out, he heard these words of tender reassurance: "'My son,' the father said, 'you are always with me and everything I have is yours'" (Luke 15:31). The prodigal son only had a portion of the inheritance. The older son possessed everything. He simply forgot that.

"In a way, you have it harder," I said.

Joyce is a wise woman and, after a moment, nodded. She has always understood that, without suffering, she must live more circumspectly. More carefully. Without suffering, she could be like the prodigal's older brother who, in his trouble-free circumstances, forgot how much he had. But God has blessed Joyce "in the heavenly realms with every spiritual blessing in Christ" (Ephesians 1:3). God has nothing more beyond Christ to give those who suffer or those who do not.

Joyce has to be wise about something else. Without suffering, she could be like an unbridled horse who lacks the restraints that guide and direct. The bit, martingale, tie down, spur, and crop school the horse to listen to the rider's commands. How hard it would be for an animal, without the aid of his master, to train himself up in the way he should go. It's the same for humans. Hardship is our bit and bridle. First Timothy 4:7–8 advises, "Train yourself to be godly. For physical training is of some value, but godliness has value for all things, holding promise for both the present life and the life to come."

God has not seen fit to place the bridle and bit, as it were, on Joyce. And so, the onus is on Joyce to look to the examples of people like Karla Larson, my half-blind friend with no legs. Joyce can benefit from her. And "as you know, we consider blessed those who have persevered . . . as an example of patience in the face of suffering" (James 5:10–11).

Contentment is counting your blessings!

## THE SECRET

Sometimes I look up on my wall calendar and gaze at the blank months of years to come and I wonder, *What will it be like five years from now? Ten years? What if my husband suffers an injury and can't take care of me? Worse yet, I won't be able to take care of him!*

The enemy of contentment is worry.

In Jesus' Sermon on the Mount, the phrase he repeated most often was, "Do not worry." The Lord was wise in repeating his warnings so many times. He knows the devastating affects of anxiety and how it can corrode faith like acid; robbing you of joy and stealing your hope.

I'm sure this is why Jesus said in the same sermon, "Therefore do not worry about tomorrow, for tomorrow will worry about itself. *Each day has enough trouble of its own"* (Matthew 6:34). The secret of being content is to take one day at a time. Not five years or ten at a time, but one *day.*

Like the manna that fell fresh from heaven each morning, God supplies the needs of his children with the dawning of each day. "Because of the LORD's great love, we are not consumed, for his compassions never fail. They are new every morning; great is your faithfulness" (Lamentations 3:22–23). The sufficiency of Christ is more than enough to meet the needs of a lifetime, but life can only be lived one day, one moment, at a time. "Since we live by the Spirit, *let us keep in step with the Spirit"* (Galatians 5:25). When you're suffering, life is lived in steps. Very small steps.

Shawna Leavell is taking life in measured moments. She is the young woman who was sentenced to prison after she drove her car, in a drunken stupor, the wrong way on the Hollywood Freeway and killed a man. I'm amazed at what contentment looks like on her.

Dear Joni,

I was moved into a new cell with two lifers in for murder. I was so oppressed. When I got together with some others for a Bible study, we talked about responding to hard situations. I cried so much the floor was wet. I was expecting God to deliver a miracle like I was ordering fast food.

He told me to lay *all* my worries at his feet and let him take care of the problem in his way and timing. I let go—it was awesome. I let go of the room always being dark. I let go of the radio, music and TV, and when I did my bunkie happened to give me ear plugs! My whining is disappearing.

I'm like the thief who was on the cross next to Jesus who said he was there because of his sin. I recognize I already am responsible for killing one man—an innocent man—Jesus, but because of my old hard heart, I now have the blood of two innocent men on my hands. It's a major reason for my striving for obedience and servitude to Christ—it's too bad I didn't recognize that sacrifice for all it was before.

Love,
Shawna

Shawna faces a long, dreary stretch behind bars. She is learning the secret of the sufficiency of Christ one day at a time. In a way, we "mark time," as well, with suffering making us move through our days in measured steps.

Satisfaction in life arises from knowing you are where you belong. Discontented people strive to be somewhere else or someone else. Contentment comes from many great and small *acceptances* in life. "Every day we experience something of the death of Jesus, so that we may also show the power of the life of Jesus in these bodies of ours" (2 Corinthians 4:10 PHILLIPS).

When life isn't the way you like it, like it the way it is . . . one day at a time with Christ. And you will be blessed.

# *Twelve*

# SUFFERING GONE MALIGNANT

It's time for the "H" word.

For eleven chapters we've looked at the hell-on-earth that many people go through. But there may be an even bigger problem. What if, as the Bible teaches, there is also a hell *after* earth? Sounds too awful to ponder, doesn't it? Yet according to historic Christianity, hell holds the key to many mysteries about our earthly sufferings. Without hell, the "why" behind so much pain will never be resolved. Without hell, there is ultimately no justice or fairness. For God to be God, for heaven to be heaven, there *must* be a hell.

Someone is rolling his eyes at that last paragraph. Maybe that someone is you ...

---

Traffic has slowed to a crawl. A furniture truck has nudged its way in, blocking your view ahead, but you check the rearview mirror and notice cars backed up roughly to the planet Mercury. You hit the radio to see if the Action News helicopter with the Traffic-Cam that "gets you where you want to go" really will. Whoa! Your hand shoots back to the volume knob as fast as a surprised roach making for the floor crack—your ears are splitting from some screaming electric guitar begging to be put out of its misery. Cranking down the volume you find your station. Lisa what's-her-name, "Live on the scene," is giving the doleful news. You check your watch, sigh, and hit the scan button to kill time.

186

A funky rap number threatens to knock the begeebers out of your speakers. You flip the button. An advertisement. The button again. Another ad—"unbelievably low prices." More buttons. Elevator music. An angry talk-show caller (Republican, you gather). Some country artist getting rich singing about how great it is to be poor. Ad. Ad. But then . . . some real entertainment.

The Reverend Doctor Somebody is deep into his sermon and has found his rhythm. You can hear the pages of his Bible flipping, only he pronounces it Bi-eee-ble. His doctorate apparently was not in grammar.

"Ooh," you smile to yourself, "this guy is good."

The sermon is on hellfire and damnation. He makes the sizzle as real as if you were at home in your kitchen frying bacon. The occasional honking of horns around you becomes the moaning of lost souls. "Can you picture, beloved, the terror that awaits the unsaved in the Great Beyond?"

"Yes, brother!" you holler, hand raised in oh-so-sincere devotion.

As he wheezes into the microphone you can almost picture his waistline straining at the buttons of a green-and-yellow sport coat. When he hits the high note to say "Jeeeeezus" you'd be willing to bet your eternal salvation that he rises on his toes behind that pulpit. Yes, for all his mournful wailing the good doctor seems to be enjoying himself as he holds forth about hell. But hey, what's this? Traffic seems to be moving again just as the sermon is ending and the quartet comes to sing.

"Yes, Reverend," you croon devoutly, "send me that free literature." *Another bozo ranting about hell.* You punch in a soft rock station and slip the car into gear.

---

It is 1946, a Tuesday noontime at the Eagle and Child pub in St. Giles, England—affectionately known as the "Bird and Baby," not far from the spires of Oxford University. To the congenial background of a crackling fire and the tinkling of glasses, friendly conversation murmurs about the room. In the corner at the rear nests a group of weekly usuals from the university. Formidable minds, these. Lounging around the table, they draw thoughtfully on their pipes between sips of bitters. They discuss literature and quote poetry, much of it their own, going at it "hammer and tongs" as one would later say—debating ideas, critiquing each other's manuscripts, matchings wits, reveling in the good-hearted swordplay.

All are respected academics. One of their number, J. R. R. Tolkien, will one day be loved worldwide as author of *The Hobbit* and the *Lord of the Rings* trilogy. But the gentleman seated across from him will become legendary. Himself an Oxford don, that gentleman has already turned heads as the atheist-become-Christian who convincingly defended his faith over nationwide BBC broadcasts during the recent war. His fame is growing yearly for his scholarly publications in literature and thought-provoking books on Christianity. By this time next year his face will front *Time* magazine. He will eventually be seated as Professor of Medieval and Renaissance English at Cambridge and earn the universal respect of his peers, even those opposed to his religious notions. Within three decades after his death his printed books in many languages will number well over forty million, making him the best-selling Christian author of all time.

His name is C. S. Lewis.

Mr. Lewis is known for his conservative tweed sport coat, not a green and yellow one. Yet he too believes in hell. He has written the following about the doctrine of eternal punishment: "There is no doctrine which I would more willingly remove from Christianity than this, if it lay in my power. But it has the full support of Scripture and, specially, of Our Lord's own words; it has always been held by Christendom; and it has the support of reason."[1]

In fact, he has penned an entire book examining the reality of that awful place.

No enjoyment here in holding forth about hell.

---

So it's not just bozos who believe in a place of torment after death—Oxford profs do too. It's not just sophisticates driving Volvos who shake their heads at hellfire sermons—the tattooed, tobacco-chewing driver of that furniture truck also turned the radio preacher off. The issue is not primarily intellectual. It's spiritual. Many people reject the biblical notion of hell simply because they find it too horrible to entertain. Would a merciful God draw such a place on the map? If so, it's . . . well . . . absolutely hellish—an endless extension of earth's worst moments. A miserably written final chapter with no THE END. Imagining it drains the blood from us.

So understandably, hell's stock has fallen lately from lack of public confidence. Of course atheists have never bought into "the place down-stairs." For them, belief in an afterlife is roughly equivalent to having faith in Bart Simpson. But thousands, perhaps millions, reject hell as a myth yet *still believe in heaven* and cherish fond hopes of going there. This kind of one-sided optimism is straight out of Oz. It defies expla-nation. No ostrich has more sand in his eyes than these people. What straws are they grasping? Some cling hopefully to the Kubler-Ross phenomenon—reports of people clinically dead who revived telling of blissful beyond-the-grave experiences. But there are also docu-mented reports of people whose dance on the edge of eternity left them terrified beyond words.[2] Are these reports being taken seriously? Others draw comfort from the Bible—its descriptions of a compas-sionate God and the joys awaiting his children in the world to come. Surely if *we* hate suffering, God must hate it worse and could never have founded an institution as horrible as described in Dante's *Inferno*. But the same Jesus who gave heaven a five-star rating also described an otherworldly chamber of horrors. And he made clear that Satan doesn't top the list of people to be feared. For the determined evil-doer, *God* is the one to shudder at. "[Hell] has long been prepared; it has been made ready. . . . Its fire pit has been made deep and wide, with an abundance of fire and wood; *the breath of the LORD*, like a stream of burning sulfur, sets it ablaze" (Isaiah 30:33).[3]

Have we really grasped the fact that God runs hell? We tend to think of that lower world as Satan's neighborhood—he's the tough guy who prowls the streets and calls the shots. But Satan will be yesterday's news in hell—the once-feared bully who's been thrashed and sent to his room by a strapping big Dad you don't want to mess with. His screaming and wailing will be heard from outside his window for blocks. "And the devil, who deceived them, was thrown into the lake of burning sulfur. . . . [He] will be tormented day and night for ever and ever" (Revelation 20:10). God, not Satan, will send ripples of fear through everyone there. "They called to the mountains and the rocks, 'Fall on us and hide us from the face of him who sits on the throne'" (Revelation 6:16).

Have you ever seen an uncomplaining, long-suffering person finally vent a righteous rage? It's more sobering than watching a foul-tempered factory boss cuss out his workers for the sixth time in one morning. In hell, God won't be the baby Jesus, meek and mild; he will be the hulking male warrior come to do battle. He will be patience exhausted.

What could be more horrifying than having as your prosecutor, judge, jury, and jailer a Father whose son you murdered? Someone you've ignored and offended all your days? Someone whose mercies you have ungratefully inhaled over a lifetime—like the spoiled kid on Christmas morning tearing through his gifts with no thought about who gave them? Someone whose interests and reputation you have only cared about when it served your purposes? Someone to whom you made promises when in trouble, but forgot them the minute things got better? Someone with meticulous knowledge of your every wicked thought, selfish motive, unkind word, and shady deed from your earliest days? Someone who can never be outwitted, sweet-talked, or negotiated into accepting a plea bargain? Someone who cannot be talked into showing mercy, because the time for mercy has passed? Someone who is serving justice—doing what is *right*—to inflict eternal misery on you? Someone who will touch off praises in Paradise for rewarding you in kind for your sins? For the Scripture says: "*Rejoice* over [unrepentant people destroyed in hell], O heaven! *Rejoice*, saints and apostles and prophets! God has judged [them] for the way [they] treated you" (Revelation 18:20).

But don't misunderstand, as if God were rubbing his hands together thinking of more inmates arriving at the furnace doors. God didn't make hell for people. Jesus said it was "prepared for the devil and his angels" (Matthew 25:41). It's *unnatural* for humans to be there—as unnatural as our turning our backs on a Creator who loved us—as unseemly as our shrugging the Father's kind arm from our shoulders while caressing Eden's serpent coiled around our hearts. God takes no joy in sending anyone to eternal misery; his Son was a lifeguard, urgently warning swimmers of treacherous waters. But in dozens of passages God warns that he will hurl everyone into that unthinkable pit who persists in challenging or ignoring him.

"Say it ain't so," we yell like the shocked young baseball fan earlier this century who couldn't believe some unwelcome news about his team. But it is so. Jesus himself told us, or we'd never believe it. He mentioned it more frequently than heaven. And he was blunt. His pleas were so urgent because hell's pains are so unbearable.

Hell is *spiritually and psychologically* unbearable. Jesus likened it to being "outside"—the warmth and partying is indoors but the door is slammed on us. He described it as "outer darkness" (Matthew 8:12).[4] Darkness makes people lonely. Nighttime makes them afraid. No shimmering dance of candle there—no promising sunrises. No welcoming glow of Christmas lights through the windows. No sun-washed vistas of ocean or landscape. No lovely or pleasant faces. Eventually, no memory of what a smile ever looked like—just the disorientation of cave explorers whose flashlight batteries have run out. In abject darkness, people can do nothing but think. Jesus taught movingly about our thoughts in hell—remorse for missed opportunities, memories of friends and family we knew on earth, concern for those we loved whose destinies our bad examples may have affected. Our terrors and strong pangs of conscience will have no distractions or entertainments to drown them, no pleasant company. There will be company in hell, but none of it pleasant.

Hell is also *physically* unbearable. Jesus once said, "Do not be amazed at this, for a time is coming when all who are in their graves will hear his voice and come out . . . and those who have done evil will rise to be condemned" (John 5:28–29). Never mind the task God will have raising people long buried, or those whose ashes have been scattered to the seven seas—God is omnipotent. But why raise the bodies of his enemies except to punish them through their five senses? "Do not be afraid of those who kill the body but cannot kill the soul. Rather, be afraid of the One who can destroy both soul *and body* in hell" (Matthew 10:28).

Jesus was specific about this. He likened hell to being cut into pieces. Better to be tossed in the ocean with a mill stone hung around your neck than set foot in there, he warned. Better to be maimed—hand and foot sawed off, eye gouged out—than to wake up in that inescapable prison (Matthew 24:50–51; 18:6, 8–9). Worse, if possible, are his earnest and repeated warnings of fire. No bodily injury matches severe burning. Yet this gentle teacher warned of the "fire of Gehenna." Gehenna was a ravine to the southwest of Jerusalem where trash burned perpetually. By Jesus' day it had become the standard figure for hell, and Jesus agreed with that usage.

"But aren't these descriptions just figurative?" we ask.

Whenever the biblical writers describe the afterlife, you sense that they are straining for adequate words. The realities are *greater* than the figures. Heaven is better than gold streets and pearly gates. If hell is not literal fire, it's not because Jesus was exaggerating. It's because hell is worse.

What makes hell supremely worse than any earthly pain is how long it lasts. Many sufferings in this life eventually go away. A pregnant woman in delivery keeps sane only by telling herself that all the pant-pant-blowing will soon end. The broken bone will mend. The headache will pass. Temporary relief is only an aspirin or a hit of morphine away—at least the edge will be gone. Boot camp will be over and I can go home on leave. It may take years, but gradually the misery will subside. But people with chronic physical or emotional pain lead the most desperate lives on earth. No break, no rest. That's why some jump off bridges—to find relief at least in death.

But the person in hell will never know relief. *People who have been there for thousands of years are not a day closer to the end of their sentence than when they entered.* Hell is, in the sobering words of Jesus, "eternal fire." He called it eternal in the same breath that he called heaven eternal (Matthew 25:41, 46). Unless God is lying about heaven, hell lasts forever.[5]

Okay, so this is what hell is like. But how does the existence of such an awful place explain any mysteries about our earthly sufferings?

## HELL WILL SERVE JUSTICE TO THE WORLD'S HITLERS

Unless hell exists, there is no justice in the world. Consider the rise of the Nazi party in Germany, culminating in World War II. Could anyone begin to tally the suffering caused just from that awful conflict? Think of Poland carved up like a piece of meat—half tossed to the dogs of Germany, half to the wolves of Russia. Think of the children made fatherless, the wives made widows, the pain of tens of thousands of soldiers writhing on the battlefields with limbs blown off. Think of the fear of simple civilians whose towns were overrun. The women raped. The six million Jews murdered—gassed, shot, cremated.

Think of the evil festering in Hitler's own mind and heart. He was never brought to justice—according to what most believe, he committed suicide. Yes, he was pressured into suicide by the encroaching Allied armies. But why should the butcherous Führer get off with sipping some strychnine in a glass a wine, in the comforting presence of his mistress? And what of his high-ranking followers? For every war criminal found guilty at the Nuremberg tribunal and hung, there were thousands of lesser players who committed unthinkable atrocities who were never caught—who fled to obscurity in South America or elsewhere and lived a normal life span in comparative ease.

How can this be fair? Even for those who were tried and executed, hanging was too good for them. It was a merciful end. These people were never paid back remotely in proportion to the pain they caused. If there is no hell, they are sleeping peacefully this moment after causing millions of others sleepless or nightmare-filled nights. Only the existence of hell brings some semblance of sense to the misery of World War II. Hell ensures that all will be repaid in full. No one will plea-bargain a reduced sentence. No dream-team of lawyers will enable these people to walk. Justice *will* be served.

## HELL EXPLAINS WHY "GOOD" PEOPLE SUFFER

In 1981 Rabbi Harold Kushner published his national best-seller, *When Bad Things Happen to Good People*. Almost everyone who picks up a copy can relate to the title. "I'm a good person. I'm a good neighbor. I pay my taxes. I don't deserve the trials I'm going through." You can't read this book without immediately liking the author. Although a man of learning, he doesn't flaunt his scholarship; his whole tone is humble and compassionate. Perhaps part of the reason is that he has suffered.

When their son Aaron was three, the Kushners learned that their boy had a rare condition called progeria, "rapid aging." They were told that Aaron would never grow much taller than three feet, would have little hair on his head or body, would appear elderly while still a child, and would live only to his early teens. Aaron did die at age fourteen. Rabbi Kushner wrote the book out of that experience.

For a Christian, reading the book is bittersweet. It is so well-written, so interestingly illustrated with true stories, so sympathetic of the human dilemma—yet so unfaithful to the Bible, both the New Testament (which is understandable) and the Hebrew Bible (which is not).

The book's thesis is this: since good people suffer unfairly, God must lack either goodness or power. The author opts to believe in God's goodness but to abandon belief in his power—God is good, he hates suffering, he would like for all humans to live healthy, happy lives, but he cannot arrange for this. Yet God can strengthen people in their sorrow and do many helpful things as a compassionate deity.

What's fascinating is that Mr. Kushner never entertains the possibility that we suffer because we are sinners. Understand, he doesn't *refute* the idea that people are sinful and deserve suffering; he *assumes* that it's not true.[6] At times he almost appears to mock the idea. He writes his book "for all those people whose love for God and devotion to Him led them to blame themselves for their suffering and persuade themselves that they deserved it." He has seen "the wrong people get sick, the wrong people be hurt, the wrong people die young." He maintains that in God's eyes "we are good and honest people who deserve better."[7]

But the doctrine of hell pours sand on this mirage. It slaps the sleeping in the face and says, "Don't you realize the nonsense you're entertaining? Don't you see the seriousness of your self-righteousness? *You* may think you're measuring up. But God is angry enough to punish you eternally. He is holy beyond your wildest dreams, and you have offended him beyond your imagination. Your trials, even the worst of them, are merely a preview of what's in store—they are spoonfuls of hell come early. Wake up! Examine yourself! Seek God!" In short, grant the Bible's teaching that we all deserve hell—even the "best" of us— and the problem of why we suffer dissolves. Because we merit hell, the hell-on-earth we suffer is fair.

We hear an objection. "But I know some very good people who suffer terribly. If you only knew the woman down the street who has terrible arthritis. She may not claim to be religious—may not go to church—but she's the most Christian person I know." But God says otherwise. According to him, "There is no one righteous, not even one; there is no one who understands, no one who seeks God. All have turned away, they have together become worthless; there is no one who does good, not even one" (Romans 3:10–12).

Perhaps this thought may clarify. Either of two factors make an act sinful—a wrong action or a wrong motive. Often our actions are good but our motives are a universe away from righteousness. To illustrate, take a man who works as the cook and doctor on a pirate ship. He has never picked up a sword a day in his life. He stays on the ship and cooks nourishing meals for the other men when they come back from a hard day's pillaging and looting. He is there to heal their cuts and put salve on their scrapes. What could be more innocent? But if the British crown captures the ship, the doctor-cook will swing from a rope just like his cutthroat shipmates. Why? Because he was doing good things in an evil cause.

This is the way God looks at our lives. We may be model citizens—working hard, driving our kids to soccer practice, keeping our lawns spruced, and waving cheerily to our neighbors as we pass. But God has said that the first and greatest commandment is to love him with all our heart, soul, and strength. That is, to do everything out of a motive of pleasing him. Yet for the unbeliever, each act in his life is only to serve his own interests—to help *his* kids, to give *himself* a sense of hard work and a job well done, to make his neighborhood an attractive place to drive home to. As Jay Adams has said, each of us is a sinner, but we all have developed our unique styles of sinning. For some it is drug addiction, drive-by shootings, and prostitution rings. For others it is a respectable lifestyle—doing all the right things while disregarding God. God hates both—finds them equally offensive—and says that both deserve hell.

Jonathan Edwards, an outstanding New England pastor from the eighteenth century, gave another explanation for why we deserve hell when we think we don't. His argument goes like this. A crime is more or less heinous according to the obligation it violates. Is there an infinite obligation to obey someone? Then I become infinitely guilty if I disobey. Now, our obligation to obey anyone is proportionate to his worthiness, authority, and honorableness. God is infinitely so, therefore crimes against him are a violation of infinite obligation. Such crimes are infinitely heinous. They deserve infinite punishment.

The eternity of our punishment is what makes it infinite.

Picture it this way. In mathematics, a line has no width whatsoever, yet it stretches out in each direction to infinity. If that line were made just the tiniest bit thick, it would cover an infinite amount of area, because it stretches for eternity. The line's width is small—perhaps just a millimeter—but its other dimension, its length, is infinite, and thus it covers an infinite area. Any individual sin of ours may seem small enough—it is like the millimeter width of a line. But because that sin is against an infinitely holy and gracious God, it is infinitely heinous, and therefore deserves infinite punishment. Since no human can experience punishment of infinite intensity, our punishment must be made infinite in duration. That is, it must last forever.

So why do bad things happen to good people? The more basic question is: Why is hell awaiting good people? The Bible's sobering answer is that we are not good. God is just to send his rebellious creatures to hell—thus, he is fair to start that hell in this life.

But there's a hidden mercy here. By tasting hell in this life we are driven to ponder what may face us in the next. In this way, our trials may be our greatest mercies. For some of us, they become God's roadblocks on our headlong rush to hell. The depressed young homemaker reaches for an answer. The cancer-ridden patient makes peace with his Creator. The ladder-climbing executive slips and falls into the arms of God.

## HELL EXPLAINS WHY CHRISTIANS SUFFER

Someone objects: "But the sins of Christians are paid for by Christ's death. They will never experience hell. What does hell-on-earth have to do with them?"

Plenty. Human suffering in this life is merely the splashover from hell. Yes, you would think Christians would be exempt. But this whole book has tried to show why God allows the splashover anyway. God's plan for us in this life is to give us the benefits of heaven only gradually. By letting us struggle with the remnants of a sinful nature, and by letting us know pain, he reminds us of the hell we are being saved from.

If we had an easy life, we would soon forget that we are eternal creatures. But hell's splashover won't allow that. It persistently reminds us that something immense and cosmic is at stake—a heaven to be reached, a hell to be avoided. Human souls are the battle ground on which massive spiritual battles are being waged. The stakes are enormous. The winner takes all and the loser loses everything. Every day of our short lives has eternal consequences for good or ill. Eternity is being affected. Right now counts forever. Thus, it is only fitting that God should give us some sense of the stakes involved, some sense of the war's magnitude. He does this by giving us foretastes of heaven in the joys we experience, and foretastes of hell in our suffering.

If we are thinking clearly, each taste of hell that we have drives us to reach out toward our unbelieving friends and neighbors. Perhaps we have cancer. Our bodies are racked with pain. The Christian should think to himself, "How horrible that our sins should bring such suffering to a world that God made perfect! But how wonderful that I am going to heaven and will be rescued from the horrible pain I deserve. Yet my neighbor down the street, whom I very much like, does not believe in Jesus. He is headed for eternal pains far worse than I am experiencing now. Lord, give me the courage, tact, and wisdom to reach out to him with the truth of the gospel."

All the while that we are experiencing such pain, these trials are making us more like Christ. They are refining our character and, thus, winning us eternal rewards. As Paul says, "Our light and momentary troubles are achieving for us an eternal glory that far outweighs them all" (2 Corinthians 4:1). In other words, by tasting a small bit of hell now, our heaven is becoming more heavenly. Our neighbors and friends are more likely to join us there. And our gratitude for our salvation overflows. "I deserve to go to hell," we admit, "but I'm going to heaven anyway—no one has more reason to rejoice than I!"

And twenty minutes of heaven will make up for everything.

# Thirteen

# SUFFERING GONE

Last weekend I took some out-of-town friends up to the coastal hills to see the Reagan Library, set low and serene on a plateau like a California mission. A lazy hawk glided on warm, dry wind gusting from the valley floor, and we leaned over the wall to admire the arid landscape below.

"This way," directed a guide once inside the library. I wheeled into an exhibit area that set the tumultuous stage onto which President Reagan walked, first, as California's governor. I stopped at the entrance, letting the images bombard me. Flower-power and anti-war posters, pictures of Twiggy, beads and bangles. A Volkswagen Beetle splattered with iridescent yellow paint squatted in the middle of the room. Next, a display of newspaper headlines: KING ASSASSINATED and BOBBY KENNEDY SHOT. After that, photos of sullen-faced Beatles, a sour-faced Janis Joplin, and sad-faced Mamas and Papas. I slowly wheeled by mannequins kneeling in military uniform, holding guns, portraying a scene from Vietnam—these were young men who had a reason to be sad. Me too. It was the era in which I was injured.

My friends wandered off to other exhibits in lovely, orderly rooms, showcasing the humble beginnings of a young Reagan growing up on a shady street in a little Illinois town. I stayed behind, staring at a cover of an old Simon and Garfunkel album. I had played that thing in the hospital over and over, grinding the sad lyrics into my mind like grooves on the record, filling the empty moments with noise, trying to obliterate the horror of entrapment inside a useless body.

Rarely do I think—really think—about those rough, early days. But the exhibit—as well as a fast approaching milestone of three decades in my chair—forced me to bear down on my brain to revive the images in the emergency room and hospital hallways. I could recall nurses looking out my window at the tanks rumbling down the streets of Baltimore. The faces of angry, black aides after a city-wide curfew was imposed. I remembered my hospital room, a few conversations I had with friends, and in my mind's eye, I could see my high school boyfriend walk out the door, leaving me behind for college. But that was it. I could not revive the real horror. I couldn't call up heart-wrenching anguish over torn relationships or gasping for breath when I learned I'd always be in a wheelchair. The mental movies I tried to run were full of blips and blank spaces—nowhere near the painful human drama of thirty years ago.

I moved on to the next room, relieved that all along there existed sane families living in small Midwest towns, raising sons and daughters to be teachers and preachers, hardware store owners and graduates of ivy-towered universities.

Time is slippery stuff. The past always looks different than it did back when. Memory is selective. It chooses only a few highlights of lasting importance from all that happened. When we recall pain in the past, we do so with a perspective we simply didn't have when going through it. We didn't understand how it would all pan out. In the middle of suffering we see only confusion. For me it was a bizarre mix of tie-dyed T-shirts, the smell of pot in the hallways of the state institution, and thoughts of suicide.

If we were looking for roads that lead somewhere through the pain, we were doing just that—looking, not finding them. Later, it's different. In my case, thirty years later, I'm finally understanding. I have found the path. All because I see things differently.

It depends on our perspective—where in time we are looking from. When looking back on heartache, the pain fades like a hazy memory. The trauma has dulled like an old photograph. Only the results survive, the things of lasting importance—like the good marriage, the successful career, or in my case, the acceptance of a wheelchair. These are the events that rise and remain, like stepping-stones above raging waters. These are the things that carry us to the other side of suffering, to the present—the place where we have a sense of "arrival," the place where we are more "us" than we were years earlier.

When we come "through the valley of the shadow of death," we are different people. Better, stronger, and wiser. It's what happens on the other side. He "prepares a table before me in the presence of my enemies;" like me wheeling placidly by a faded poster of a huge marijuana leaf. He "anoints my head with oil; my cup overflows" with the satisfaction of surviving suffering with a smile (Psalm 23:4–5).

The Bible constantly tries to get us to look at life this way. It steadfastly tries to implant the perspective of the future into our present, like a voice counseling us, "This is the way it's all going to turn out, this is how it will all seem when it's over, a better way, I promise." It's a view that separates what is lasting from what will fall by the wayside.

Scripture can do no less. It only deals in realities, always underscoring the final results—the heart settled, the soul rejoicing. And so Scripture urges: "Consider it pure joy, my brothers, whenever you face trials of many kinds" (James 1:2). It reminds us:

> "It was good for me to be afflicted so that I might learn your decrees" (Psalm 119:71).
>
> "For our light and momentary troubles are achieving for us an eternal glory that far outweighs them all" (2 Corinthians 4:17).
>
> "Not only so, but we also rejoice in our sufferings" (Romans 5:3).
>
> "'For I know the plans I have for you,' declares the LORD, 'plans to prosper you and not to harm you, plans to give you hope and a future'" (Jeremiah 29:11).
>
> "Blessed [happy] is the man you discipline, O LORD, the man you teach from your law; you grant him relief from days of trouble" (Psalm 94:12–13).

Human nature gags on such a perspective. It tries to rivet you to the pain of the present, blinding you to the realities of the future. Human nature would rather lick its wounds and sneer, "That's pie in the sky. The future doesn't count." But it does count. So much so that "everything else, no matter how real it seems to us, is treated as insubstantial, hardly worth a snort." Tim Stafford, in *Knowing the Face of God,* continues: "That is why Scripture can seem at times so blithely and irritatingly out of touch with reality, brushing past huge philosophical problems and personal agony. That is just how life is when you are looking from the end. Perspective changes everything. What seemed so important at the time has no significance at all."[1]

The Bible blatantly tells us to "rejoice in suffering" and "welcome trials as friends" because God wants us to step into the reality he has in mind for us, the only reality that ultimately counts. It requires gutsy faith to do so, but as we trust God, we move beyond the present into the future. In fact, we enter the very future God intends for us. "Your new life, which is your *real* life—even though invisible to spectators—is with Christ in God. *He* is your life. When Christ (who is your real life, remember) shows up again on this earth, you'll show up, too—the real you, the glorious you" (Colossians 3:3 THE MESSAGE).

"Real life which is invisible" seems as impossible to comprehend as "rejoicing in suffering" seems impossible to do. But don't forget, "Faith is being sure of what we hope for and certain of what we do not see" (Hebrews 11:1). Like watching a Polaroid snapshot develop before your eyes, the "we" God intends us to be as a result of suffering emerges when we "welcome trials." "We share in his sufferings in order that we may also share in his glory . . . the glory that will be revealed *in us*" (Romans 8:17–18).

The future is straining to get out. To be revealed in us: "The creation waits in eager expectation for the sons of God to be revealed" (Romans 8:19). We have seen the future and it is us—Christ in us and us in Christ. "*If,* indeed, we share in his sufferings."

As we do, our perspective is changed.

This is what God wants—hearts burning with a passion for future things, on fire for kingdom realities that are out of this world. God wants his people aflame with his hope. A "consider it pure joy" outlook affects the way we live on earth. Though we still suffer, we become "cities on a hill" and "lights on a lamp stand" (Matthew 5:14–15) for all to see and thus be encouraged. People whose hearts are ignited for heaven make good inhabitants of earth. These, said C. S. Lewis, do earth a world of good.

It doesn't happen without suffering. Affliction is what fuels the furnace of this heaven-hearted hope. People whose lives are unscathed by affliction have a less energetic hope. Oh, they are glad to know they are going to heaven; for them, accepting Jesus was a guarantee of no hell and all heaven, like a buy-and-sell agreement—place your sins on the counter and get an asbestos-lined soul. Once that's taken care of, they feel they can get back to life as usual—dating and marrying, working and vacationing, spending and saving.

But suffering makes the Christian experience more than signing the dotted line on an eternal health-care contract. Suffering gives the covenant life. It turns our hearts toward the future, like a mother turning the face of her child, insisting, "Look this way!" The apostle Paul said as much to his friends as the first waves of persecution were sweeping through the church:

> Since, then, you have been raised with Christ, set your hearts on things above, where Christ is seated at the right hand of God. Set your minds on things above, not on earthly things. For you died, and your life is now hidden with Christ in God. When Christ, who is your life, appears, then you also will appear with him in glory." (Colossians 3:1–4)

Once heaven has our attention, a fervid anticipation for God's ultimate reality—appearing with him in glory—begins to glow, making everything earthly pale in comparison. Earth's pain keeps crushing our hopes, reminding us this world can never satisfy; only heaven can. And every time we begin to nestle too comfortably on this planet, God cracks open the locks of the dam to allow an ice-cold splash of suffering to wake us from our spiritual slumber.

## WHAT IS OUR HOPE?

Suffering keeps swelling our feet so that earth's shoes won't fit. My atrophied legs and swollen ankles, curled fingers and limp wrists are visual aids in a children's Sunday school lesson on Isaiah 40:6, 8: "All flesh is grass . . . the grass withereth, the flower fadeth: but the word of our God shall stand for ever." (KJV). So I can, along with others who suffer,

"Strengthen the feeble hands, steady the knees that give way; say to those with fearful hearts, 'Be strong, do not fear; your God will come . . . he will come to save you.' Then will the eyes of the blind be opened and the ears of the deaf unstopped. Then will the lame leap like a deer, and the mute tongue shout for joy. . . . Gladness and joy will overtake them, and sorrow and sighing will flee away" (Isaiah 35:3–6, 10).

For me, verses like this are not cross-stitched promises nostalgic of a vague, nebulous and distant era. It's part of the hope I'm already stepping into, the time when Jesus will "transform our lowly bodies so that they will be like his glorious body" (Philippians 3:21). I like that part about new bodies.

But my hope isn't centered around a glorious body.[2] It goes far beyond that.

The New Testament writers, bruised and battered, felt the same. There was something more grandiose about the hope of heaven that stoked the fire in their bones—their writings are laced with constant references to the second coming of *Christ,* the time when heaven will burst over the horizon. Continually they were praying, "Maranatha! Come, *Lord Jesus!*" It was said of the early Christians, "You eagerly wait for our *Lord Jesus Christ* to be revealed" (1 Corinthians 1:7). They likened themselves to soldiers poised on the watchtower, workers hoeing for the harvest, athletes straining toward the finish line, and virgins waiting and watching at night, lamps trimmed, hearts afire, and eyes scanning the horizon for someone special.

The world was no party. They were waiting for the party.

It was clear to them that although the King had begun to set up his kingdom, he hadn't finished. Jesus himself asked his Father, "May Thy kingdom come . . . as it is *in heaven."* He had begun to reverse the effects of sin and its results—pain, death, and disease—but it was just that, a beginning. When the Savior ascended to heaven, no lambs were nuzzling lions yet, no swords were being beaten into plowshares. A few could recall fondly the time Jesus touched their blind eyes and gave them sight, but the eyes of all the blind weren't opened yet, the ears of all the deaf weren't unstopped, and most of the lame were a far cry from leaping like deer.

New Testament writers realized that the final brick had not been cemented into the kingdom building (Ephesians 2:20). Successive generations knew this. Saints—who through the ages would see persecution and pestilence, holocaust and heartache—realized they were living stones being trowelled into the kingdom building (1 Peter 2:5). They understood that suffering was, at times, sickening, but life was worth living if it meant more time granted for the world to hear the Good News. They knew the biting reality of their suffering; but they also remembered the enormously high price Jesus placed on a soul—suffering is bad, but a soul lost is worse (Matthew 16:26). And so, "The Lord is not slow in keeping his promise, as some understand slowness. He is patient . . . not wanting anyone to perish, but everyone to come to repentance" (2 Peter 3:9). Past generations realized God was permitting something he hated (their pain and persecution) so that something he prized (more souls salvaged) could be achieved. "Now I want you to know, brothers, that what has happened to me [imprisonment] has really *served to advance the gospel*" (Philippians 1:12).

Our generation is standing on their shoulders. We hate hell, and because we don't want to see our loved ones go there, we persevere through the pain, not wanting anyone to perish. Our generation shares their same hope: "We . . . groan inwardly as we wait eagerly for our adoption as sons . . . For in this hope we were saved. But hope that is seen is no hope at all. Who hopes for what he already has? But if we hope for what we do not yet have, we wait for it patiently" (Romans 8:23–25).

The hope we wait for means more than splendorous bodies. It involves more than sorrow and sighing fleeing away. And it certainly encompasses more than the cataclysmic end-of-the-world clashes of Armageddon.

## COMING FULL CIRCLE

The hope we wait for is what this book has been about.

Remember when we peered into the heavenly whirlwind of joy and pleasure between the Father, Son, and Holy Spirit? Theirs was—or is—a river of joy splashing over heaven's walls onto us. And remember how suffering sandblasts us to the core, removing sin and impurities so that intimacy with Jesus is possible? Do you recall the

suffering and the sacrifice Jesus offered that we might know this intimacy and his joy? It was the Savior's mission: "I have told you this so
that my joy may be in you" (John 15:11).

Misery may love company, but joy craves a crowd. The Father, Son,
and Holy Spirit's plan to rescue humans was not only for man's sake.
It is for God's sake. The Father is gathering a crowd—an inheritance,
pure and blameless—to worship his Son in the joy of the Holy Spirit.
"God is love" (John 4:16), and the wish of love is to drench with
delight those for whom God has suffered.

Soon the Father, the Son, and the Holy Spirit will get their wish.

Soon, perhaps sooner than we think, "the day of our Lord Jesus
Christ" will arrive and "all who have longed for his appearing" will be
stripped of the last vestige of sin. God will close the curtain on sin,
Satan, and suffering, and we will step into the waterfall of the joy and
pleasure that is the Trinity.

Better yet, we will become part of a Niagara Falls of thunderous joy
as "God is all and in all" for "when he appears we shall be like him for
we shall see him as he is." God in us and we in him. No longer will we
be "hidden with Christ." "Now we see but a poor reflection; then we
shall see face to face. Now I know in part; then I shall know fully, even
as I am fully known" (1 Corinthians 13:12)—the apostle Paul who
wrote this, who ached to *know* Christ through sharing in the fellowship of his sufferings, will finally get his wish, or *has* his wish now. He
is perfectly bonded. Completely united. He not only knows God, he
*knows* God in that deep, personal union, that utter euphoria of experiencing him. Paul tasted it in the pain of earth, but now he "eats of the
tree of life" in the pleasure of heaven (Revelation 22:2).

Our hope is not a "what," but a "Who." The hope we wait for, our
*only* hope, is the "blessed hope—the glorious appearing of our great
God and Savior, Jesus Christ" (Titus 2:13). Heaven is not a place we are
waiting to see; we wait for a Person. It is Jesus we've travailed through
all this suffering for. Our hope is for the Desire of the Nations, the
Healer of Broken Hearts, the Friend of Sinners. True, we are waiting
for the party. But more accurately, we are waiting for the Person who
will make it a party.

## HOW MUCH PLEASURE?

Can heaven's joy, can eternal intimacy with God be *that* pleasurable? It's human to think this way. The pursuit of pleasure is an earthly fixation. But pleasure is not earth's invention; God invented every delight, every delectable sensual experience, "Every good and perfect gift is from above, coming down from the Father of the heavenly lights" (James 1:17). It is natural to whine and wonder whether or not our cravings will be satisfied (earth is the culprit that keeps itching, tickling, and teasing our desires, all the while diminishing the possibilities of fulfillment). Sin always gets worse because it never finds satisfaction. As the song goes, "Kicks just keep getting harder to find."

Will heaven be different?

Consider this unusual but excellent analogy by C. S. Lewis:

> I think our present outlook might be like that of a small boy who, on being told that the sexual act was the highest bodily pleasure, should immediately ask whether you ate chocolates at the same time. On receiving the answer "no," he might regard absence of chocolates as the chief characteristic of sexuality. In vain would you tell him that the reasons why lovers in their carnal raptures don't bother about chocolates is that they have something better to think of. The boy knows chocolate: He does not know the positive thing that excludes it.
>
> We are in the same position. We know the sexual life; we do not know, except in glimpses, the other thing which, in Heaven, will leave no room for it. Hence where fulness awaits us we anticipate [loss].[3]

Earth has conditioned us to think heaven is a place of less, not more.

But enraptured in heaven's joy, we won't think about carnal raptures because we will have something better, something far more pleasurable to consume us. The delight I experience with my husband Ken is merely a hint, a whisper—a bite of chocolate—compared to the resounding joy that, in heaven, will sweep me away in a deluge of ecstasy. "There is scarce anything that can be conceived or expressed about the degree of the happiness of the saints in heaven," asserts

Jonathan Edwards.[4] It's a matter of faith, and I believe the Bible when it says: "No eye has seen, no ear has heard, no mind has conceived what God has prepared for those who love him" (1 Corinthians 2:9).

Every good pleasure on earth is but a shadow of its fulfillment in heaven. The best of friendships are embryonic on earth, snatching only a few short years to mature. There's never enough time. Words can never convey what overflows our hearts. I experience this bittersweet sadness with intimate friends. I love them so much that I want to pass through them, reach the other side, to know them fully, be one with them. Not to possess but to meld with them. I can't on earth. I'm on the outside of their heart's door, always wanting to get in, get closer, even while relishing in their company. My longings are eased knowing that in heaven I will "get in." Jesus has deigned it: "Holy Father, protect them ... so that *they may be one as we are one*" (John 17:11).

Do you recall the definition we've used for suffering? It's wanting what you don't have and having what you don't want. In heaven, you will finally possess what you've always wanted: fulfillment of your deepest desires. And you will always be satisfied with what you have: no boredom and no envy.

Lewis once told a tale of a woman who, after she was thrown into a dungeon, bore and reared a son. The child grew up seeing nothing but the dungeon walls, straw on the floor, and a little patch of sky through the grating above. His mother, an artist, tried to teach her son about the outside world by sketching for him pictures of fields, rivers, mountains, and cities. The boy did his best to believe his mother when she told him the outer world was far more interesting and glorious than her drawings. "What?" asked the boy. "No pencil marks out there?" His whole notion of the outer world became blank, for the pencil lines were not part of the real world. The boy believed the real world was somehow less visible than his mother's pictures. But really, the world outside lacked lines because it was incomparably more visible.

Lewis concluded, "So with us. Our natural experiences (sensory, emotional, imaginative) are only like penciled lines on flat paper. If they vanish in the risen life, they will vanish only as pencil lines vanish from the real landscape."[5]

Words don't do heaven justice. Try as I may to talk of raptures and ecstasies, I fall short. "The most artful composition of words would be to darken and cloud it, to set forth very low shadows of the reality; and all we can say [about heaven] by our best rhetoric is really and truly vastly below the truth. If St. Paul who had seen [heaven] thought it but in vain to utter it, much less shall we pretend to do it," sighed Edwards.[6]

## HOW MUCH TIME?

Heaven will not only be more than we can imagine, the "more" will go on forever. It will be timeless. It has to be; joy flows from God, God is eternal; therefore, so is joy. You instinctively know this when you are gripped by a timeless moment, an experience so precious, so perfect you wish it would last forever.

One early summer morning my sister Jay and I drove down to the little Maryland farming community of Sykesville to visit Grandma Clark. She wasn't really my grandmother; she and Jay had become friends at their tiny stone church on top of the hill, and we had been invited to her big farmhouse for tea. I wheeled into the kitchen and was greeted by the aroma of hot cake from the oven. Grandma had placed white crisp linen on a table by an open window. A breeze lifted lace curtains and wafted in the scent of hydrangeas.

Jay and I sipped tea from delicate cups. My eyes followed Grandma Clark. She leaned back, smoothed the tablecloth with her hand, and spoke of heaven in grand and wistful terms.

A gust of wind suddenly whipped the curtains, tossing her gray hair; she held up her hand, smiling and squinting against the stiff breeze. Whoosh!—it eddied around the table, dizzying and lifting our spirits. The moment was delightfully strange; but as quickly as it came, it vanished, settling us back down and becoming timeless, leaving in its wake peace and joy. I can still taste the cakes and tea, inhale the spring flowers, see the curtains snap and dapples of sun on the tablecloth.

Moments like these remind us of some other time or place. We say the same of childhood memories: lazy, late afternoons licking Popsicles on a back step, listening to a lawnmower up the street, and feeling a breeze cool our brow. Or running out the screen door after dinner to collect fireflies. Or by a campfire, hugging our knees, watching the sparks fly upward, becoming stars. If we could be transported back, we'd discover that even as children, we felt the same nostalgia, the "remembering" of another time or place.

It's that ancient longing I wrote of earlier. It's a yearning to pass through and reach the other side, as C. S. Lewis said. These moments—whether having tea on a spring afternoon or licking Popsicles and feeling safe—are whispering, "One day you will bathe in peace like this . . . satisfaction will shower you . . . this joy will last forever." This is what we as children feel. It's another hint of heaven, like choosing the happiest point in your life and having time stand still. Lewis wrote:

> And in [heaven], we shall eat of the tree of life. . . . The faint, far-off results of those energies which God's creative rapture implanted in matter when he made the worlds are what we now call physical pleasures; and even thus filtered, they are too much for our present management.
>
> What would it be to taste at the fountain-head that stream of which even these lower reaches prove so intoxicating? Yet that, I believe, is what lies before us [in heaven]. The whole man is to drink joy from the fountain of joy. In the light of our depraved appetites we cannot imagine this.[7]

In the light of my depraved appetites, I can barely imagine ecstasy going on forever. It's always something I want to grasp, but can't. I hear inklings in Dvořák's *New World Symphony*. I glimpse it in the soft gaze of someone I love. I smell it in the air at the ocean when the sky is gray and violent in the distance. I felt it once when I was nine years old, holding on to the guardrail by the Grand Canyon because if I let go, I was certain I would fly away across the wide expanse.

If these are mere omens, what will the real thing be like?

What's more, the pleasure and the joy will continue to increase in heaven. The perfection of happiness does not mean idleness; on the contrary, it very much consists in action—"Man is rational and must, to be happy, be rationally active. . . . In heaven, 'tis the directly reverse of what 'tis on earth; for in heaven, by length of time things become more and more youthful, that is, more vigorous, active, tender and beautiful," Jonathan Edwards asserts.[8] In heaven, we keep getting smarter, wiser, younger, and happier. We keep falling more in love. The unfolding of the story of redemption will have us taking one gasp after another, our joy and amazement ever increasing.

## IS SUFFERING WORTH IT?

Is all the bleeding worth the benefit?

More than we realize. "For our light and momentary troubles are achieving for us an eternal glory that far outweighs them all" (2 Corinthians 4:17). Heaven knows its pleasures and joys, the ecstasy and elation. As far as heaven is concerned, our troubles are "light" in comparison. This is another verse written in end-time perspective, telling us, "This is the way it will all turn out, this is the way it will be, you'll see!" Again, it's a matter of faith. A pile of problems are on one side of the scale; heaven's glory, the other.

If the problem-side of the scale seems heavy, then focus your faith on the glory-side. When you do, you're a Rumpelstiltskin weaving straw into gold; like a divine spinning wheel, your affliction "*worketh . . . a far more exceeding and eternal weight of glory*" (2 Corinthians 4:17 KJV). It's as J. B. Phillips paraphrases, "These little troubles (which are really so transitory) are winning for us a permanent, glorious and solid reward out of all proportion to our pain" (2 Corinthians 4:17 PHILLIPS).

It's not merely that heaven will be wonderful *in spite* of our anguish; it will be wonderful *because* of it. Suffering serves us. A faithful response to affliction accrues a *weight* of glory. A bounteous reward. God has every intention of rewarding your endurance. Why else would he meticulously chronicle every one of your tears? "Record my lament; list my tears on your scroll—are they not on your record?" (Psalm 56:8).

Every tear you've cried—think of it—will be redeemed. God will give you indescribable glory for your grief. Not with a general wave of the hand, but in a considered and specific way. Each tear has been listed; each will be recompensed. We know how valuable our tears are in his sight—when Mary anointed Jesus with the valuable perfume, it was her tears with which she washed his feet that moved him most powerfully (Luke 7:44). The worth of our weeping is underscored again in Revelation 21:4 where "he will wipe every tear from their eyes." It won't be the duty of angels or others. It'll be God's.

"Weeping may endure for a night, but joy cometh in the morning" (Psalm 30:5 KJV).

Our reward will be our joy. The more faithful to God we are in the midst of our pain, the more our reward and joy. The Gospels are packed with parables of kings honoring servants for their diligence, landlords showering bonuses on faithful laborers, monarchs placing loyal subjects in charge of many cities. Whatever suffering you are going through this minute, your reaction to it affects the eternity you will enjoy. Heaven will be more heavenly to the degree that you have followed Christ on earth. "I consider that our present sufferings are not worth comparing with the glory that will be revealed in us" (Romans 8:18).

It has been said that something so grand, so glorious is going to happen in the world's finale, something so awesome and wonderful—the dénouement of the Lord Jesus—that it will suffice for every hurt, it will compensate for every inhumanity, and it will atone for every terror. His glory will fill the universe and hell will be an afterthought compared to the resplendent brightness of God's cosmos and "the Lamb who gives it light." Heaven's joy far outweighs hell's dread. Heaven has no opposite, just as God has no opposite (the Devil is a created being, and a fallen one at that).

## A FINAL WORD

You will see your daughter unfettered from her cerebral palsy. You will know the freedom of a heart pure and blameless. You will see your husband walk without a limp. You will know family members and friends as God intended them to be all along, their best attributes shining clearly, and their worst traits gone with the wind. No bruises on your daughter, free from the shackles of an abusive marriage. No confused thoughts, no mental illness, no Alzheimer's disease.

You will see what lessons the angels and the demons learned about God from observing him at work in your mother, languishing in that nursing home. You will stand amazed at how your perseverance through pain sent repercussions rumbling through the lives of people you didn't know were watching, forcing them to make tough decisions about God and suffering.

You will experience love like you never dared imagine. This is good news for people who have never been "the most important person" in anyone's life. But in heaven, "All shall have as much love as they desire ... as much as they can bear. Such will be the sweet and perfect harmony among the heavenly saints, perfect love reigning in every heart toward every other, without limit or restriction or interruption."[9] If you've never known love, never been married, don't worry: you'll be loved more than you can bear.

Karla Larson, who lost legs and kidneys and fingers, will receive a brilliant splendorous body that will be more "Karla" than she ever was on earth. The same for John McAllister. Greg and his ex-wife will find out who they really are in Christ. Ryan will rejoice with them as he races into their arms and says his first words to them, "We knew it would be great, but *this* great ...!"

And for those whose suffering was most confounding, such as Paul Ruffner, God will personally flip right-side-up the tangled embroidery of his life to reveal the delicate and beautiful pattern he never saw on earth. He and millions like him, martyred or tortured, will stand and adore God for his plan and purpose in their suffering.

Most of all, God will not be weeping. Yes, our sufferings matter to the Almighty and he has wept in empathy, crying at the graveside of Lazarus; he often wept when he prayed, pouring out tears in the garden of Gethsemane. But heaven will reveal something different. An eternal plan that was never threatened, never in jeopardy of collapsing, never on the edge of defeat.

There will be no need for tears. "Then one of the elders said to me, 'Do not weep! See, the Lion of the tribe of Judah ... has triumphed.'" But it is not a *lion* that commands center stage: "Then I saw a *Lamb*, looking as if it had been slain, standing in the center of the throne.... Then I heard every creature in heaven and on earth ... singing: 'To him who sits on the throne and to the Lamb be praise and honor and glory and power, for ever and ever!'" (Revelation 5:5–6, 13).

God may have wept, but the suffering of his Son had an eternal perspective too. He will be honored as the slain Lamb. The sufferings of Jesus will never ever be forgotten. Unlike us, he will always visibly bare his wounds to the universe, and for that, God the Father, Son, and Holy Spirit will enjoy a cacophony of praise and worship as never before. If any dark demon in any corner of the universe ever doubted the righteousness of God in stooping to rescue debased and defiled sinners, he'll be set straight. The sacrifice and suffering of Jesus was of such massive worth, such supreme value, that God's righteousness will shine even brighter. God was able to rescue sinners, redeem suffering, crush the rebellion, restore all things, vindicate his holy name, provide restitution . . . and come out all the more glorious for it! Heaven will show this. "Worthy is the Lamb who was slain, to receive power and wealth and wisdom and strength and honor and glory and praise!" (Revelation 5:12).

Finally, you step forward onto heaven's courts.

You drop to your knees to express thanks and gratitude. The Man of Sorrows walks from his throne and approaches you. He has absolutely no doubt of your appreciation, for he knows what you've suffered. He reaches toward you with his nail-scarred hands, and when you feel your hands in his, you are not embarrassed. Your own scars, your anguish, all those times you felt rejection and pain, have given you at least a tiny taste of what the Savior endured to purchase your redemption. Your suffering, like nothing else, has prepared you to meet God—for what proof could you have brought of your love if this life left you totally unscarred?

You have something eternally precious in common with Christ—suffering! But to your amazement, the fellowship of sharing in his sufferings has faded like a half-forgotten dream. Now it is a fellowship of sharing in his joy and pleasure. Pleasure made more wonderful by suffering.

*Oh, the pain of earth,* you half sigh. Then you smile, rising to your feet to live the life God had been preparing for you all along. Weeping may have endured for a night, but it is morning.

And the joy has come.

# BEFORE YOU PUT THIS BOOK DOWN

It's a promise we've staked our lives on for years. "And we know that in all things God works for the good of those who love him, who have been called according to his purpose. For those God foreknew he also predestined to be conformed to the likeness of his Son . . ." (Romans 8:28–29).

The idea of God being in control can sound alarming, but once we settle into the promise, it begins to feel immensely comfortable. If God didn't restrain evil, then suffering would come barreling at us, uncontrolled. His decrees and ordinances shape good and evil in such a way as to warn us of hell, woo us toward heaven, and fit us for life here and in the hereafter. All inspired by his love, pure and passionate.

Such love, you can't ignore. You can't sit on a fence or put it off until later. Love like this begs a response. Besides, remember the promise. It's conditional. This God of love controls the circumstances that touch the lives of *those who love him.*

What to do about that promise? Through this book, have you found yourself drawn to him? Is your anger moving God-ward? Do you see the convincing truth of the Scriptures quoted? In short, is your heart warmed toward him?

Because this book is about him, it's about decisions. Always when we discover something new in his Word, he backs us up against spiritual walls, forcing us to make tough decisions about himself, as well as choices in our suffering. Pressed against our limitations, we come face-to-face with an awesome yet loving God. Yes, you may still have questions, but a choice to trust him can never be wrong. When you say yes to Christ, the wall behind you collapses, sashes are thrown open, and windows are raised to let in a fresh breeze of possibilities. "Where the Spirit of the Lord is, there is freedom."

If you sense your heart burning more brightly by the things you've read on these pages, if you hear the ring of truth, then it is God who is saying to you, "I am the answer to your deepest longings. Trust me. See, the nail prints in my hands. I have suffered for you. And I have permitted in your life what I hate, so that something eternal and wonderful can be achieved—life, rich and meaningful on earth, and life in heaven, free of pain and full of joy."

If you feel up against a wall, if your sin is heavy on your heart, let Christ come into the corner with you. Feel free to borrow the following words and make them your personal prayer . . .

> Lord Jesus, I have not allowed my suffering to draw me to you. Instead, I have resisted you. I see now how my sin has separated me from you. Please forgive me. Sit on the throne of my life as I lay before you my old way of doing things, and help me to live a life that pleases you. As you help me, I will wait patiently to see how you work through my trials. Thank you for the difference you will make in my life. Amen.

If this is your prayer, then the next step is to find a church where Christian friends can embrace you and help you through your painful times. No one should suffer alone—this is a big reason why God instituted the church. Find a church where believers lift up the Word of God, such as you've been hearing from these pages. Step-by-step, you will grow to know God better and discover the fellowship of sharing in his sufferings, as well as the enjoyment of being with other Christians.

We look forward to the day when "the eyes of the blind will be opened . . . and the lame shall leap like deer." Like you, we are anxious for "sorrow and sighing [to] flee away." When that happens, we will embrace each other, free of pain, and marvel how God worked it all, everything, lock stock and barrel, for our good and his glory. Until that day, until God drops the curtain on suffering, let's commit ourselves to trusting him, the One who holds all the answers in his hands.

Joni Eareckson Tada and Steven Estes
JAF Ministries
P.O. Box 3333
Agoura Hills, CA 91301
www.jafministries.com

*Section IV*

# APPENDICES

# *Appendix A*

# SCRIPTURE ON GOD'S HAND IN OUR SUFFERINGS

What is it about lemonade that appeals to us on a hot August afternoon? Other drinks are just as cold, just as wet. Surely it's that winning combination of sweet and sour that we love. But imagine someone handing you a frosty cold glass of pure sugar-water. Sickening. Or envision sucking a raw lemon. Unbearably tart. (We realize a few of you out there enjoy lemons like this, but we're talking about sane people.) Neither sugar-water nor lemon-juice tastes very good, but the mixture is a summer classic.

For decades now, many Christians have been sipping sugar-water almost exclusively when it comes to thoughts about God. God's kindness, God's goodness, God's tenderness is all they know. But there's a rugged side of God, a masculine side, that's often avoided—his holy, powerful, sovereign, sin-destroying nature. To come to grips with these will not make us hate him; it will make us *worship* him. It will have us on our faces in awe. It will make Christ's death for us a wonder beyond expressing.

This book has tried to reintroduce some of God's lemon to our thinking without ignoring his sweetness. Below is a collection of passages for quick reference that teach his sovereignty over our sufferings—that remind us how nothing pleasant or difficult crosses our path apart from his decree. Most people who believe the Bible can see God's hand in their *mercies*. Therefore, we've primarily focused in this appendix on his hand in life's *afflictions*. If you study this outline without keeping

God's gentleness in mind—gentleness discussed throughout this book, particularly in chapters 2 and 3—you'll feel like you're sipping lemon-water. The balancing sweetness is found in his love, compassion, and wisdom. Please remember this as you read.

---

Many things cause us to suffer. Most, perhaps all, can be boiled down to a few major categories as follows:

- Other people (deliberate actions, negligence)
- Satan and demons
- Animals and plants (mosquitoes biting, farm animals not cooperating, rabid dogs attacking, trees falling, poison mushrooms killing, pollen causing allergies, etc.)
- Nature's inanimate forces (weather, earthquakes, etc.)
- Man-made machinery, tools, and technology (a tire goes flat, a bridge collapses, a space shuttle explodes, etc.)
- Bodily afflictions (illness, disabilities, genetic disorders)
- Psychological/Spiritual afflictions (depression, fear, sorrow, guilt, nightmares, etc.). This category usually overlaps those above, often in ways we don't understand.

The verses below assert God's reign over each—always for the ultimate good of his people. "God has put everything under the control of Christ. He has made Christ the head of everything *for the good of the church*" (Ephesians 1:2, GOD'S WORD translation).

## I. GOD'S HAND OVER OTHER PEOPLE

A. Even though humans have an intelligence and will of their own, God ultimately governs all they do—even their "accidental" actions.

    1. Proverbs 16:9: *In his heart a man plans his course, but the LORD determines his steps.*

    2. Proverbs 19:21: *Many are the plans in a man's heart, but it is the LORD's purpose that prevails.*

    3. Proverbs 20:24: *A man's steps are directed by the LORD. How then can anyone understand his own way?*

4. Proverbs 21:1: *The king's heart is in the hand of the LORD; he directs it like a watercourse wherever he pleases.*

5. Daniel 5:23: [Daniel speaking to the pagan king Belshazzar] *"But you did not honor the God who holds in his hand your life and all your ways."*

6. 2 Chronicles 18:33–34: [God has decreed that Ahab, king of Israel, will die in battle. Ahab tries to avoid this by disguising himself as a common soldier] *But someone drew his bow at random and hit the king of Israel between the sections of his armor . . . All day long the battle raged, and the king of Israel propped himself up in his chariot facing the Arameans until evening. Then at sunset he died.*

7. Numbers 35:9–10: [Concerning "accidents"] *Then the LORD said to Moses: "Speak to the Israelites and say to them: 'When you cross the Jordan into Canaan, select some towns to be your cities of refuge, to which a person who has killed someone accidentally may flee.'"* Compare Exodus 21:12–13: *Anyone who strikes a man and kills him shall surely be put to death. However, if he does not do it intentionally, but God lets it happen, he is to flee to a place I will designate.*

B. Most Christians willingly acknowledge God's hand in people's good deeds, even the good deeds of total pagans.

1. Philippians 2:13: *For it is God who works in you to will and to act according to his good purpose.*

2. 2 Corinthians 8:16: *I thank God, who put into the heart of Titus the same concern I have for you.*

3. Acts 16:14: *One of those listening was a woman named Lydia . . . The Lord opened her heart to respond to Paul's message.*

4. 1 Corinthians 15:10: [Paul speaking] *I worked harder than all [the other apostles]—yet not I, but the grace of God that was with me.*

5. Ezra 1:1: [Regarding the Persian decree allowing Jewish exiles to return home and rebuild the temple in Jerusalem] *The LORD moved the heart of Cyrus king of Persia to make a proclamation throughout his realm and to put it in writing.*

6. Genesis 20:3–6: [Abimelech, pagan king of Gerar, has taken Sarah, wife of Abraham, into his harem] *But God came to Abimelech in a dream one night and said to him, "You are as good as dead because*

*of the woman you have taken; she is a married woman." Now Abimelech had not gone near her, so he said, "Lord, will you destroy an innocent nation? Did [her husband Abraham] not say to me, 'She is my sister,' and didn't she also say, 'He is my brother'? I have done this with a clear conscience and clean hands." Then God said to him in the dream, "Yes, I know you did this with a clear conscience, and so I have kept you from sinning against me. That is why I did not let you touch her."*

C. But God also oversees people's wicked actions. No sin happens that he doesn't deliberately allow. Don't misunderstand—he is not the source of people's evil deeds, for he despises sin. James 1:13 says that God never tempts anyone. Rather, he steers the sin already in their hearts so that sinners unwittingly fulfill his plans and not merely their own. He accomplishes this by infinite wisdom beyond our grasp.

1. Proverbs 16:4: *The LORD works out everything for his own ends— even the wicked for a day of disaster.*

2. Ezekiel 32:32: [God, speaking of Pharaoh's cruelty] *"I had him spread terror in the land of the living . . ." declares the Sovereign LORD.*

3. Acts 4:28: [The early Christians, speaking to God about the men who unjustly had Jesus murdered] *"They did what your power and will had decided beforehand should happen."*

4. Genesis 45:7–8: [Joseph, speaking to his brothers about their selling him into slavery] *But God sent me ahead of you to preserve for you a remnant on earth and to save your lives by a great deliverance. So then, it was not you who sent me here, but God.*

5. 1 Samuel 2:25: [Regarding the warnings of the high priest, Eli, to his sons that they stop sinning] *His sons, however, did not listen to their father's rebuke, for it was the LORD's will to put them to death.*

6. 2 Chronicles 25:20: [Regarding a warning to Amaziah, king of Judah, not to enter battle] *Amaziah, however, would not listen, for God so worked that he might hand them over to Jehoash [the enemy king], because they sought the gods of Edom.*

7. Judges 14:3–4: [Samson rejects his parents' pleas that he not marry an idol-worshiping Philistine] *"Must you go to the uncircumcised Philistines to get a wife?" But Samson said to his father, "Get*

*her for me. She's the right one for me." (His parents did not know that this was from the* LORD, *who was seeking an occasion to confront the Philistines; for at that time they were ruling over Israel.)*

8. Exodus 14:17: [God telling Moses that he is going to drown the Egyptians in the Red Sea] *I will harden the hearts of the Egyptians so that they will go in after [the Israelites]. And I will gain glory through Pharaoh and all his army, through his chariots and his horsemen.*

9. Psalm 105:25 (NASV): *He turned [the Egyptians'] heart to hate His people.*

10. Deuteronomy 2:30: *But Sihon king of Heshbon refused to let us pass through. For the* LORD *your God had made his spirit stubborn and his heart obstinate in order to give him into your hands.*

11. Joshua 11:20 [Regarding the Canaanites, whose land Israel conquered] *For it was the* LORD *himself who hardened their hearts to wage war against Israel, so that he might destroy them totally, exterminating them without mercy, as the* LORD *had commanded Moses.*

12. Isaiah 10:5–7, 15: [God is sending the wicked Assyrians to punish his people Israel, who have sinned so badly they are called "a godless nation." The Assyrians are clueless about being used as God's tools]

> *Woe to the Assyrian, the rod of my anger,*
> *in whose hand is the club of my wrath!*
> *I send him against a godless nation,*
> *I dispatch him against a people who anger me,*
> *to seize loot and snatch plunder,*
> *and to trample them down like mud in the streets.*
> *But this is not what he [the Assyrian king] intends,*
> *this is not what he has in mind;*
> *his purpose is to destroy,*
> *to put an end to many nations . . .*
> *Does the ax raise itself above him who swings it,*
> *or the saw boast against him who uses it?*
> *As if a rod were to wield him who lifts it up,*
> *or a club brandish him who is not wood!*

D. He deludes evil people, confusing their thinking, thereby frustrating their rebellious plans.

1. 2 Thessalonians 2:10—11: *They refused to love the truth ... For this reason God sends them a powerful delusion so that they will believe the lie.*

2. John 12:39—40: *For this reason they could not believe, because, as Isaiah says elsewhere: "He has blinded their eyes and deadened their hearts, so they can neither see with their eyes, nor understand with their hearts, nor turn—and I would heal them."*

3. 2 Samuel 17:14: [Ahithophel, universally admired for his wisdom, gives some sound military advice to wicked throne-usurper Absalom. Hushai, a less-respected but more godly advisor, gives deliberately bad advice that will hamper Absalom's plans] *Absalom and all the men of Israel said, "The advice of Hushai the Arkite is better than that of Ahithophel." For the LORD had determined to frustrate the good advice of Ahithophel in order to bring disaster on Absalom.*

4. Jeremiah 4:10: [God has allowed false prophets to predict peace when war is imminent] *Then I said, "Ah, Sovereign LORD, how completely you have deceived this people and Jerusalem by saying, 'You will have peace,' when the sword is at our throats."*

## II. GOD'S HAND OVER SATAN AND DEMONS

1. Luke 22:31: [Satan needs permission to act] *Simon, Simon, Satan has asked to sift you as wheat.*

2. Job 2:6 (NASV): [God grants Satan permission to harm Job, but imposes definite limits] *"Behold, he is in your power, only spare his life."*

3. Matthew 8:31—32: [Demons need Jesus' permission] *The demons begged Jesus, "If you drive us out, send us into the herd of pigs." He said to them, "Go!" So they came out and went into the pigs, and the whole herd rushed down the steep bank into the lake and died in the water.*

4. 1 Kings 22:22: [A demon's conversation with Jehovah] *"I will go out and be a lying spirit in the mouths of [Ahab's] prophets," he said. "You will succeed in enticing him," said the LORD. "Go and do it."* Compare 1 Kings 22:23: [The godly prophet Micaiah to wicked king Ahab] *So now the LORD has put a lying spirit in the mouths of all these prophets of yours. The LORD has decreed disaster for you.*

5. 1 Samuel 16:14: *Now the Spirit of the LORD had departed from Saul, and an evil spirit from the LORD tormented him.*

6. Matthew 4:10–11: *Jesus said to [Lucifer], "Away from me, Satan! . . ." Then the devil left him.*

7. Mark 1:23–27: *Just then a man in their synagogue who was possessed by an evil spirit cried out, "What do you want with us, Jesus of Nazareth? Have you come to destroy us? I know who you are—the Holy One of God!" "Be quiet!" said Jesus sternly. "Come out of him!" The evil spirit shook the man violently and came out of him with a shriek. The people were all so amazed that they asked each other, "What is this? A new teaching—and with authority! He even gives orders to evil spirits and they obey him."*

Sometimes by looking at distant verses side-by-side we can see how Satan is unwittingly forced to serve God's decrees:

8. 1 Chronicles 21:1: *Satan rose up against Israel and incited David to take a census of Israel.* Compare 2 Samuel 24:1: *Again the anger of the LORD burned against Israel, and he incited David against them, saying, "Go and take a census of Israel and Judah."* [God accomplished his purpose of punishing Israel by letting Satan plant a wicked thought in David's mind]

9. 2 Corinthians 4:4: *The god of this age [i.e., Satan] has blinded the minds of unbelievers, so that they cannot see the light of the gospel of the glory of Christ.* Compare John 12:39–40: *For this reason they could not believe, because, as Isaiah says elsewhere: "He [i.e., God] has blinded their eyes and deadened their hearts, so they can neither see with their eyes, nor understand with their hearts, nor turn—and I would heal them."*

## III. GOD'S HAND OVER ANIMALS AND PLANTS

1. Matthew 10:29: *Are not two sparrows sold for a penny? Yet not one of them will fall to the ground apart from the will of your Father.*

2. Numbers 22:28: *Then the LORD opened the donkey's mouth, and she said to Balaam, "What have I done to you to make you beat me these three times?"*

3. 2 Kings 17:25: *When they first lived there, they did not worship the* LORD; *so he sent lions among them and they killed some of the people.*

4. 1 Kings 17:2–4: *Then the word of the* LORD *came to Elijah: "Leave here, turn eastward and hide in the Kerith Ravine . . . I have ordered the ravens to feed you there."*

5. Jonah 1:17; 2:10: *But the* LORD *provided a great fish to swallow Jonah . . . And the* LORD *commanded the fish, and it vomited Jonah onto dry land.*

6. Jonah 4:6: *Then the* LORD *God provided a vine and made it grow up over Jonah to give shade for his head to ease his discomfort.*

7. Jonah 4:7: *But at dawn the next day God provided a worm, which chewed the vine so that it withered.*

8. Leviticus 14:34–35: [God addressing Israel] *When you enter the land of Canaan . . . and I put a spreading mildew in a house in that land, the owner of the house must go and tell the priest.*

9. 2 Samuel 24:15: *So the* LORD *sent a plague on Israel . . . and seventy thousand of the people from Dan to Beersheba died.*

10. Exodus 8:1–2: [God speaking to Pharaoh via Moses] *This is what the* LORD *says: "Let my people go, so that they may worship me. If you refuse to let them go, I will plague your whole country with frogs."*

11. Exodus 8:21, 24: [God to Pharaoh] *"If you do not let my people go, I will send swarms of flies on you . . ." And the* LORD *did this.*

12. Exodus 10:13: *The* LORD *made an east wind blow across the land . . . By morning the wind had brought the locusts.*

## IV. GOD'S HAND OVER NATURE'S (SMALL "N"!) INANIMATE FORCES

1. Psalm 147:15–18: *He sends his command to the earth; his word runs swiftly. He spreads the snow like wool and scatters the frost like ashes. He hurls down his hail like pebbles. Who can withstand his icy blast? He sends his word and melts them; he stirs up his breezes, and the waters flow.*

2. Psalms 148:8: *. . . lightning and hail, snow and clouds, stormy winds that do his bidding.*

3. Amos 4:7–10: [God addressing Israel] *"I also withheld rain from you when the harvest was still three months away. I sent rain on one*

town, but withheld it from another ... Many times I struck your gardens and vineyards, I struck them with blight and mildew ... yet you have not returned to me," declares the LORD.

4. Jonah 1:4: *Then the LORD sent a great wind on the sea, and such a violent storm arose that the ship threatened to break up.*

5. Genesis 6:17: *I am going to bring floodwaters on the earth to destroy all life under the heavens, every creature that has the breath of life in it. Everything on earth will perish.*

6. Genesis 19:24: *Then the LORD rained down burning sulfur on Sodom and Gomorrah.*

7. Mark 4:37–41: *A furious squall came up, and the waves broke over the boat, so that it was nearly swamped ... He got up, rebuked the wind and said to the waves, "Quiet! Be still!" Then the wind died down and it was completely calm. ... [His disciples] were terrified and asked each other, "Who is this? Even the wind and the waves obey him!"*

8. Exodus 9:23: *When Moses stretched out his staff toward the sky, the LORD sent thunder and hail, and lightning flashed down to the ground. So the LORD rained hail on the land of Egypt ... The only place it did not hail was the land of Goshen, where the Israelites were.*

9. Exodus 14:21, 27: *All that night the LORD drove the sea back with a strong east wind and turned it into dry land. The waters were divided. ... At daybreak the sea went back to its place. The Egyptians were fleeing toward it, and the LORD swept them into the sea.*

10. Numbers 16:28–33: *Then Moses said, " ... If the LORD brings about something totally new, and the earth opens its mouth and swallows them, with everything that belongs to them, and they go down alive into the grave, then you will know that these men have treated the LORD with contempt." As soon as he finished saying all this, the ground under them split apart and the earth opened its mouth and swallowed them.*

## V. GOD'S HAND OVER MAN-MADE MACHINERY, TOOLS, AND TECHNOLOGY

1. Exodus 14:25: *He made the wheels of their chariots come off so that they had difficulty driving. And the Egyptians said, "Let's get away from the Israelites! The LORD is fighting for them against Egypt."*

2. 2 Kings 6:5–6: *As one of them was cutting down a tree, the iron axhead fell into the water. "Oh, my lord," he cried out, "it was borrowed!" The man of God asked, "Where did it fall?" When he showed him the place, Elisha cut a stick and threw it there, and made the iron float.*

3. Proverbs 16:33: *The lot is cast into the lap, but its every decision is from the* LORD.

4. Daniel 3:27–28: [Shadrach, Meshach, and Abednego are thrown into a blazing furnace by King Nebuchadnezzar for refusing to bow down to an idol] *The satraps, prefects, governors and royal advisers crowded around them. They saw that the fire had not harmed their bodies, nor was a hair of their heads singed; their robes were not scorched, and there was no smell of fire on them. Then Nebuchadnezzar said, "Praise be to the God of Shadrach, Meshach and Abednego, who has sent his angel and rescued his servants!"*

## VI. GOD'S HAND OVER OUR BODILY AFFLICTIONS

1. Psalm 103:2–3: *Praise the* LORD, *O my soul, and forget not all his benefits—who forgives all your sins and heals all your diseases.*

2. Mark 1:32–34: *That evening after sunset the people brought to Jesus all the sick . . . The whole town gathered at the door, and Jesus healed many who had various diseases . . .*

3. Exodus 4:11: *The* LORD *said to him, "Who gave man his mouth? Who makes him deaf or mute? Who gives him sight or makes him blind? Is it not I, the* LORD?"

4. 2 Kings 15:5: *The* LORD *afflicted the king with leprosy until the day he died.*

5. Psalms 38:3: [David speaking to God] *Because of your wrath there is no health in my body; my bones have no soundness because of my sin.*

6. Deuteronomy 28:27, 35: [God promising sickness if Israel disobeys] *The* LORD *will afflict you with the boils of Egypt and with tumors, festering sores and the itch, from which you cannot be cured . . . The* LORD *will afflict your knees and legs with painful boils that cannot be cured, spreading from the soles of your feet to the top of your head.*

7. Deuteronomy 28:58–59: [More warnings] *If you do not carefully follow all the words of this law, which are written in this book, and do*

*not revere this glorious and awesome name—the LORD your God— the LORD will send fearful plagues on you and your descendants, harsh and prolonged disasters, and severe and lingering illnesses.*

8. Exodus 15:26: [On the other hand, if Israel obeys . . . ] *If you listen carefully to the voice of the LORD your God and do what is right in his eyes, if you pay attention to his commands and keep all his decrees, I will not bring on you any of the diseases I brought on the Egyptians, for I am the LORD, who heals you.*

    Of course Satan sometimes causes illness (Job 2:7; Luke 13:16)—but there, as everywhere, Satan unwittingly serves God's ends (section II above). Note also the following verses showing that mature Christians can become sick even while living close to God. The passages show that sickness stems not merely from specific sin or from "lack of faith."

9. 1 Timothy 5:23: [Paul to Timothy] *Stop drinking only water, and use a little wine because of your stomach and your frequent illnesses.*

10. 2 Timothy 4:20: [Paul to Timothy] *I left Trophimus sick in Miletus.*

11. Philippians 2:27: [Concerning Epaphroditus, who hand-delivered Paul's Philippian epistle] *Indeed he was ill, and almost died.*

12. Galatians 4:13: [After Paul's apparent detour into Galatia to recuperate] *As you know, it was because of an illness that I first preached the gospel to you.*

## VII. GOD'S HAND OVER OUR PSYCHOLOGICAL/ SPIRITUAL AFFLICTIONS

1. Galatians 5:22–23: *But the fruit of the Spirit is . . . joy, peace.*

2. Psalm 30:11–12: [David praying] *You turned my wailing into dancing; you removed my sackcloth and clothed me with joy, that my heart may sing to you and not be silent.*

3. Psalms 4:7–8: [David praying] *You have filled my heart with greater joy than when their grain and new wine abound. I will lie down and sleep in peace, for you alone, O LORD, make me dwell in safety.*

4. Lamentations 3:32: *. . . he [the Lord] brings grief.*

5. Psalms 6:3–4: [David praying] *My soul is in anguish. How long, O LORD, how long? Turn, O LORD, and deliver me; save me because of your unfailing love.*

6. Psalms 13:1–3: *How long, O LORD? Will you forget me forever? How long will you hide your face from me? How long must I wrestle with my thoughts and every day have sorrow in my heart? . . . Look on me and answer, O LORD my God. Give light to my eyes.*

7. Deuteronomy 28:28, 34: [God threatens Israel if they disobey] *The LORD will afflict you with madness, blindness and confusion of mind . . . The sights you see will drive you mad.*

8. Deuteronomy 28:65–67: [Israel again warned] *The LORD will give you an anxious mind, eyes weary with longing, and a despairing heart. You will live in constant suspense, filled with dread both night and day . . . In the morning you will say, "If only it were evening!" and in the evening, "If only it were morning!"—because of the terror that will fill your hearts . . .*

9. Leviticus 26:36: *I will make their hearts so fearful in the lands of their enemies that the sound of a windblown leaf will put them to flight. They will run as though fleeing from the sword, and they will fall, even though no one is pursuing them.*

10. 1 Samuel 16:14: *Now the Spirit of the LORD had departed from Saul, and an evil spirit from the LORD tormented him.*

11. Proverbs 21:1: *The king's heart [includes thoughts, emotions, will] is in the hand of the LORD; he directs it like a watercourse wherever he pleases.*

12. Daniel 4:31, 16, 33–34: *A voice came from heaven, "This is what is decreed for you, King Nebuchadnezzar: 'Let his mind be changed from that of a man and let him be given the mind of an animal . . .' " . . . Immediately what had been said about Nebuchadnezzar was fulfilled. He was driven away from people and ate grass like cattle. His body was drenched with the dew of heaven until his hair grew like the feathers of an eagle and his nails like the claws of a bird. "At the end of that time, I, Nebuchadnezzar, raised my eyes toward heaven, and my sanity was restored."*

13. 2 Corinthians 12:7: [Paul speaking] *To keep me from becoming conceited because of these surpassingly great revelations, there was given me a thorn in my flesh, a messenger of Satan, to torment me."* [It's not clear whether Paul's torment, sent by God but brought by Satan, was physical or psychological]

## VIII. IN SUMMARY, NO TRIAL REACHES US APART FROM GOD'S EXPLICIT DECREE AND SPECIFIC PERMISSION

1. Amos 3:6: *When disaster comes to a city, has not the LORD caused it?*
2. Lamentations 3:38: *Is it not from the mouth of the Most High that both calamities and good things come?*
3. Isaiah 45:7: *I form the light and create darkness, I bring prosperity and create disaster; I, the LORD, do all these things.*
4. 1 Samuel 2:6–7: *The LORD brings death and makes alive; he brings down to the grave and raises up. The LORD sends poverty and wealth; he humbles and he exalts.*
5. 1 Thessalonians 3:3: *You know quite well that we were destined for [trials].*
6. Ephesians 1:11: *[God] works out everything in conformity with the purpose of his will.*

In conclusion, God may not *initiate* all our trials—but by the time they reach us, they are his will for us. When Satan, other people, or just plain "accidents" bring us sorrow, we can answer like Joseph to his brothers who sold him into slavery, "As for you, you meant evil against me, but God meant it for good" (Genesis 50:20, NASV).

# *Appendix B:*

# SCRIPTURE ON GOD'S PURPOSE IN OUR SUFFERINGS

Discovering God's hand in hardship is really a discovery of God's Word. The following verses underscore a few of the benefits derived from our pain and problems. These power-packed verses serve as a lens through which we gain a clearer perspective on our afflictions.

**Suffering is used to increase our awareness of the sustaining power of God to whom we owe our sustenance**

1. Psalm 68:19: *Praise be to the Lord, to God our Savior, who daily bears our burdens.*

**God uses suffering to refine, perfect, strengthen, and keep us from falling**

1. Psalm 66:8–9: *Praise our God, O peoples, let the sound of his praise be heard; he has preserved our lives and kept our feet from slipping.*
2. Hebrews 2:10: *In bringing many sons to glory, it was fitting that God, for whom and through whom everything exists, should make the author of their salvation perfect through suffering.*

**Suffering allows the life of Christ to be manifested in our mortal flesh**

1. 2 Corinthians 4:7–11: *But we have this treasure in jars of clay to show that this all-surpassing power is from God and not from us. We are hard pressed on every side, but not crushed; perplexed, but not in despair; persecuted, but not abandoned; struck down, but not destroyed. We always carry*

*around in our body the death of Jesus, so that the life of Jesus may also be revealed in our body. For we who are alive are always being given over to death for Jesus' sake, so that his life may be revealed in our mortal body.*

## Suffering bankrupts us, making us dependent on God

1. 2 Corinthians 12:9: *"My grace is sufficient for you, for my power is made perfect in weakness." Therefore I will boast all the more gladly about my weaknesses, so that Christ's power may rest on me.*

## Suffering teaches us humility

1. 2 Corinthians 12:7: *To keep me from becoming conceited because of these surpassingly great revelations, there was given me a thorn in my flesh, a messenger of Satan, to torment me.*

## Suffering imparts the mind of Christ

1. Philippians 2:1–11: *If you have any encouragement from being united with Christ, if any comfort from his love, if any fellowship with the Spirit, if any tenderness and compassion, then make my joy complete by being like-minded, having the same love, being one in spirit and purpose. Do nothing out of selfish ambition or vain conceit, but in humility consider others better than yourselves. Each of you should look not only to your own interests, but also to the interests of others. Your attitude should be the same as that of Christ Jesus: Who, being in very nature God, did not consider equality with God something to be grasped, but made himself nothing, taking the very nature of a servant, being made in human likeness. And being found in appearance as a man, he humbled himself and became obedient to death—even death on a cross! Therefore God exalted him to the highest place and gave him the name that is above every name, that at the name of Jesus every knee should bow, in heaven and on earth and under the earth, and every tongue confess that Jesus Christ is Lord, to the glory of God the Father.*

## Suffering teaches us that God is more concerned with character than comfort

1. Romans 5:3–4: *Not only so, but we also rejoice in our sufferings, because we know that suffering produces perseverance; perseverance, character; and character, hope.*

2. Hebrews 12:10–11: *Our fathers disciplined us for a little while as they thought best; but God disciplines us for our good, that we may share in his holiness. No discipline seems pleasant at the time, but painful. Later on, however, it produces a harvest of righteousness and peace for those who have been trained by it.*

## Suffering teaches us that the greatest good of the Christian life is not absence of pain but Christ-likeness

1. 2 Corinthians 4:8–10: *We are hard pressed on every side, but not crushed; perplexed, but not in despair; persecuted, but not abandoned; struck down, but not destroyed. We always carry around in our body the death of Jesus, so that the life of Jesus may also be revealed in our body.*

2. Romans 8:28–29: *And we know that in all things God works for the good of those who love him, who have been called according to his purpose. For those God foreknew he also predestined to be conformed to the likeness of his Son, that he might be the firstborn among many brothers.*

## Suffering can be a chastisement from God for sin and rebellion

1. Psalm 107:17: *Some became fools through their rebellious ways and suffered affliction because of their iniquities.*

## Obedience and self-control is learned from suffering

1. Hebrews 5:8: *Although he was a son, he learned obedience from what he suffered.*

2. Psalm 119:67: *Before I was afflicted I went astray, but now I obey your word.*

3. Romans 5:1–5: *Therefore, since we have been justified through faith, we have peace with God through our Lord Jesus Christ, through whom we have gained access by faith into this grace in which we now stand. And we rejoice in the hope of the glory of God. Not only so, but we also rejoice in our sufferings, because we know that suffering produces perseverance; perseverance, character; and character, hope. And hope does not disappoint us, because God has poured out his love into our hearts by the Holy Spirit, whom he has given us.*

4. James 1:2–8: *Consider it pure joy, my brothers, whenever you face trials of many kinds, because you know that the testing of your faith develops*

perseverance. Perseverance must finish its work so that you may be mature and complete, not lacking anything. If any of you lacks wisdom, he should ask God, who gives generously to all without finding fault, and it will be given to him. But when he asks, he must believe and not doubt, because he who doubts is like a wave of the sea, blown and tossed by the wind. That man should not think he will receive anything from the Lord; he is a double-minded man, unstable in all that he does.

5. Philippians 3:10: *I want to know Christ and the power of his resurrection and the fellowship of sharing in his sufferings, becoming like him in his death.*

## Voluntary suffering is one way to demonstrate the love of God

1. 2 Corinthians 8:1–2, 9: *And now, brothers, we want you to know about the grace that God has given the Macedonian churches. Out of the most severe trial, their overflowing joy and their extreme poverty welled up in rich generosity . . . For you know the grace of our Lord Jesus Christ, that though he was rich, yet for your sakes he became poor, so that you through his poverty might become rich.*

## Suffering is part of the struggle against sin

1. Hebrews 12:4–13: *In your struggle against sin, you have not yet resisted to the point of shedding your blood. And you have forgotten that word of encouragement that addresses you as sons: "My son, do not make light of the Lord's discipline, and do not lose heart when he rebukes you, because the Lord disciplines those he loves, and he punishes everyone he accepts as a son." Endure hardship as discipline; God is treating you as sons. For what son is not disciplined by his father? If you are not disciplined (and everyone undergoes discipline), then you are illegitimate children and not true sons. Moreover, we have all had human fathers who disciplined us and we respected them for it. How much more should we submit to the Father of our spirits and live! Our fathers disciplined us for a little while as they thought best; but God disciplines us for our good, that we may share in his holiness. No discipline seems pleasant at the time, but painful. Later on, however, it produces a harvest of righteousness and peace for those who have been trained by it. Therefore,*

*strengthen your feeble arms and weak knees. "Make level paths for your feet," so that the lame may not be disabled, but rather healed.*

## Suffering is part of the struggle against evil men

1. Psalm 27:12: *Do not turn me over to the desire of my foes, for false witnesses rise up against me, breathing out violence.*
2. Psalm 37:14–15: *The wicked draw the sword and bend the bow to bring down the poor and needy, to slay those whose ways are upright. But their swords will pierce their own hearts, and their bows will be broken.*

## Suffering is part of the struggle for the kingdom of God

1. 2 Thessalonians 1:5: *All this is evidence that God's judgment is right, and as a result you will be counted worthy of the kingdom of God, for which you are suffering.*

## Suffering is part of the struggle for the Gospel

1. 2 Timothy 2:8–9: *This is my gospel, for which I am suffering even to the point of being chained like a criminal. But God's word is not chained.*

## Suffering is part of the struggle against injustice

1. 1 Peter 2:19: *For it is commendable if a man bears up under the pain of unjust suffering because he is conscious of God.*

## Suffering is part of the struggle for the name of Christ

1. Acts 5:41: *The apostles left the Sanhedrin, rejoicing because they had been counted worthy of suffering disgrace for the Name.*
2. 1 Peter 4:14: *If you are insulted because of the name of Christ, you are blessed, for the Spirit of glory and of God rests on you.*

## Suffering indicates how the righteous become sharers in Christ's suffering

1. 2 Corinthians 1:5: *For just as the sufferings of Christ flow over into our lives, so also through Christ our comfort overflows.*
2. 1 Peter 4:12–13: *Dear friends, do not be surprised at the painful trial you are suffering, as though something strange were happening to you. But rejoice that you participate in the sufferings of Christ, so that you may be overjoyed when his glory is revealed.*

## Endurance of suffering is given as a cause for reward

1. 2 Corinthians 4:17: *For our light and momentary troubles are achieving for us an eternal glory that far outweighs them all.*
2. 2 Timothy 2:12: *If we endure, we will also reign with him. If we disown him, he will also disown us.*

## Suffering forces community and the administration of our gifts for the common good

1. Philippians 4:12–15: *I know what it is to be in need, and I know what it is to have plenty. I have learned the secret of being content in any and every situation, whether well fed or hungry, whether living in plenty or in want. I can do everything through him who gives me strength. Yet it was good of you to share in my troubles. Moreover, as you Philippians know, in the early days of your acquaintance with the gospel, when I set out from Macedonia, not one church shared with me in the matter of giving and receiving, except you only.*

## Suffering binds Christians together into a common or joint purpose

1. Revelation 1:9: *I, John, your brother and companion in the suffering and kingdom and patient endurance that are ours in Jesus, was on the island of Patmos because of the word of God and the testimony of Jesus.*

## Suffering produces discernment, knowledge, and teaches us God's statutes

1. Psalm 119:66–67, 71: *Teach me knowledge and good judgment, for I believe in your commands. Before I was afflicted I went astray, but now I obey your word . . . It was good for me to be afflicted so that I might learn your decrees.*

## Through suffering, God is able to obtain our broken and contrite spirit, which he desires

1. Psalm 51:16–17: *You do not delight in sacrifice, or I would bring it; you do not take pleasure in burnt offerings. The sacrifices of God are a broken spirit; a broken and contrite heart, O God, you will not despise.*

## Suffering causes us to discipline our minds by making us focus our hope on the grace to be revealed at the revelation of Jesus Christ

1. 1 Peter 1:6, 13: *In this you greatly rejoice, though now for a little while you may have had to suffer grief in all kinds of trials . . . Therefore, prepare your minds for action; be self-controlled; set your hope fully on the grace to be given you when Jesus Christ is revealed.*

## God uses suffering to humble us so he can exalt us at the proper time

1. 1 Peter 5:6–7: *Humble yourselves, therefore, under God's mighty hand, that he may lift you up in due time. Cast all your anxiety on him because he cares for you.*

## Suffering teaches us to number our days so we can present to God a heart of wisdom

1. Psalm 90:7–12: *We are consumed by your anger and terrified by your indignation. You have set our iniquities before you, our secret sins in the light of your presence. All our days pass away under your wrath; we finish our years with a moan. The length of our days is seventy years—or eighty, if we have the strength; yet their span is but trouble and sorrow, for they quickly pass, and we fly away. Who knows the power of your anger? For your wrath is as great as the fear that is due you. Teach us to number our days aright, that we may gain a heart of wisdom.*

## Suffering is sometimes necessary to win the lost

1. 2 Timothy 2:8–10: *Remember Jesus Christ, raised from the dead, descended from David. This is my gospel, for which I am suffering even to the point of being chained like a criminal. But God's word is not chained. Therefore I endure everything for the sake of the elect, that they too may obtain the salvation that is in Christ Jesus, with eternal glory.*

2. 2 Timothy 4:5–6: *But you, keep your head in all situations, endure hardship, do the work of an evangelist, discharge all the duties of your ministry. For I am already being poured out like a drink offering, and the time has come for my departure.*

## Suffering strengthens and allows us to comfort others who are weak

1. 2 Corinthians 1:3–11: *Praise be to the God and Father of our Lord Jesus Christ, the Father of compassion and the God of all comfort, who comforts us in all our troubles, so that we can comfort those in any trouble with the comfort we ourselves have received from God. For just as the sufferings of Christ flow over into our lives, so also through Christ our comfort overflows. If we are distressed, it is for your comfort and salvation; if we are comforted, it is for your comfort, which produces in you patient endurance of the same sufferings we suffer. And our hope for you is firm, because we know that just as you share in our sufferings, so also you share in our comfort. We do not want you to be uninformed, brothers, about the hardships we suffered in the province of Asia. We were under great pressure, far beyond our ability to endure, so that we despaired even of life. Indeed, in our hearts we felt the sentence of death. But this happened that we might not rely on ourselves but on God, who raises the dead. He has delivered us from such a deadly peril, and he will deliver us. On him we have set our hope that he will continue to deliver us, as you help us by your prayers. Then many will give thanks on our behalf for the gracious favor granted us in answer to the prayers of many.*

## Suffering is small compared to the surpassing value of knowing Christ

1. Philippians 3:8: *What is more, I consider everything a loss compared to the surpassing greatness of knowing Christ Jesus my Lord, for whose sake I have lost all things. I consider them rubbish, that I may gain Christ.*

## God desires truth in our innermost being, and one way he does it is through suffering

1. Psalm 51:6: *Surely you desire truth in the inner parts; you teach me wisdom in the inmost place.*
2. Psalm 119:17: *Do good to your servant, and I will live; I will obey your word.*

## The equity for suffering will be found in the next life

1. Psalm 58:10–11: *The righteous will be glad when they are avenged, when they bathe their feet in the blood of the wicked. Then men will say, "Surely the righteous still are rewarded; surely there is a God who judges the earth."*

## Suffering is always coupled with a greater source of grace

1. 2 Timothy 1:7–8: *For God did not give us a spirit of timidity, but a spirit of power, of love and of self-discipline. So do not be ashamed to testify about our Lord, or ashamed of me his prisoner. But join with me in suffering for the gospel, by the power of God.*
2. 2 Timothy 4:16–18: *At my first defense, no one came to my support, but everyone deserted me. May it not be held against them. But the Lord stood at my side and gave me strength, so that through me the message might be fully proclaimed and all the Gentiles might hear it. And I was delivered from the lion's mouth. The Lord will rescue me from every evil attack and will bring me safely to his heavenly kingdom. To him be glory for ever and ever. Amen.*

## Suffering teaches us to give thanks in times of sorrow

1. 1 Thessalonians 5:18: *Give thanks in all circumstances.*
2. 2 Corinthians 1:11: *Then many will give thanks on our behalf for the gracious favor granted us in answer to the prayers of many.*

## Suffering increases faith

1. Jeremiah 29:11: *"For I know the plans I have for you," declares the Lord, "plans to prosper you and not to harm you, plans to give you hope and a future."*

## Suffering allows God to manifest his care

1. Psalm 56:8: *Record my lament; list my tears on your scroll—are they not in your record?*

## Suffering stretches our hope

1. Job 13:14–15: *Why do I put myself in jeopardy and take my life in my hands? Though he slay me, yet will I hope in him; I will surely defend my ways to his face.*

# Appendix C

# CAN GOD EXPERIENCE GRIEF?[1]

In Chapter 2 we saw that God is eternally joyful and contented. Yet this book is entitled *When God Weeps*, and throughout it we have spoken of God as mourning over human sin and suffering. If God is always happy, can he truly grieve?

A common answer to this dilemma is to take God's sorrow as figurative. The Bible often speaks figuratively of God. For example, God has no body, yet we read of his all-seeing eyes and outstretched hand (2 Chronicles 16:9; Proverbs 15:3; Isaiah 40:12; Zephaniah 1:4). God is everywhere and knows everything, yet in Genesis 18:21 he says he will "go down [to Sodom and Gomorrah] to see if what they have done is as bad as the outcry that has reached [heaven]." We also read about God "repenting"—for instance, of his decision to wipe out Israel after the golden-calf incident, or to devastate the nation's crops with locusts in the time of Amos (Exodus 32:14; Amos 7:3).[2] Such repentings must be figurative. Did God sin in these incidents and then later feel bad about it? No. Did he have a change of opinion? No, it's almost blasphemous to speak of God having an "opinion" about anything— it implies that he makes judgment calls without knowing all the facts, or that his preferences are mere tastes that may not reflect what is actually superior. Did God repent in the sense of deciding one way yesterday and another way today? No, for he knows everything from the beginning, including how he will act in all future situations. Rather, as humans change, God shows them different "sides" of his character appropriate to their behavior. His wrath shows itself when people rebel, his kindness when they turn again—kindness that he had all along. Thus it appears to *us* that he has repented or reconsidered.

Could the passages quoted in this book about God grieving over human sin and suffering be merely figurative as well? Consider Genesis 6:6 where we read in the New International Version, "God was grieved that he had made man on the earth." Interestingly, "grieved" is the NIV's translation of the Hebrew word for "repent" discussed above. We've already concluded that God's repenting in the sense of changing his mind is figurative—what about his grieving here? Is it unworthy of an eternally blessed God to say that he grieves, other than poetically? Many superb theologians whom we greatly admire say yes. Does God actually feel emotional pain? These scholars say no, and seem to limit any suffering on God's part to what Jesus endured while on earth. These writers hold the Bible in esteem, and have the following over-arching Scriptural reasons for their position: 1) The Bible clearly teaches that God is "blessed" or happy; 2) Acts 14:15 may imply that God does not have emotions; 3) Just as the parables of Jesus are usually meant to teach a single truth, but are often stretched by interpreters, so the passages about God's "emotions" may intend to teach only that his actions parallel ours when our feelings are running high.

Let's hear directly from some of these thinkers:

Professor A. A. Hodge:

> When he is said to . . . be grieved, or to be jealous, it is only meant that he acts towards us as a man would when agitated by such passions. These metaphors occur principally in the Old Testament, and in highly rhetorical passages of the poetical and prophetical books.[3]

John Calvin:

> [Commenting on Genesis 6:6—"And the Lord was sorry that he had made man on the earth, and his heart was filled with pain."] Since we cannot comprehend [God] as he is, it is necessary that, for our sake, he should, in a certain sense, transform himself [by using figures of speech about himself]. . . . Certainly God is not sorrowful or sad; but remains forever like himself in his

celestial and happy repose: yet because it could not otherwise be known how great is God's hatred and detestation of sin, therefore the Spirit accommodates himself to our capacity. . . . God was so offended by the atrocious wickedness of men, [he speaks] *as if* they had wounded his heart with mortal grief.[4]

The *Westminster Confession of Faith* (II.1.):

There is but one . . . true God, who is infinite in being and perfection, a most pure spirit, invisible, without body, parts, *or passions* . . .

In support of God being without passions, the *Westminster Confession* quotes Acts 14:15 in the King James Version, spoken by Paul and Barnabas to a crowd who mistook them for gods. "Sirs, why do ye these things? We also are men of *like passions* with you, and preach unto you that ye should turn from these vanities unto the living God . . ." Were Paul and Barnabas implying that "passions"—that is, emotions—are partly what distinguishes humans from God?

## WHY WE THINK GOD'S GRIEF IS REAL

Despite our deep respect for the theologians quoted above and for their views in general, we think the Bible does teach that God feels grief over human sinfulness and suffering. Here are our reasons:

**1. Passages about God repenting in the sense of "changing his mind" are clearly *limited and narrowed* in meaning by other Scriptures. But passages about God repenting in the sense of "grieving" over sin and suffering are *expanded* by other Scriptures.**

1 Samuel 15:29 could not be clearer: "He who is the Glory of Israel does not lie or change his mind." Repeatedly the Bible claims that God does not change in any way (Numbers 23:19; Psalm 110:4; Malachi 3:6; Hebrews 13:8; James 1:17). Such verses force us to take God's "changes of mind" as figurative.[5]

In contrast, many passages flesh out God's strong emotional response to human sin. In Isaiah 1:11–14 God says that because Judah rebelled he took "no pleasure" in their sacrifices, their worship was "meaningless" to him, their incense "detestable." What does he say about their religious festivals? "I am weary of bearing them"—"My soul hates" them—"I have had more than enough"—"They have become a burden to me," he complained. Elsewhere he became "displeased" (Isaiah 59:15) and "provoked" (Hosea 12:14). He turned from Judah "in disgust" (Ezekiel 23:18) because her conduct was "like a woman's monthly uncleanness in his sight" (Ezekiel 36:17). He couldn't wait to "get relief" from it all (Isaiah 1:24).

As with human sin, so with human sorrow—*many* passages elaborate on how it touches God's heart. We have quoted them abundantly throughout this book. The very passages that speak specifically of God's grief add to the impression of something more than poetic language. In Genesis 6:6 God was not only "grieved" at humanity's wickedness—the verse intensifies this by adding, literally, "and he was hurt to his heart." The Hebrew word here for "hurt " is used elsewhere in the Bible of a deserted wife, of young men learning of their sister's rape, of Jonathan realizing that his father wants to murder Jonathan's best friend.

Nor is mention of God's grief limited to the poetry of the Old Testament. In the cool logic of his epistles Paul urges us not to "grieve" the Holy Spirit (Ephesians 4:30).

## 2. Other emotions of God seem to be non-figurative.

The Son of God entered our world "so that my *joy* may be in you and that your joy may be complete" (John 15:11). Is this joy only figurative? Is "joy" used only to describe Jesus acting "as a man would when agitated by such passions," to use Hodge's words? What about God's love? Jesus expressed a desire for the disciples to love him in the same way his father loved him; he once prayed "that the love you [the Father] have for me may be in them ..." (John 17:26). Thus, isn't our love for Christ (which certainly includes emotions) only a mirror of what God the Father feels?

We're clearly told in Ephesians 5:22–30 that God designed marriage to teach us about Christ's relationship to the church. Don't we learn, however dimly, something of his love for us as we experience love with our spouse and children? Don't we cherish the notion that God actually *feels* a certain delight in his people when he calls them "the apple of his eye" (Zechariah 2:8)? His love actually makes him sing over us (Zephaniah 3:17). Of course, the pinnacle of God's heart going out was seen at the cross: "God so *loved* the world that he gave his one and only Son"

(John 3:16). He was willing to watch his son being murdered for us. But what love does this show if it cost the Father nothing emotionally—if the Father felt no grief as he watched the scene at Calvary?

### 3. The emotions of Jesus show that the Father feels as well.

Jesus said, "I and the Father are one" and "Anyone who has seen me has seen the Father" (John 10:30; 14:9). If Jesus' heart went out to people in a variety of emotions, the Father's heart does also.

Consider the grief shown by Jesus in the gospels. See him with Mary, the sister of Lazarus, at the tomb of her brother. "When Jesus saw her weeping, and the Jews who had come along with her also weeping, he was deeply moved in spirit and troubled. 'Where have you laid him?' he asked. 'Come and see, Lord,' they replied. Jesus wept" (John 11:33–35).

Did only his human nature weep, and not his divine? No, for Jesus said, "I tell you the truth, the Son can do nothing by himself; he can do only what he sees his Father doing . . ." (John 5:19).

Remember his lament over the holy city? "O Jerusalem, Jerusalem, you who kill the prophets and stone those sent to you, how often I have longed to gather your children together, as a hen gathers her chicks under her wings, but you were not willing" (Matthew 23:37). He is a mother whose children refuse to come—there is an aching. Did Jesus long only in his humanity, not in his divinity? No, his ardor mirrored Jehovah's toward Judah six centuries earlier: "Repent! Turn away from all your offenses; then sin will not be your downfall . . . . Why will you die, O house of Israel? For I take no pleasure in the death of anyone, declares the Sovereign LORD. Repent and live!" (Ezekiel 18:30–32).

The grief Jesus showed on earth reflects not only the Father's heart, but also the Holy Spirit's—for we learn in Isaiah 63:10 of the Spirit's reaction to a straying Israel: "They rebelled and grieved his Holy Spirit . . ." Thus the entire Trinity grieves over human sin and its results.

### 4. Acts 14:15 doesn't necessarily teach that passions and emotions are foreign to God.

Paul and Barnabas once tried to fend off pagans who wanted to worship them by saying, "We also are men of like passions with you." Were they saying that God, in contrast, doesn't have passions and feelings?

What complicates the issue is uncertainty about the origin of the Greek word translated "like passions." It is a combination of two words. The first is agreed upon by all and means "like, similar, same." The second word is unclear—either of two similarly spelled Greek words could fit: a word meaning "passion," or a word meaning "suffering."[6] One's choice might make a difference. Are similar *passions and feelings* what distinguish Paul and Barnabas and their hearers from the true God? Or are similar *sufferings and experiences*—that is, mortality—the difference?

Interestingly, even though language authorities disagree on the word's origin, the vast majority seem to agree that, over time, the word came to have the broad meaning of "having a similar nature as someone." Thus, M. R. Vincent says in his *Word Studies in the New Testament*: "There is some danger of a misunderstanding of this rendering ["like passions"], from the limited and generally bad sense in which the word *passions* is popularly used. The meaning is rather of *like nature and constitution*."[7]

The *New International Dictionary of New Testament Theology* agrees. After offering its opinion that word means literally "suffering the same," it adds that the word is used more generally to mean "of similar disposition" (II. 501). With the exception of Abbott-Smith, the standard lexicons for New Testament studies that we checked concur. This is why the NIV translates Acts 14:15: "We too are only men, *human like you*." Most English versions render it similarly. The point of the verse, then, is not that God doesn't have feelings, as do humans. The point is that he is high above us, on a totally different level. Paul and Barnabas were saying in effect, "Don't worship us; we're just human—not even in God's league."

## 5. God's emotions, unlike ours, are sinless.

Those who consider God's grief as figurative are rightly trying to avoid attributing to him the sins and weaknesses that so often plague human emotions. But these human failings stem from our fallenness, not from the nature of emotions themselves. Nothing but perfectly righteous and honorably expressed feelings come from a holy God.

Our emotions are hopelessly contaminated by a heart that is "more deceitful than all else and . . . desperately sick" (Jeremiah 17:9, NASV). Our feelings goad us into losing control, wringing our hands, getting depressed, giving up, dumping on others, or acting in an undignified way. But God's emotions, unlike ours, are not connected to flawed wiring.

For example, God's contentment is not that of the spoiled rich kid with bedroom floor-to-ceiling TV screens and an indoor pool. His happiness isn't that of the easy chair, the absence of chores, and endless snacks between meals. His delight is in his own goodness and wisdom, in the beautiful character of his Son, and in the complexity and wonder of all he has made. His is not a complacent, lazy joy—his is the rugged joy of the warrior returned home, the admiral sailing into port flying colors of victory, the bone-tired, soot-faced (hand-scarred!) but grinning hero carrying the child to safety from the burning building.

God's *anger* is also righteous. In this connection, it's interesting to note the word usually used by the Greek New Testament when speaking of God's wrath. Except for the book of Revelation, the New Testament generally avoids the word meaning "rage" (from the root "to rush along fiercely," "to be in a heat of violence," "to breathe violently"). Rather, it favors a word stemming from the root "to grow ripe." The idea is that God's wrath slowly builds over a long period of time. It stems from perfect reasoning and consideration. It is "not so much a flaring up of passion which is soon over, as a strong and settled opposition to all that is evil arising out of God's very nature."[8] The relevant point for us is that God's anger is not a knee-jerk reaction as ours often is—it flows from holy, studied wisdom.[9]

As with his contentment, joy, and anger, God's grief as the Bible describes it is a worthy emotion—without weakness, without impurity, without anything uncomely. It never paralyzes him, and it did not lead him sentimentally to ignore justice when seeking the salvation of his creatures. The bottom line is this: when it is right to grieve, when grieving is the perfect response—that is what God does, because he is perfect.

## 6. Grief and joy can be experienced simultaneously.

Can God laugh and weep in the same moment? Jesus himself was "full of joy," and prayed that "the full measure of my joy" might be in the disciples—yet Isaiah called him "a man of sorrows, and acquainted with grief" (Luke 10:21; John 17:13; Isaiah 53:3).

We mortals—made in God's image—also know joy and pain together. A father stands at the altar and sighs deeply as he gives his daughter's hand to the perfect future husband. A woman finally lands that long-coveted job, but in taking it must leave familiar friends and the town she loves. A mother watches her son languish behind prison bars, but sees the experience bring the rebellious young man to genuine repentance and salvation. The apostle Paul was "sorrowful, yet always rejoicing" (2 Corinthians 6:10).

Of course, no human analogy is ever sufficient when talking about God. We find life bittersweet, yet it is almost certainly wrong to think that God finds anything actually "bitter." The Bible speaks of God in far too glorious a manner for this—his sorrows have a triumph to them that we can't imagine.

How can this be? How does it all work in the mind of God? God is inscrutable, and guesses can be hazardous. But perhaps the answer lies in his ability to know all things and to see the eternal picture.

God does look down on his world and weep. But its twistedness did not catch him by surprise. He knew that humans would fall into sin. He knew the immeasurable sorrow this would let loose. He knew the suffering it would cost his own Son. But he decreed to permit this fall because he knew how he would resolve it: that Jesus would die, that his church would eventually triumph through innumerable trials, that Satan's fingers would be pried off the planet, that justice would be served at the final judgment, that heaven would make up for all, and that God would receive more glory—and we would know more joy— than if the Fall had never happened. Can anyone but God see enough of this coming ecstasy to make sense out of our present agony? *God sees this glorious end as clearly as if it were today.*

This, in our opinion, is how he can be truly "blessed," and truly weep.

# NOTES

## Chapter One: I'm Hurting Bad

1. During debate, Jesus' opponents implied that he was of illegitimate birth. See John 8:19, 41.

## Chapter Two: Ecstasy Spilling Over

1. *American Bible Union Version*, cited by Curtis Vaughan, ed. *The New Testament from 26 Translations* (Grand Rapids: Zondervan, 1967), p. 960.

2. Writing in the eighteenth century, Jonathan Edwards did special justice in several places to the topic of God's happiness. Easier to read is John Piper's outstanding *The Pleasures of God: Meditations on God's Delight in Being God* (Portland: Multnomah, 1991). Run, don't walk, to buy this remarkable work.

3. From the sermon "The Condescension of Christ" in *Spurgeon's Sermons, Vol. 4* (Grand Rapids: Baker, 1989), pp. 366–367. Originally published as *Sermons of Rev. C. H. Spurgeon of London* (New York: Robert Carter & Brothers).

4. The phrase "God the only Son" is from the first edition of the *New International Version* and appears to be an informal rendering of *monogenes theos*—the best-attested Greek reading. The more literal and traditional translation is "only begotten God."

## Chapter Three: The Suffering God

1. Herodotus, *Histories* (New York: Penguin), p. 459.

2. We call him Abraham to avoid confusion. He was actually still named Abram at this time.

3. Deuteronomy 1:31; Isaiah 46:3; Ex 2:24–25; Psalm 44:3; Isaiah 49:16; Psalm 149:4; Judges 10:16; Psalm 106:46; Jeremiah 23:1; Ezekiel 16:32; Psalm 28:9; Zechariah 2:8; Psalm 148:14; Isaiah 49:15.

4. In John 1:33, John the Baptist says, "I would not have known him, except that the one who sent me to baptize with water told me, 'The man on whom you see the Spirit come down and remain is he who will baptize with the Holy Spirit.'" No doubt this means that John wasn't aware of Jesus' identity as messiah until the moment of Jesus' baptism. But it may also mean that the two had never met, which is the view taken by our chapter. Although their mothers were "relatives" (the word in Luke 1:36 is broad) and had visited when both boys were still in the womb, John and Jesus lived in different parts of the country. No other contact before Jesus' baptism is recorded.

5. The literal "stay awake" (not in the NIV) seems more in keeping with the context than "keep [spiritual] watch," although the latter becomes the more natural translation in verse 41. William Hendriksen, R.V. G. Tasker, and many others hold this view.

6. It goes without saying that Christ was completely innocent of these things. Peter wrote that Jesus "committed no sin . . ." Hebrews boasts that he was "without sin," while positively lauding him as "holy, blameless, pure, set apart from sinners . . ." All of Scripture agrees. Old Testament guilt and sin offerings had to be "without defect" because they symbolized the morally perfect Lamb of God who would take away the sins of the world (1 Peter 2:22; Hebrews 4:15, 7:26; Leviticus 4 and 5).

But in the most glorious mystery of all time, the Father transferred our sins onto his holy Son. Just as Christ's righteousness is credited to our account as believers, so our sins were credited (imputed) to his account. "The LORD has laid on him the iniquity of us all" (Isaiah 53:6). "God made him [Jesus] who had no sin to be sin for us . . ." (2 Corinthians 5:21). God treated his beloved Son as *if* Jesus had been a sinner, as *if* he were personally guilty—yet on the cross Jesus remained the spotless Lamb of God, steadfastly righteous in character.

The point of pages 53–54 is this: the experience of being identified with human sin was infinitely repulsive to Christ's holy nature; enduring the wrath of his beloved Father (in our stead) far outweighed the physical pains of crucifixion. Yet we must keep in mind that Father and Son had planned the atonement *together* and were working *in concert* on that Good Friday. God loved the Son even as he punished him on our account. Does this boggle our minds? It was meant to.

## Chapter Four: Does He Really Expect Me to Suffer?

1. "Disease" here is used for all medical problems, whatever their cause—microbodies, genetic disorders, accidents, etc.

2. Ephesians 1:7 and Colossians 1:14 contrasted with Romans 8:23 and Ephesians 1:14.

3. 2 Timothy 1:9 contrasted with 1 Corinthians 1:18 and 2 Corinthians 2:15.

4. Matthew 1:21; 1 John 1:8.

5. Philippians 2:27; Romans 9:2; 2 Corinthians 6:10.

6. Luke 6:21; James 4:10.

7. 1 Timothy 5:23; Philippians 2:27; 2 Timothy 4:20; Galatians 4:13.

8. Acts 16:7; 2 Corinthians 12:9; James 4:15.

9. For more about early Christian poverty see Acts 6:1; 11:28–29; 1 Corinthians 1:26; 4:11; 2 Corinthians 8:2. James and Peter—Acts 12:2–3. Stephen—Acts 6:12–7:60. John—Revelation 1:9. Jerusalem Christians—Acts 8:1. Acquila and Priscilla—Acts 18:1. John Mark—Acts 13:13. Christians of Asia Minor—1 Peter 1:6 (see the whole epistle). Slaves—1 Corinthians 7:22; Ephesians 6:5–8; Titus 2:9. Women with unbelieving husbands—1 Corinthians 7:13–14; 1 Peter 3:1–6. Singles—1 Corinthians 7:8–9, 25–27. Insults, persecution, property taken—Hebrews 10:32–34. Sickness—1 Timothy 5:23; Philippians 2:27; 2 Timothy 4:20; Galatians 4:13. Temptation, sin, conscience—Luke 22:62; 1 Corinthians 5:1, cf. 2 Corinthians 2:7 and 10:8–11;

Galatians 1:11–13; plus passages describing the believer's soul conflict in Romans 7:14–25; Galatians 5:16–17; and Ephesians 6:10–18. Churches with problems; the need for encouragement—read any NT epistle! Paul's "diary"—2 Corinthians 11:23–27.

## Chapter Five: All Trials Great and Small

1. Our account doesn't say the event occurred in our day, only that the Middle East is associated with terrorism in our day. The Sanhedrin's court proceedings were illegal. The soldiers' delight in their work shows they were thugs. Crucifixion victims were stretched/positioned so as to make breathing excruciating. Please forgive us this device for the sake of our point.

2. The words rendered "spreading mildew" by the NIV have been understood by commentators to mean any number of growths, fungi, dry rot, etc.—possibly even a type of lichen.

## Chapter Six: Heaven's Dirty Laundry?

1. Harold S. Kushner, *When Bad Things Happen to Good People* (New York: Avon, 1983), pp. 43, 81.

2. John Boykin, *Circumstances and the Role of God* (Grand Rapids: Zondervan, 1986), p. 42.

3. Phrase adapted from Charles Swindoll. We can't recall the reference.

4. Israelites were forbidden to marry any inhabitants of Canaan, although they could marry women from outside Israel's borders who were captured in war (Deuteronomy 7:1–4; 21:10–11). The forbidden peoples listed by God were "the Hittites, Girgashites, Amorites, Canaanites, Perizzites, Hivites and Jebusites"—Philistines are not mentioned. However, the Philistines lived in Canaan when Israel entered it (Exodus 13:17), were well-established there by Joshua's old age (Joshua 13:2–3), and were Israel's overlords in the very land God had promised to the Jews. Thus, by Samson's day, marrying a Philistine was apparently considered a violation of the spirit of God's law at the very least.

5. Of the many examples of this principle, here are a few: God promised to "raise up for himself" an Israelite king to wipe out the dynasty of Jeroboam (1 Kings 14:14–16), yet destroyed Baasha for fulfilling this decree (1 Kings 16:1–3, 7). God sent lying prophets with a false message of "peace in our times" to rebellious Israel (Jeremiah 4:10), then claimed, "I did not send them" and promises to judge them (Jeremiah 14:13–16). God vows to punish Assyria for overrunning Israel, after having clearly "sent" and "dispatched" it (Isaiah 10:5–19). In each case, the punished party had no intention of serving God.

6. The KJV's rendering "with them that met with him" doesn't seem to do justice to the Greek *paratunchano*, which means "to chance to be by, to happen to be present, to meet by chance" (Thayer's lexicon and others).

7. C. S. Lewis, *The Lion, the Witch, and the Wardrobe* (New York: Macmillan, 1950), p. 64.

## Chapter Eight: The Best Answer We Have

1. J. B. Phillips, *The New Testament in Modern English* (New York: Macmillan Publishing Company, 1972), p. 478.

2. "There Is a Balm in Gilead," *The Hymnal for Worship & Celebration* (Waco: Word Music, 1986), p. 423.

3. For more reading on this theme, we recommend Dr. Peter Kreeft's book *Making Sense Out of Suffering* (Ann Arbor, Mich.: Servant Books, 1986).

## Chapter Nine: Making Sense of Suffering

1. The idea in this paragraph came from Tim Stafford, *Knowing the Face of God* (Colorado Springs: NavPress, 1996), p. 16.

2. Robert K. Brown and Mark R. Norton, *The One Year Book of Hymns* (Wheaton, Ill.: Tyndale House, 1995), April 11.

3. Thomas Merton, "No Man Is An Island," *The Word of the Cross* (New York: Harcourt, Brace and Co., 1955), p. 84.

4. Dr. Peter Kreeft, *Making Sense Out of Suffering* (Ann Arbor, Mich.: Servant Books, 1986), p. 153.

## Chapter Ten: Cry of the Soul

1. The ideas on the following pages have been gleaned from Dr. Dan Allender & Dr. Tremper Longman III, *The Cry of the Soul: How Our Emotions Reveal Our Deepest Questions About God* (Colorado Springs: 1994), p. 150. We highly recommend this excellent book for understanding how the Psalms expose the nature of our emotional responses as they relate to God. Dr. Allender and Dr. Longman have written this exhaustive text from their combined studies in Theology and Psychology. There's not a better book around on the subject.

2. Ibid., p. 150.

3. Ibid., p. 25.

4. Ibid., p. 74.

5. Ibid., p. 72.

6. Fanny J. Crosby, "He Hideth My Soul," (public domain).

7. Glenda Revell, *Glenda's Story* (Lincoln: Gateway to Joy Publishers, 1994). The story on these pages, only half-told here, is shockingly true. The adversary will try to discredit the goodness of God as well as weaken the faith of believers with stories of abuse and torture; yet Glenda Revell's testimony stands as evidence of God's power to redeem an almost unbelievably painful situation. We highly recommend her book.

8. Thomas Merton, *No Man Is an Island* (New York: Harcourt, Brace and Co., 1955), p. 94.

## Chapter Eleven: Gaining Contentment

1. Quote by George Herbert, Edythe Draper, *Edythe Draper's Book of Quotations for the Christian World* (Wheaton, Ill.: Tyndale House, 1992), p. 101.

2. The idea for this story came from Carol Turkington in the Washinton State School for the Deaf Newsletter.

3. Jeremiah Burroughs, *The Rare Jewel of Christian Contentment* (Carlisle, Penn.: The Banner of Truth Trust, 1992), p. 46.

4. Ibid., pp. 42–43.

5. Dr. John Piper, *The Pleasures of God* (Portland: Multnomah Press).

6. Burroughs, *The Rare Jewel,* p. 57.

## Chapter Twelve: Suffering Gone Malignant

1. C. S. Lewis, *The Problem of Pain* (New York: Macmillan, 1962), 118.

2. Dr. Maurice Rawlings, a cardiologist, became a Christian largely because of interviews with such people—some of whom he personally revived from heart attacks suffered while undergoing stress tests in his office. He has written of these experiences in several books, most recently in *To Hell and Back* (Thomas Nelson & Sons, 1993).

3. Literally, "Topheth has long been prepared; etc." Topheth was the shrine outside Jerusalem in the valley of Hinnom where child sacrifices were offered to the idol Molech. The city's refuse was also burned there, the fires going continuously. Thus Topheth and the Valley of Hinnom (Greek: "Gehenna") became symbols for eternal torment.

4. The NIV gives another possible translation: "outside, into the darkness."

5. Theologically liberal scholars have traditionally questioned hell's very existence, or at least its eternal nature. But in recent years, even some evangelical scholars have published similar misgivings about the classic, orthodox view of hell as expressed in this chapter. Their views are well catalogued and answered in John Blanchard's excellent *Whatever Happened to Hell?*—published by Crossway Books in the United States and by Evangelical Press in Great Britain.

6. Lest anyone misunderstand, John 9:1–3 and the Book of Job make clear that our sufferings don't bear a one-to-one correspondence to our sins. In other words, just because I am diagnosed with cancer today doesn't mean that I recently sinned worse than my neighbor who is healthy. But we are all sinners by both birth and choice, and so experience the sentence of suffering pronounced upon our race by God in Eden. God's reasoning in deciding how to distribute suffering is often a mystery.

A related issue is the question of why suffering comes to small children who are too young to have deliberately sinned. Romans 5:12–19 addresses this. God chose Adam to be mankind's representative in the garden of Eden. When Adam sinned, we sinned "in" him and are thus all guilty of his transgression from birth (Psalm 51:5). This concept may seem less foreign when we consider that our nation's leaders routinely make huge decisions in our stead that affect us greatly, including making treaties and declaring war. Children need the blood of Christ to cover their inherited sin just as much as adults need it to cover their deliberate sins. An excellent treatment of this doctrine, known as "original sin," is found in Martyn Lloyd-Jones's *Romans: An Exposition of Chapter 5:1–21,* published by Zondervan.

7. Harold S. Kushner, *When Bad Things Happen to Good People* (New York: Avon, 1983), pp. 4, 7, 44.

## Chapter Thirteen: Suffering Gone

1. Tim Stafford, *Knowing the Face of God* (Colorado Springs: NavPress, 1996), 221. A few of the ideas in this chapter find a broader discussion in Tim's book. We recommend it.

2. I wrote more on this subject in *Heaven . . . Your Real Home* (Grand Rapids: Zondervan, 1996).

3. C. S. Lewis, *The Inspirational Writings of C. S. Lewis* (New York: Inspirational Press, 1991), p. 361.

4. Dr. John H. Gerstner, *The Rational Biblical Theology of Jonathan Edwards* (Orlando: Berea Publications, Ligonier Ministries, 1993), p. 543.

5. Lewis, *The Inspirational Writings of C. S. Lewis,* p. 363.

6. Gerstner, *The Rational Biblical Theology of Jonathan Edwards,* p. 544.

7. C. S. Lewis, *The Weight of Glory* (Grand Rapids: Eerdmans, 1949), p. 14.

8. Gerstner, *The Rational Biblical Theology of Jonathan Edwards,* pp. 556–57.

9. Jonathan Edwards, *Heaven: A World of Love* (Amityville, N.Y.: Calvary Press, 1992), p. 26.

## Appendices

1. Turned off by appendices that are too technical? Then skip directly to page 247 and at least read point number 6.

2. The King James Version uses the word "repent" of God. Newer versions, following contemporary English usage, tend to say explicitly what kind of repentance is meant in each context—such as grief, or an apparent change of mind.

3. A. A. Hodge, *Outlines of Theology* (reprint ed., Edinburgh: The Banner of Truth Trust, 1983), p. 132.

4. John Calvin, *Calvin's Commentaries*, 22 vols. (reprint ed., Grand Rapids: Baker Book House, 1979), 1:1:249.

5. 1 Samuel 15 presents an interesting question. In verse 11 we read that God repents (NIV: is "grieved") over making Saul king. Yet in verse 29 we learn that "God does not repent." Could verse 29 mean that God does not grieve, and thus that God's grief in verse 11 *must* be taken figuratively? No, for the two verses carry different nuances. In verse 11, "repent" seems clearly to mean "to grieve." In verse 29, it means "to change one's mind"—this is clear from the fact that in verse 29 God's not "repenting" is expressed in parallel with his not lying.

6. "Like passions" is a translation of *homoiopathes*—a combination of *homoios* ("like, similar, same") and either *pathos* ("passion") or *pathema* ("suffering, misfortune").

7. M. R. Vincent, *Word Studies in the New Testament*, 2nd ed. (reprint ed., Wilmington, Del.: Associated Publishers and Authors, 1972), p. 364.

8. James Montgomery Boice, *Foundations of the Christian Faith: A Comprehensive and Readable Theology* (Downers Grove, Ill.: Inter-Varsity Press, 1986), p. 250, citing Leon Morris, *The Apostolic Preaching of the Cross* (Grand Rapids: Eerdmans, 1956), pp. 162–63. Dr. Boice's book first brought the distinction between these two words to our attention, even as it admitted that they sometimes are used interchangeably.

Trench's *Synonyms of the New Testament* also argues that their occasional ability to be interchanged does not erase their distinctives. The word for "rage" is *thumos*—the less passionate word is *orgē*.

9. Of course, even when God pours out rage it is not a knee-jerk reaction.

For More Information:

JAF Ministries
PO Box 3333
Agoura Hills, CA 91301
http://www.jafministries.com/

We want to hear from you. Please send your comments about this
book to us in care of the address below. Thank you.

ZondervanPublishingHouse
*Grand Rapids, Michigan 49530*
http://www.zondervan.com